WHICH SIDE ARE YOU ON?

WHICH SIDE ARE YOU ON?

20th Century American History in 100 Protest Songs

James Sullivan

Foreword by the Reverend Lennox Yearwood
and Bill McKibben

OXFORD
UNIVERSITY PRESS

OXFORD
UNIVERSITY PRESS

Oxford University Press is a department of the University of Oxford. It furthers
the University's objective of excellence in research, scholarship, and education
by publishing worldwide. Oxford is a registered trade mark of Oxford University
Press in the UK and certain other countries.

Published in the United States of America by Oxford University Press
198 Madison Avenue, New York, NY 10016, United States of America.

Library of Congress Cataloging-in-Publication Data
Names: Sullivan, James, 1965 November 7- author.
Title: Which side are you on? : 20th century American history in 100 protest
songs / James Sullivan ; foreword by Reverend Lennox Yearwood and Bill McKibben.
Description: New York, NY : Oxford University Press, 2019. | Includes
bibliographical references and index.
Identifiers: LCCN 2018012412| ISBN 9780190660307 (hardcover : alk. paper) |
ISBN 9780190660321 (epub)
Subjects: LCSH: Protest songs—United States—20th century—History and
criticism. | Music—Political aspects—United States—History—20th century.
Classification: LCC ML3917.U6 S85 2019 | DDC 782.42/15920973—dc23
LC record available at https://lccn.loc.gov/2018012412

9 8 7 6 5 4 3 2

Printed by Sheridan Books, Inc., United States of America

To the ReSisters

CONTENTS

FOREWORD

Neither of us are musicians, but both of us have some experience with protest, and we can say with assurance that if you're not singing—or dancing, or using the tools that culture has to offer—you're not doing it right.

We say this for several reasons. One is internal. Movements are made up of human beings, and human beings are braver and more unified when they are singing. If, say, you are sitting someplace you're not supposed to be, waiting to get arrested, you can't help but feel a little worried. But if you're all singing "We Shall Not Be Moved," or "We Shall Overcome," it's easier to remind yourself that you're part of a tradition, that you have friends all around you, that you are stronger than you think. And in jail? The civil rights movement made clear that songs of freedom keep you strong, especially when you are alone and feeling discouraged, and we've found that to be true.

But at least as important, music helps other people understand what you're up to. The point of movements is to shift the zeitgeist, to persuade onlookers (and most people are onlookers) that change must come. Some of this persuasion is done with statistics and arguments—you have to win the argument. But you can win the argument and lose the fight, because fights are often about power. The status quo can usually count on money as its ally; those trying to force change have to find other weapons. And some of the strongest weapons are music and art—an appeal to that half of the human brain that does not respond to bar graphs and pie charts.

One of the finest things about music is the way it can bridge the gulfs that have divided Americans and kept them from cooperating for change. We know, for instance, that when people think about music for environmentalists, they tend to imagine a white guy in a sweater with a guitar strapped around his neck. John Denver, say. But the finest and most important environmental anthem in American history is almost certainly Marvin Gaye's "Mercy Mercy Me (The Ecology Song)." It's a reminder that in 1970 the environment seemed as much a project of inner-city America as of the wilderness. If we'd kept that link stronger, we might have avoided abominations like Flint's water crisis. That's why it's so powerful right now to see hip-hop and R&B musicians writing the next wave of environmental songs.

This volume is a powerful reminder of just how crucial music has been over the long history of American protest. And it's a reminder too of the way that America has specialized in protest—one of the great gifts we've given to the rest of the world has been the long and rich history of people standing up to power. America was born in protest against the greatest empire on earth, and protesters have tried to fix some of its grave defects ever since. This book emerges in a moment of great upheaval, as many Americans try to come to terms with the radical presidency of Donald Trump. More than ever, we need hearts and minds moved simultaneously. We have a great tradition to draw on!

Rev. Lennox Yearwood, Hip Hop Caucus
Bill McKibben, 350.org

INTRODUCTION

The Star-Spangled Banner

Though this book is about the power of words, the American protest song that spoke the loudest may be the one that was played without them.

When Jimi Hendrix wrung the notes of "**The Star-Spangled Banner**" from his white Fender Stratocaster from the Woodstock stage on a breaking Sunday morning in August 1969, he bombarded the melody with eruptions of feedback. Those amplified sound effects echoed the war that was tearing apart the country of Vietnam, and, closer to home, the American family: the cluster-bombing, the machine-gun fire, the slapping helicopter blades, the screaming napalm victims.

Hendrix himself had been a candidate for duty in Vietnam, having enlisted in the US Army at the age of eighteen and been assigned to the 101st Airborne Division at Fort Campbell, Kentucky. He never made it to the field of battle. An indifferent soldier, he was honorably discharged following an ankle injury on a training jump.

A few weeks after the Woodstock Music & Art Fair—the cultural event in Upstate New York that would define a generation—Hendrix made a rare appearance on a television talk show, sitting down with interviewer Dick Cavett for his prime-time ABC program. When Cavett asked about the "controversy" the guitar's rendition of the national anthem had evoked, Hendrix replied, "I don't know, man. I'm American, and so I played it. . . . They made me sing it in school, so it was a flashback."

Persisting gently, Cavett noted the unorthodoxy of Hendrix's approach to the song.

"That's not unorthodox," the soft-spoken musician responded. "I thought it was beautiful."

Ask Johnny Cash to choose, and he'd take the side of the disadvantaged every time. In a field of music dominated by cowboys, the country singer told tales of the Native Americans they'd vanquished. He sang of the farmhands and the assembly line workers. He recorded his fabled live albums at Folsom Prison and San Quentin because he felt a kinship with the inmates and the outlaws. He sang for the forgotten, the outsiders, the ones who have no voice.

On this day in early 1970, however, Johnny Cash was going to the White House. He'd been invited by President Nixon, who'd heard impressive things about the singer from the Reverend Billy Graham, a mutual friend. At the height of his career, with a weekly network television show and a long string of hit records dating back to the mid-1950s, Cash was an entertainment king.

Nixon had a few requests. The president wanted to hear Cash sing "A Boy Named Sue," his oddball hit written by Shel Silverstein; "Welfare Cadillac," a wry poke at federal handouts by the songwriter Guy Drake; and "Okie from Muskogee," Merle Haggard's classic song about the great divide between traditional American values and the counterculture of the 1960s. Cash did play "A Boy Named Sue," but he politely declined to perform the others: he didn't know them, he claimed. During a forty-minute appearance, Cash and his accompanists performed songs including "Five Feet High and Rising," "Jesus Was a Carpenter," and the gospel standard "Peace in the Valley."

Cash also played a new song that, like Haggard's, addressed the generation gap then roiling the country. "What Is Truth" was inspired by comments Cash heard on the set of his television show, when a fellow country music veteran complained that he couldn't make sense of the loud rock music the younger generation was making. Cash had written his latest single at the urging of Graham, the evangelical minister, who'd suggested the youth of America needed some guidance. Instead, the song attempted to explain their side to his own peers. "Maybe I was trying to be a kid again," he told the guests at the White House.

> *A little boy of three sittin' on the floor*
> *Looks up and says, "Daddy, what is war?"*
> *"Son, that's when people fight and die"*
> *A little boy of three says, "Daddy, why?"*

"What Is Truth" went on to remind those in power that the young were destined to have their day: "The ones that you're callin' wild/Are going to be the leaders in a little while." After he finished delivering the song, Cash quietly told the president that he hoped the soldiers who were overseas could come home as soon as possible. The two hundred guests responded with a sincere, sustained round of applause.[1]

A year later, Cash released another purposeful new single, this one called "Man in Black." He'd written it after meeting with students at Vanderbilt University to discuss a range of issues. Asked why he wore black clothing onstage, he used his answer as the song's theme. He wore black, he wrote, as a comment on the world's inequities. He chose to wear somber colors to honor the poor, the hungry, the elderly, the "beaten down." He dressed in black for those who hadn't heard Jesus' message of love and charity, and for the thousands who died in wartime, "believing that the Lord was on their side." Some troubles may never be solved, Cash knew, but we could surely make some things right. "Till things are brighter," he rumbled, "I'm the man in black."

The hardest song to write is a protest song, Joan Baez once said, though few of her contemporaries seemed to think so. The 1960s—so full of disruption that the adjectives "turbulent" and "tumultuous" are practically synonymous with the decade—were consumed with a spirit of popular protest. Folk, rock, and soul musicians wrote and performed songs that condemned segregation and bigotry, the war in Vietnam, the second-class status of women, the plunder of Mother Earth. Some of those words have proven timeless.

> How many roads must a man walk down before you call him a man?
> There's a man with a gun over there, telling me I got to beware.
> War—what is it good for?

From the American Revolution to the twenty-first century, every social debate in America—about war, class, gender, race, the environment—has been set to song. "This machine kills fascists," as Woody Guthrie inscribed on his guitar—but his familiar model of the guitar-strumming dissident is only one of many. Protest music has spanned nearly every style of American music, from the town common to the digital commons.

The United States was born out of protest, and many of the country's greatest artistic contributions have come as protest in one form or another. Woody Guthrie wrote "This Land Is Your Land" about freedoms not granted, but restricted. Spirituals and blues lamented racial inequality. Rock 'n' roll originated as the voice of an underestimated youth movement. Hip-hop, too, emerged from an overlooked segment of society as an urge to be heard.

The nineteenth century saw the dawning of social movements to demand the abolition of slavery and the end of segregation; equal rights for women, including the right to vote; and overdue safeguards for the working class, from shorter workdays and compensation for injuries sustained on the job to the curtailing of child labor practices.

"Write and sing about it," urged Joshua McCarter Simpson, a freeborn man who composed dozens of antislavery songs. "You can sing what would be death to speak."

The right to protest was ingrained in the American experiment from its very inception. New World colonists demonstrated against the duties imposed on them as English subjects, arguing that they had no voice in Parliament. "No taxation without representation," as the Congregational minister Jonathan Mayhew put it in a sermon in Boston in 1750, coining the phrase that would help spark the American Revolution.

Like many of his fellow Bostonians at the time, Andrew Oliver felt that the British Parliament's Stamp Act of 1765 would be an onerous burden on commerce in the New World. But Oliver, scion of a merchant family, was not one to protest.

As a public official, having served as Boston's town auditor, Oliver dutifully accepted when he was appointed to administer the Stamp Act, which levied taxes on the distribution of newspapers, legal documents, and even playing cards in the colonies. The edict was an unpopular one, to say the least. During the night leading into August 14, 1765, a group of Boston's most vehement Stamp Act opponents hung Oliver in effigy from a sturdy American elm standing at the edge of Boston's South End, near the Boston Common. In the morning, Thomas Hutchinson, the patriarch who would become governor of the province of Massachusetts Bay, called for the removal of the effigy. But a gathering mob guarded the scene around the symbolic meeting point, which they'd named the Liberty Tree.[2]

As the day progressed, the demonstration led to a march through the streets, during which the protesters destroyed a building rumored to be one of the new stamp distribution centers. Then they set upon Oliver's private home, stomping through his garden and ransacking the interior. When Hutchinson tried to intervene, they threw stones. Within days, Oliver had resigned from his post.

That year produced one of the first musical salvos of the colonists' resentment toward the British crown. Written by a Connecticut schoolteacher named Peter St. John, "American Taxation" (sung to the tune of the traditional marching song "The British Grenadiers") accused King George of enacting laws "of the blackest kind."[3] Soon the Boston agitators were promoting a boycott on imported British goods, particularly fabrics. In the popular ballad "To the Ladies," American women were implored to spurn British fashion in favor of "clothes of your own make and spinning." The boycott resulted in an estimated $3 million drop (more than $85 million in today's dollars) in British exports to the colonies in the year 1769.

Around the time the boycott was established, Philadelphia's John Dickinson celebrated the resistance in a poem. Dickinson, later known as the "Penman of the Revolution" for his series of essays "Letters from a Farmer in Pennsylvania," would serve as a delegate to the First Continental Congress. Though he would decline to sign the Declaration of Independence, favoring mediation over open revolution, Dickinson wrote "The Liberty Song" as a rallying cry against submission to England's oppressive legislation: "For shame is to freemen more dreadful than pain."[4] He set his verse to the tune of "Hearts of Oak," a beloved British military song that celebrated the British navy's victorious campaigns overseas. Dickinson's song quickly drew a rejoinder from the Loyalist side, "Parody upon a Well-Known Liberty Song." First printed in the *Boston Gazette*, the satire took aim at the "numskulls" and "pumpkins" who resorted to demonstrating in the streets against the Crown: "All ages shall speak with contempt and amaze/of the vilest banditti that swarmed in these days."[5]

But the protesters were to gather again. Eight years after the first mob action against the Stamp Act, Boston's Sons of Liberty demanded that a prominent tea merchant appear under the Liberty Tree to recuse himself of his contract with the East India Company. The Tea Act of 1773 had granted the merchant's troubled company a virtual monopoly on the tea trade in the North American colonies. "Fail not upon your peril," wrote the protesters in their demand. When the merchant did not show up, the Boston Tea Party began in earnest.

By then, the Liberty Tree was a symbol of the colonists' "glorious cause," their fight for home rule. Occupying British soldiers ridiculed the tree. When they detained an aspiring Minuteman who tried to arrange to buy arms from an undercover British soldier, they tarred and feathered him and carted him to the Liberty Tree. As they marched, a fife and drum corps playing a derisive rendition of "Yankee Doodle."

Finally, in August 1775, a group of British loyalists chopped down the old elm, using the logs for firewood. For years the stump remained, a reminder of the revolution the Sons of Liberty helped incite. In memory of the tree, hundreds of seedlings—the new Liberty Trees—were planted on commons across the colonies. A pine tree flag, often bearing the inscription "An Appeal to Heaven," became a familiar sight during the Revolutionary War.

Thomas Paine, the political philosopher who wrote the pro-independence pamphlet "Common Sense," found the inspiration of the Liberty Tree worthy of his own poem. He published the verse in *Pennsylvania Magazine* during the summer of 1775. (Sometime after the first publication, Paine added a subtitle: "A Song, Written Early in the American Revolution.") Set to a pastoral air, "Liberty Tree" helped spread early word that the revolution was imminent. It eventually became a rallying cry for the American rebels.

From the east to the west blow the trumpet to arms
Through the land let the sound of it flee
Let the far and the near all unite with a cheer
In defense of our Liberty Tree.[6]

Few songs from the time of the Revolutionary War survived much beyond the period. Music itself played a complicated role in everyday life in colonial America; the descendants of the original settlers were often still influenced by the Puritans' disavowal of entertainment in any form. And much of the music that did become familiar to the colonists tended to be based on British ballads. But Paine's verse, like those of St. John and Dickinson, was an early example of the American protest song: an exercise, set to rhyme and melody, of the First Amendment's guarantee "to petition the government for a redress of grievances."

"The duty of youth is to challenge corruption," said the late Kurt Cobain. And not just the young. More than two centuries after the revolutionaries won independence, the folk singer Pete Seeger, then in his late eighties, performed a rendition of Paine's song at the dedication of the New York Liberty Tree at Washington's Headquarters, the Hudson Valley farm where the first president once lived. New York's Liberty Tree was one of thirteen saplings harvested from the oldest surviving Liberty Tree, planted in each of the original thirteen colonies by an environmental conservation group.

"In the largest sense," Seeger once said, "every work of art is protest. . . . A lullaby is a propaganda song, and any three-year-old knows it."

The songs covered in this book—one hundred of them that span a century of petition in the name of social progress—are more eloquent than speech. They were written and performed by artists both popular and unpopular, famous and unknown, commercially successful and unrecorded. Published at a time of notable unrest, just like many others in our collective history, *Which Side Are You On?* will tell the story of modern American democracy, and the music that had the audacity to speak up and take a side.

This book is a selective survey. A hundred songs is a lot of songs, but there were dozens more considered, and still more hundreds that might have been. In focusing on American issues, I have chosen not to include the brilliant protest music of the Clash, Bob Marley, Fela Kuti, or Victor Jara, to name a few of the many omissions some readers may note. Neither should the book be read as a comprehensive history of the social movements described in each chapter. These are introductions only.

The lessons handed down from the major social movements of the twentieth century—from organized labor, civil rights, women's liberation, opposition to war—have left a proliferation of causes that sometimes feels too multifarious, too factionalized, for any kind of meaningful gain. There are many distinct definitions of feminism, for instance; those who identify as environmentalists range from organic consumers to ecoterrorists; various groups call themselves libertarians, socialists, anti-globalists, anarchists. "At times," writes the longtime activist and journalist L. A. Kauffman, "it can seem like the number of recent radicalisms stands in inverse proportion to their overall influence."[7]

The 1960s were a heyday of protest against which all future dissenting voices would be measured. Every new cause for demonstration in recent years, be it climate change, police brutality, or a legislative assault on the social safety net, has invited questions about the supposed scarcity of modern protest songs. In fact, however, protest music thrives. In February 2017, two weeks after the presidential inauguration, the chameleonic pop star Lady Gaga appeared during the NFL Super Bowl halftime show in Houston. A year after Beyoncé's halftime performance, which was seen in part as a statement against racial profiling, some critics saw Lady Gaga's performance as refreshingly apolitical. But to those who recognize the legacy of protest song in this country, her opening rendition of Woody Guthrie's "This Land Is Your Land," paired with Irving Berlin's "God Bless America," suggested otherwise.

WHICH SIDE ARE YOU ON?

War protesters, c. 1940.

1 NONVIOLENCE

I-Feel-Like-I'm-Fixin'-to-Die Rag – Handsome Johnny – With God on Our Side – I Ain't Marching Anymore – Three-Five-Zero-Zero – Kill for Peace – The Strange Death of John Doe – Waist Deep in the Big Muddy – I Didn't Raise My Boy to Be a Soldier – God Bless America

"War is hell," said, among many, William Tecumseh Sherman.

"I am tired and sick of war," he once confessed. "Its glory is all moonshine. It is only those who have neither fired a shot nor heard the shrieks and groans of the wounded who cry aloud for blood, for vengeance, for desolation."

Sherman's Union troops almost surely sang a similar sentiment. "We are tired of war," as one verse begins in "Tenting on the Old Camp Ground," one of the most popular songs to be produced during the war meant "to preserve the Union." Written in 1863 by New Hampshire native Walter Kittredge, the song was conceived, as its composer noted, while he was "soon expecting to go down South to join the boys in blue."[1]

One hundred years after Sherman, the fierce debate across the United States over the purpose of another war—this time the one in Vietnam—felt like its own kind of hell. By the late 1960s there appeared to be no end in sight in the battle against communist influence in Asia, which the adversary was conducting in an unconventional style that bewildered the American generals. Back at home in America, the country convulsed in recrimination and mistrust. What were we fighting for?

One conscientious objector encouraged his peers to raise their own voices in outrage, creating one of the enduring images of politically charged popular music. For the generation of military draft-age young adults who were mobilizing the opposition, the Woodstock Music & Art Fair was a cultural event that came to symbolize a true political awakening. In an early afternoon solo set on muddy farmland in Upstate New York, Country Joe McDonald goaded his vast audience of bleary-eyed listeners, who were just waking up after the first night of the soon-to-be-legendary weekend festival. "Listen, people, I don't know how you expect to ever stop the war if you can't sing it any better than that," he chastised as the crowd half-heartedly sang along. "There's about three hundred thousand of you fuckers out there. I want you to start singing! *Come on*!"

Wearing an unbuttoned, olive drab Army surplus shirt and a bandanna folded into a headband around his long, wavy hair, McDonald coaxed his crowd—young, shirtless men in the midday sun, young women in peasant blouses—to climb to their feet and join in to the bitter satire of his **"I-Feel-Like-I'm-Fixin'-to-Die Rag."**

> *Well it's one, two, three, what are we fighting for?*
> *Don't tell me I don't give a damn*
> *Next stop is Vietnam*
> *And it's five, six, seven, open up the pearly gates*
> *Well, there ain't no time to wonder why*
> *Whoopee! We're all gonna die!*

McDonald was the second act on Saturday, the second day of the festival. Early Sunday evening he performed again, this time with his band, and reprised his anti-war "rag."

The defiant tone of the festival had been set when the folk singer Richie Havens inaugurated the weekend's events at five o'clock on Friday afternoon. A familiar presence on the Greenwich Village folk scene, Havens opened his acoustic performance with "Minstrel from Gaul," an original song that alluded to the war with an image of a soldier who "came down from Dien Bien Phu with silence in his eyes." In the last verse, Havens evoked the Ten Commandments ("a man came down from Sinai mountain with words of truth for us all") before concluding that God's lessons had gone unheeded. "When it came to listening," he sang, "we listened little, if at all, if at all."

Havens, who had family roots in the Blackfoot tribe and the British West Indies, was born and raised in Brooklyn. In 1966 he released his debut album, *Mixed Bag*, which included the anti-war song **"Handsome Johnny,"** which he performed near the end of his set at Woodstock. Havens co-wrote the song with the actor Louis Gossett, Jr., then known for his roles on and off Broadway. Each verse imagined an American soldier marching off to war: there's Handsome Johnny marching off to Concord "with a musket in his hand." There he is marching to Gettysburg with a flintlock in his hand.

Our man Johnny goes off to Dunkirk and Korea and Vietnam, and the result, the lyrics imply, is always the same—always tragic. "Hey, what's the use of singing this song/Some of you are not even listening," Havens scolded. But the song did have an effect, as he wrote in his 1999 autobiography, when he performed it on *The Tonight Show* the year before Woodstock. "The live audience was mostly made up of visiting tourists from the Midwest," Havens remembered. "To my surprise, the audience understood perfectly what was being said about the war." When he finished, they stood and applauded.[2]

If Richie Havens took a somber approach to the absurdity of war, Country Joe met that absurdity on its own terms. Joseph Allen McDonald was raised by parents who were Communist Party members in their youth. They'd named their son, who was born in Washington, DC, after Joseph Stalin. McDonald served three years in the US Navy beginning at age seventeen. After his discharge, he made his way from Southern California to Berkeley, where he busked on Telegraph Avenue, amid growing student dissent over the conflict overseas and the Free Speech Movement that was polarizing the nearby UC–Berkeley campus.

Formed out of the irreverent folk music revival that produced the Jim Kweskin Jug Band and the groups that would soon become the Lovin' Spoonful and the Grateful Dead, Country Joe and the Fish evolved in 1965 from McDonald's earlier group, the Instant Action Jug Band, which he'd formed with the guitarist Barry Melton. Besides making music, for a year or two McDonald published an underground paper called *Rag Baby*. His publishing partner, Eugene "ED" Denson, was then a music columnist for the *Berkeley Barb*; he'd cofounded the independent Takoma Records label with guitarist John Fahey.

Denson helped McDonald record an audio version of their publication in the form of a limited-edition, extended-play vinyl recording. The EP *Rag Baby Talking Issue No. 1*, one hundred copies of which were sold in the autumn of 1965, featured two topical songs by a local folk musician named Peter Krug, one of them called "Johnny's Gone to the War." The flip side was pressed with two songs by the group now billed as Country Joe and the Fish. The band name referenced both Stalin's World War II nickname, which McDonald adopted as his own, and a favored expression of another Communist giant, the Chinese leader Mao Zedong, who once referred to revolutionaries as those who "must move amongst the people as the fish swims in the sea."[3]

Those two songs by Country Joe and the Fish included a jab at President Lyndon B. Johnson called "Superbird" and the antiwar ditty—written in a half hour, McDonald has claimed—that he called his "I-Feel-Like-I'm-Fixin'-to-Die

Rag." "Be the first on your block to have your boy come home in a box!" he sang like some sort of deranged huckster, savaging the law-abiding citizens who had yet to come around to the idea that the war in Vietnam was unsupportable.

The band featured a new version of their anti-war broadside—sometimes called the "Fish Cheer" for its invitation to audiences to spell out F-I-S-H—on their second album, which took the song's name as its title. By 1969, the war resistance that had begun in the leftist corners of college campuses had grown into a mass movement. The Woodstock generation would be defined by its scruffy style, its mind-altering substances and the art forms that accompanied those trips, and, most of all, its pacifist, hedonistic activism.

The era produced the most sustained wave of issue-oriented popular music that the recording industry has ever supported. Most famously, Bob Dylan seized the attention of his peers with topical songs that expressed the anxieties of the Cold War and the looming threat of nuclear annihilation, among them "Blowin' in the Wind," "A Hard Rain's a-Gonna Fall," and "Masters of War," all of which appeared on his second album, *The Freewheelin' Bob Dylan*. But it was the young balladeer's **"With God on Our Side,"** the third song on his next release, *The Times They Are a-Changin'*, that seemed to speak directly to the escalating tensions in Vietnam, though Dylan didn't mention the conflict by name.

Like "Handsome Johnny" and Buffy Sainte-Marie's "Universal Soldier," another song (released in 1964) that questioned the motives behind all wars, "With God on Our Side" spans hundreds of years of conflict. Dylan's verses march forward from the extermination campaigns of Native Americans to the Spanish-American War, the Civil War, and more recent times when the country's young men fought "with God on our side."

"You never ask questions when God's on your side," he suggested—before doing just that.

The words fill my head
And fall to the floor
That if God's on our side
He'll stop the next war

The debut of Dylan's song brought about an early instance of the sourcing disputes that would become a familiar part of his legacy. The song borrowed liberally from "The Patriot Game," a contemporary Irish ballad about a deadly

Irish Republican Army raid in the 1950s. The folk singer Dominic Behan, in turn, drew his own melody from older sources, such as the traditional tune "The Merry Month of May."

Whatever the provenance, Dylan's antiwar song was a thing of beauty to Joan Baez, who found it to be the first modern protest song she felt compelled to sing. "It was a song that, as the Quakers say, spoke to Joan's condition," as David Hajdu would write.[4] The two sang it together for the first time at the Monterey Folk Festival in May 1963, marking Dylan's West Coast debut. When Dylan took the stage by himself, the crowd wasn't impressed. Unsure what to make of him, they chatted and laughed through his short set. But when Baez strode up to join him, she urged the audience to listen closely to this young man, who had something to say. By the time they finished singing "With God on Our Side" together, the newcomer was ready to join Baez as an idol of the folk scene.

Twenty years after Dylan renounced his short-lived role as a "protest" folk singer, he added a new verse about the Vietnam War for his occasional live renditions of "With God on Our Side." Just as Country Joe McDonald would demand, Dylan's question is simple and direct: "Can somebody tell me what we're fighting for?"

So many young men died
So many mothers cried
Now I ask the question
Was God on our side?

One of Dylan's most polemical peers, Phil Ochs, who brought a journalist's sensibility to the coffeehouse folk scene, released an album in 1965 named for its title track, **"I Ain't Marching Anymore,"** which quickly became the singer's signature song. "It's always the old who lead us to war, always the young to fall," Ochs sang over his own acoustic guitar accompaniment, picking the strings like a one-man fife and drum corps. His lyrics, too, imagined a universal soldier who represented generations of casualties, from the Battle of New Orleans during the War of 1812 and Custer's last stand in the Battle of Little Bighorn to the world war "that was bound to end all wars"—and the enlistees the US government was sending overseas two decades later. The many songs Ochs ripped from the headlines (in fact, he named his debut album *All the News That's Fit to Sing*) featured themes such as labor struggle, institutional racism, and political apathy. At a time when the Vietnam War was just beginning to intensify, he recorded a song called "The War Is Over," which presented a case for the power of wishful thinking: "The gypsy fortune teller told me that we'd been deceived/You only are what you believe." He chose to believe that the war was, in fact, over.

Still, Ochs continued to agitate through his music. When he performed "I Ain't Marching Anymore" for the throng of protesters gathered outside the Democratic National Convention in Chicago in 1968, scores of young men burned their draft cards. For the rest of his short life, Ochs would consider that moment the highlight of his career.[5]

A few months before the appalling violence that gripped the Democratic National Convention in 1968, the drama that would define the generation gap hit the stage. In April 1968, the rock musical *Hair* (bearing the descriptive subtitle *The American Tribal Love-Rock Musical*) opened at New York City's Biltmore Theater after a short, celebrated run off-Broadway. Among the many memorable songs in the show, several—"Aquarius," "Easy to Be Hard," "Good Morning Starshine"—became major pop hits. *New York Times* critic Clive Barnes was enthusiastic about the show, though he felt compelled to inform his readers that the book featured "frequent approving references . . . to the expanding benefits of drugs." The American flag, while not exactly desecrated, "is used in a manner that not everyone would call respectful," Barnes continued. "Christian ritual also comes in for a bad time, the authors approve enthusiastically of miscegenation, and one enterprising lyric catalogues somewhat arcane sexual practices more familiar to the 'Kama Sutra' than the *New York Times*. So there—you have been warned. Oh yes, they also hand out flowers."[6]

As risque and groundbreaking as it was, *Hair* owed a significant debt to an earlier, less successful show. The off-Broadway musical *Viet Rock* was "the first realized theatrical statement about the Vietnam war and a rare instance of theater confronting issues broader than individual psychology," wrote Michael Smith in the *Village Voice*.[7] Playwright Megan Terry, known as the "mother of American feminist drama," developed her shows through improvisational rehearsals with her actors, who were encouraged to help rework the scripts, often even after the shows had opened. Among the innovations of *Viet Rock*, as the theater historian Scott Miller has noted, were its emphasis on rock music, actors who were encouraged to leave the stage for direct interaction with their audiences, and a heavy reliance on the "cliches" of the mass media.[8] Gerome Ragni, the future co-creator of *Hair*, was one of the principal actors on *Viet Rock* through its performance runs at La MaMa Experimental Theatre Club and the Martinique Theatre. He borrowed many of Terry's ideas for the new show.

Hair's opening date on Broadway was chosen by an astrologer. The good-luck gesture apparently worked: the original show would run for 1,742 performances. One of the many elements that impressed critics was the show's use of actors who were themselves conducting their lives much like the characters in the play: "Instead of finding conventional musical-comedy performers to impersonate hippies," explained a reviewer in the *Saturday Review*, director Tom O'Horgan "has encouraged a bunch of mainly hippie performers inventively to explore their own natures with songs and dance."[9]

In Act II, the members of the "tribe" address their generation's distress over the war against the Viet Cong in the experimental song **"Three-Five-Zero-Zero."** With the title borrowed from a line in Allen Ginsberg's antiwar poem "Wichita Vortex Sutra," the song opens with the kind of searing electric guitar feedback that Jimi Hendrix would play at Woodstock in his distorted instrumental version of "The Star-Spangled Banner." Ginsberg's poem, inspired during a cross-country bus trip by the disorienting, rapid-fire news reports from the front lines of the war, was an attempt to wrest the power of words from the government's public relations machine. Several phrases—"Ripped open by metal explosion/Caught in barbed wire"— were transposed verbatim into the musical. The song, written by show co-creators Jerry Ragni and James Rado (with music by Galt MacDermot), toggles between a funereal recitation and an incongruous kind of halle-lujah chorus that highlights the folly of war. Ginsberg attributed the figure "Three-Five-Zero-Zero" to the calculations of General Maxwell D. Taylor, one of President Johnson's advisers:

> *Viet Cong losses leveling up three five zero zero per month*
> *Front page testimony February '66*
> *Here in Nebraska same as Kansas same known in Saigon*
> *in Peking, in Moscow, same known*
> *by the youths of Liverpool three five zero zero*
> *the latest quotation in the human meat market . . .*[10]

Hair was nominated for a Tony Award as the year's best musical, and the show's original cast recording won a Grammy for Best Score from an Original Cast Show Album, selling three million copies in the process. The 5th Dimension's medley version of "Aquarius/Let the Sunshine In (The Flesh Failures)" would become the number one song of 1969. On the surface a celebration of the Aquarian generation, "Let the Sunshine In" was, on a deeper level, a desperate plea for tolerance and compassion. The song's sheer exuberance sometimes masked its anguish. "Everyone always portrays it as a happy song," argues Miller, artistic director of the alternative New Line Theatre in St. Louis. In fact, he believes, the characters are "begging the audience to let the sunshine in. They're saying please, please, get rid of the darkness. Realizing that changed the show for me."

Allen Ginsberg was also an inspiration for the Fugs, the irreverent East Village band that inflicted "total assault on the culture," as the writer William S. Burroughs once described. Formed by the poets Ed Sanders and Tuli Kupferberg with drummer Ken Weaver, the Fugs took their name from the euphemism coined by Norman Mailer in his debut war novel, *The Naked and the Dead*. At the Sing-In for Peace, an all-star concert that took place at Carnegie Hall in September 1965, the Fugs subverted the solemnity that Joan Baez, Phil Ochs, civil rights activist Fannie Lou Hamer, and dozens of others brought to the program, performing their song **"Kill for Peace,"** a wicked satire of the human instinct to wage war. They left the stage, Sanders claimed, to "thunderous applause."

The Sing-In for Peace was organized by Irwin Silber, editor of *Sing Out!*, the quarterly bible of the folk scene, and the folk and jazz singer Barbara Dane. After the two-part program ended around 3 A.M., several hundred participants marched from Carnegie Hall to the Village Gate nightclub, where they continued to sing until dawn. While the concert received little media coverage due to a New York City newspaper strike, it did achieve the organizers' goal, which was to raise enough money to fund newspaper advertisements condemning the war. "American boys are dying today in Vietnam in a brutal, senseless war," read the open letter, which ran several months later in the *New York Times* and the *San Francisco Chronicle*. "Their deaths constitute a national tragedy."[11]

In February 1967, Ed Sanders appeared on the cover of *Life* magazine, representing the emerging "worldwide underground," which the publication called the "Other Culture." He was invited to make a guest appearance on Johnny Carson's *Tonight Show*, but the invitation was rescinded when Sanders insisted the Fugs be allowed to sing "Kill for Peace" on the air.

It would take *The Smothers Brothers Comedy Hour* to bring the antiwar spirit of the counterculture to prime-time television. The comic folk-singing duo Tom and Dick Smothers were raised by their mother in Southern California following the death of their father, an army officer who was captured by the Japanese during World War II. They were already familiar faces on network TV by the time they were awarded their CBS variety series, which debuted in February 1967. Their show, designed to attract a younger audience, launched the careers of an impressive list of writers and comic actors, including Steve Martin, Rob Reiner, and Albert Brooks.

The Smothers Brothers also showcased a wide variety of musical guests, among them Baez, the Doors, Buffalo Springfield, and Harry Belafonte. For their second season premiere in September 1967, the cohosts welcomed Pete Seeger, who had not been invited on network television since the earliest days of the medium. A target in the early 1950s of the House Committee on Un-American Activities, led by Senator Joe McCarthy, Seeger had spent the prime of his career rallying grass-roots audiences on behalf of social justice. With the Almanac Singers, alongside cofounders Woody Guthrie, Lee Hays, and Millard Lampell, Seeger recorded a 1941 antiwar album, *Songs for John Doe*, that reportedly raised the ire of President Roosevelt. That album produced "**The Strange Death of John Doe**," an antiwar ballad about a strong, healthy young man who dies suddenly one day, leaving just one clue—"a bayonet sticking in his side." Though the Almanacs' pacifist message had a powerful impact ("The Strange Death of John Doe," Hays wrote, "produced the most startling effect on audiences I have ever seen"), it was rendered obsolete as the American public grew to understand the inevitability of World War II. "Well, I guess we're not going to be singing any more of them peace songs," Guthrie remarked.[12] With his later group the Weavers, Seeger helped popularize another lasting antiwar song, "Last Night I Had the Strangest Dream."

> *Last night I had the strangest dream*
> *I'd never dreamed before*
> *I dreamed the world had all agreed*
> *To put an end to war*

Written in 1950 by folk singer Ed McCurdy, the song would become a worldwide call for peace, recorded in dozens of languages. (When the Berlin Wall came down in 1989, East German schoolchildren were seen on American newscasts singing the song at the demolition.)

Arriving on the set of *The Smothers Brothers Comedy Hour*, Seeger had recently written a new antiwar song called "**Waist Deep in the Big Muddy**." Inspired by a newspaper photograph of several soldiers wading across a river, the song imagined an army platoon on a training mission in the swamps of Louisiana, pushing on through the swelling water until a captain drowns. Each verse concluded with the narrating soldier recalling the captain's ill-fated admonishment: "The big fool says to push on." Before Seeger recorded it, he'd given the song the working title "General Fathead."[13]

The lyrics were inspired in part by a 1956 tragedy known as the River Creek incident, in which a Marine Corps drill sergeant stationed at Parris Island in South Carolina instructed his men to cross a tidal creek. Six recruits were killed. But Seeger acknowledged that his intent in writing the song was not so much historical as it was "an allegory, and a very obvious one."[14] Just as the soldiers in his tale were unaware of the fact that the river they were crossing would grow more treacherous, Seeger suggested that the war in Vietnam held more unforeseen danger to come than the "big fool"—President Johnson— was willing to admit.

Never a major commercial artist, the prolific Seeger hoped this topical song might find a broad audience. "Oh, don't I wish it would sell a million," he wrote in *Sing Out!*, which he'd cofounded. But despite the enthusiastic response of his live audiences, the song went nowhere, commercially speaking. He'd been dropped by Columbia Records in 1965, then reinstated at the strong urging of John Hammond, the legendary producer. Briefly, he'd allowed himself high hopes for a hit record. But when a distributor from Denver told him the single never left the shelves there, Seeger realized that his record label had no interest in promoting the song.

Regardless of its failure to sell, by the time of his appearance on *The Smothers Brothers Comedy Hour* in late 1967, the song had drawn plenty of attention. Seeger, already reviled by certain Americans as "Khrushchev's songbird," played it during a visit to Moscow, prompting the *New York Times* to complain that he'd sung an "anti-American" song in the USSR. When he was criticized by some in the folk community for accepting the CBS gig, he responded sharply: "I think all of us who love music and love America and the world must figure out how we are going to take the next steps. Unless we prefer to get off in a corner by ourselves and congratulate each other on our exclusiveness."

Relishing the opportunity to promote the song before such a big mainstream audience—"I probably reached seven million people all at once," he later enthused—he was infuriated when his performance of "Big Muddy," one of two songs he'd taped, was cut from the broadcast. Afterward, the singer bit his tongue as he thanked CBS for facilitating his return to commercial broadcasting, but he expressed concern about the network's fear of his politics. "I think the public should know that their airwaves are censored for ideas as well as for sex," he said.

Newspapers played up the dispute. "Is the presidency so teetery that it cannot withstand the musical barbs of a folk singer?" asked one.[15] Ultimately, the network gave in. On a return visit to the show in February 1968, Seeger sang a medley of historic American war songs that concluded with "Waist Deep in the Big Muddy." Opening by whistling a bit of "Yankee Doodle Dandy" ("a pop song of two hundred years ago"), Seeger pointed out that each American war had its detractors, just like the present one in Vietnam. Abe Lincoln voted against the Mexican-American War, he noted; Mark Twain thought President McKinley should be "boiled in oil" over the Spanish-American War. "1863—well, wasn't in agreement here, neither," he said in his folksy speaking style before citing the first verse of "John Brown's Body."

A few weeks later, LBJ's presumed lock on a second full term as president eroded when Senator Eugene McCarthy of Minnesota made a strong showing in the New Hampshire Democratic primary, drawing 42 percent of the vote. Sensing deepening divides in the Democratic Party, Bobby Kennedy quickly joined the race. On March 31, Johnson stunned the nation when he declared his decision to step down from the office and forgo a potential second term.

By 1968, folk music was a familiar part of the American mainstream. To some northern sophisticates, however, the bent notes and drawling vocals of country and western were the sounds of unblinking patriotism and narrow small-town values. Yet a generation committed to critical thinking increasingly saw the dominance of government and industry leading to an artificial lifestyle. Roots music, by contrast—folk and country alike—represented a pure, authentic American art form. Dylan, leading the way, recorded his classic 1966 album *Blonde on Blonde* with Nashville session musicians. In August 1968, the California rock band the Byrds, who'd had several hits with chiming versions of Dylan songs, released their sixth album, *Sweetheart of the Rodeo*, which marked a dramatic shift from psychedelic rock to songs inspired by the folklore of Woody Guthrie and the high harmonies of the Louvin Brothers.

In Cleveland, meanwhile, four young rock 'n' rollers were testing their own ragged ideas about a new kind of country-flavored rock music. "We struggled for months searching for ways to put rock grooves under country, or country-blues, material, blending traditional country and western with rock 'n' roll roots," as the band's bassist, Danny Sheridan, would recall.[16] "If we'd had the sense to call it 'country rock,' we would be legends by now." Instead, they gave their unusual music the ungainly name "country acid."

One night Sheridan received an unexpected phone call from a Capitol Records promotions man who knew the Cleveland music scene well: Roger Karshner had a million-selling single in 1966 called "Time Won't Let Me" with a local garage band called the Outsiders. Karshner had an idea. He'd been collecting topical sheet music from the two World Wars, and he wanted the Eli Radish Band, as Sheridan's group billed itself, to record some of the songs in a concept album aimed at the new generation. "He said, 'I want to put this to country music and have you maniacs play it,'" Sheridan remembered.

The album was titled after "I Didn't Raise My Boy to Be a Soldier," a popular song from 1915. Other tracks on the release included a satirical rendition of "Praise the Lord and Pass the Ammunition," a 1942 wartime tune written by Frank Loesser, the songwriter behind the Broadway smash *Guys and Dolls*, which had been recorded in several hit versions; a similarly sardonic take on George M. Cohan's flag-waving anthem "Over There"; and a cover of "The Ballad of the Green Berets," the maudlin 1966 hit (one of the rare pro-military popular songs of the 1960s) sung by an actual Green Beret, Staff Sergeant Barry Sadler. Appealing to an irreverent audience, Eli Radish intentionally cut much of the album "off-beat and out of tune," according to Sheridan. Though there'd been some precedent for music that sounded "wrong" in the freewheeling Sixties—bands such as the Fugs and Frank Zappa's Mothers of Invention had already tested their listeners' resolve with purposeful atonality—neither the Capitol Records team nor the record-buying public proved especially fond of the experiment.

Still, the Eli Radish Band met with modest success on the stages of its hometown and as an opening act on tour with the Doors, the Who, and other big-name groups. Along with Sheridan, guitarist Tom Foster and drummer Skip Heil backed the singer Kenny Frak, who earned the nickname "The Rev" for his habit of proselytizing about the war, among other topics. At one point, the band headlined a benefit concert for one of Frak's former schoolmates, an all-American boy who'd gone off to the war in Vietnam and come back missing three limbs. In Cleveland, after their album came out, the band hosted a benefit for the radical activist Angela Davis, who was on trial for her alleged involvement in the supply of firearms in a notorious courtroom kidnapping case. "I'm sure we ended up on some kind of FBI list" for their role in the fundraiser, says Frak, who went on from his brief rock 'n' roll life to become a churchgoing insurance man, raising four children in his Ohio hometown.

The song "I Didn't Raise My Boy to Be a Soldier" had been recorded first more than a half-century earlier, in April 1915. As controversial as the Vietnam War would be, as Pete Seeger would point out, the American public actually "wasn't in agreement" on most of the country's previous wars, either.

Decades before Vietnam, the campaign for pacifism achieved a kind of critical mass in the late nineteenth century. In fact, various groups had long advocated conflict resolution and the abolition of warfare. The Quakers, for instance, had emerged in reaction to the English Civil War that began in 1642.

They refused to bear arms, declaring themselves opposed to war of all kinds. "All bloody principles and practices we do utterly deny, with all outward wars, and strife, and fightings with outward weapons, for any end, or under any preten[s]e whatsoever," declared George Fox, founder of the Religious Society of Friends, and his colleagues in 1660, "and this our testimony to the whole world."

The inaugural Universal Peace Conference in Paris, which took place in 1889, was the first in what would become a long series of summit meetings in London, Rome, Chicago, and other major cities across the globe. In America, the First International Conference of American States took place in Washington, DC in January 1890. Nine years later, the organization of the Hague Convention of 1899 marked the first time in history in which multiple nations entered a series of agreements to define the rules of war.

In 1914 the United Kingdom declared war on Germany in defense of neutral Belgium. In response to England's declaration of war, many young British men began identifying themselves as conscientious objectors. They typically cited either religious beliefs, such as the Quakers' refusal to bear arms, or their Marxist opposition to the capitalist system, which, they believed, stoked aggression. While the British government established a mandatory draft in 1916, it also recognized the principle of conscientious objection. The government offered to assign young men who expressed such views to non-combat positions. Of those who continued to resist, an estimated six thousand were imprisoned. Those men were said to have filled the stone walls of England's prisons with their voices, singing Christian hymns and socialist protest songs.

America, meanwhile, heard a growing isolationist chorus of its own. Roughly 20 percent of the country's population at the time were descended from German immigrants. Another 20 percent were of Irish heritage, who were closely following the Irish campaign for independence from England and in no mood to ally with Great Britain.[17] While the United States debated whether or not to enter the war in Europe, President Woodrow Wilson hosted at least twenty meetings in the White House with peace activists. The industrialist Henry Ford, recruited to the isolationist cause, chartered an ocean liner in a scheme designed to bring American pacifists to the theater of war in Europe. Dubbed the "Peace Ship," Ford's cruise was intended to convince the soldiers already in the fight to throw down their arms. He planned, he said, to "get the boys out of the trenches by Christmas." But the voyage was disorganized and ill-fated from the start. Ford's invitations to Thomas Edison, Helen Keller, William Jennings Bryan, and others were all declined.

Then, five days into Ford's trip, President Wilson changed his tune on the "preparedness movement"—a call, led in part by the former President

Theodore Roosevelt, to train reserve officers and bolster the military in anticipation of the United States' intervention. Wilson had been an advocate of neutrality, but now, with Ford's ship full of pacifists churning across the Atlantic, the president signaled his intention to prepare the US military for the possibility of war. Upon arrival in Norway, Ford abandoned his widely ridiculed peace project, quickly boarding another ocean liner for the return trip to America. He did, however, continue to fund his peace advocates, who managed to arrange a handful of insignificant meetings with European diplomats during their stay abroad.

Back at home in America, the newly established Women's Peace Party had recently named Jane Addams its national chairwoman. Formed in part from the prominent role of women in the American Union against Militarism (AUAM), in its inaugural year the Women's Peace Party sent a delegation by ocean liner to the first International Congress of Women at the Hague, several months before Ford's "Peace Ship." Addams, who would later become the first American woman to win the Nobel Peace Prize, was a social reformer and a leading suffragist who had declared herself a pacifist after the Spanish-American War of 1898. In 1907 she published *Newer Ideals of Peace*, in which she called for social justice and a total end to war. Addams, who died at age seventy-four in 1935, left behind a long shadow of influence that includes the model for today's social work industry and the cofounding, in 1920, of the American Civil Liberties Union.

"America's future will be determined by the home and the school," Addams once wrote. "The child becomes largely what he is taught; hence we must watch what we teach, and how we live." By some accounts, her unshakeable belief in the power of women to use their maternal instincts for good was a direct inspiration on the two men behind "I Didn't Raise My Boy to Be a Soldier."

With lyrics by Alfred Bryan and music by Al Piantadosi, the song captured the country's mood at the outset of the Great War, when a majority of Americans agreed that the United States should remain neutral.

> *Ten million soldiers to the war have gone*
> *Who may never return again.*
> *Ten million mothers' hearts must break*
> *For the ones who died in vain.*

The songwriter Bryan, born in Brantford, Ontario, in 1871, had already toiled for twenty years in New York City before scoring his first big hit, "Come

Josephine in My Flying Machine." Inspired by the first female parachute jumper in America, Josephine Sarah Magner, it became a number one hit for Ada Jones with Billy Murray and the American Quartet in March of 1911. Bryan's song, set to music by Fred Fisher (later to be a fellow inductee to the Songwriters Hall of Fame), became a signature song for the Broadway star Blanche Ring. It would be parodied by Spike Jones and His City Slickers in the 1940s and revived in scenes from the blockbuster 1997 film *Titanic*.

Bryan and Fisher went on to write several more hits together, including "Peg O' My Heart," recorded by Guy Lombardo and Glenn Miller, among others. But Bryan's most successful collaboration may have been with the Tin Pan Alley composer Piantadosi. Together they wrote "I Didn't Raise My Boy to Be a Soldier," which became one of the most popular songs of 1915— and the most controversial. For one thing, Piantadosi's melody borrowed indiscreetly from an earlier song called "You Will Never Know How Much I Really Cared." Though the credit was never changed, the authors of that song eventually earned a notable settlement from the music publisher Leo Feist.

But "I Didn't Raise My Boy to Be a Soldier" was controversial for another reason. The former president Theodore Roosevelt, a vocal supporter of the Preparedness Movement and US intervention in the European conflict, was one of the song's louder detractors, of which there were plenty. He scoffed that Bryan's antiwar lyric might inspire a companion song called "I Didn't Raise My Girl to Be a Mother." (In fact, a few legitimate songwriters did write parodies of "I Didn't Raise My Boy to Be a Soldier," including "I Didn't Raise My Boy to Be a Coward" and "I Didn't Raise My Boy to Be a Slacker.") Women who opposed US involvement in the war belonged "in China," suggested the Rough Rider, "or by preference in a harem." The song had few fans in England, where the British, already battling the Germans, were angered by Washington's reluctance to join the fray. According to a report in an August 1915 issue of the *Literary Digest* newsmagazine, the Brits wondered "how America can be so sunk in pacifist conviction as to elevate such a ditty as 'I didn't raise my boy to be a soldier!' into a song of nationwide popularity."

An item in the *Daily Mail* of London suggested that Bryan's song represented "a force of American opinion such as has never yet in any country been devoted to the cause of peace"—peace, the writer added, "at any price, peace regardless of justice and national dignity and rights." While admitting that it was a catchy tune, the London *Spectator* complained that if pacifism "as enshrined in the popular verse of the moment" prevailed, "the bitter awakening will be only postponed. It is bound to come some time. Perhaps the blow will come from Germany. Perhaps it will come from Japan. Come it will, if the United States asks for it by a policy of impotence."

The songwriter Bryan, it seems, was a pacifist only inasmuch as he recognized the commercial potential of an antiwar song for the American market at a time when isolationist sentiment ran high. After Wilson won re-election in 1916, campaigning on the popular slogan "He Kept Us Out of War," the president recanted. The German torpedo that sunk the British ocean liner *Lusitania* in May 1915—the ship's 1,100 passengers included 128 Americans—effectively sank the nonintervention movement in the United States. The president would have no choice but to view another such attack as "deliberately unfriendly," he warned the Germans. German submarine attacks on US merchant ships in early 1917, combined with reports of the so-called Zimmermann telegram, in which Germany's foreign minister attempted to entice Mexico into the war by offering the country parts of United States territory, completed the reversal in US public opinion about the Great War. One month after the contents of the decrypted Zimmermann telegram were revealed, the US Congress declared war on Germany and its Quadruple Alliance (Austria-Hungary, Bulgaria, and the Ottoman Empire). "The world must be made safe for democracy," Wilson said as he asked Congress to de-clare war. Bryan joined the cause, writing the lyrics to a song called "It's Time for Every Boy to Be a Soldier."

By the time the United States declared war on Germany in 1917, there was little tolerance left for explicit antiwar songs. Al Jolson, the "World's Greatest Entertainer," had scored a melodramatic hit the previous year with "War Babies" ("Little war babies, our hearts ache for you/Where will you go to, and what will you do?"). But that was not so much an antiwar song as an emotional ballad.

One popular music-hall song of 1917, though—"Oh! It's a Lovely War!," by J. P. Long and M. Scott—became a favorite of soldiers headed to the front lines. They embraced it as a sing-along drenched in sarcasm:

> *Up to your waist in water, up to your eyes in slush*
> *Using the kind of language that makes the sergeant blush—*
> *Oh, who wouldn't join the army?*

To modern ears, the song sounds like the kind of farcical marching band music of a classic skit from the British sketch-comedy troupe Monty Python.

The Tin Pan Alley giant Irving Berlin wrote his own absurd antiwar song, "Stay Down Here Where You Belong." The song presented a clever scenario in which the Devil himself appeals to his son not to go up to Earth during wartime, an experience the son thinks might be "fun." "Stay down here where you belong," the devil urges.

> *The folks who live above you don't know right from wrong*
> *To please their king, they've all gone out to war*
> *And not one of them know what he's fighting for*

The song, not one of Berlin's favorites, was recorded in 1915 by Henry Burr, the prolific Canadian tenor who frequently collaborated with the Peerless Quartet, the act that had the biggest hit with "I Didn't Raise My Boy to Be a Soldier." Years after writing "Stay Down Here Where You Belong," Berlin would bicker with his friend Groucho Marx, the comedian, over the tune: "Any time he sees me, when I am trying to pose as a pretty good songwriter, he squares off and sings it," Berlin would write. "I've asked him how much money he will take not to do this but so far he will not be bribed."[18]

Berlin, of course, went on to great fame as the composer of a long string of songbook standards, including "White Christmas," "There's No Business Like Show Business," and **"God Bless America."** He originally wrote the latter in 1918 while stationed as an army recruit at Camp Upton in Yaphank, New York. The song was intended for a revue called *Yip Yip Yaphank*, which eventually featured several numbers (including a tongue-in-cheek soldier's song called "Oh, How I Hate to Get Up in the Morning"). But the show did not include "God Bless America."

Twenty years later, with the Nazi threat looming large overseas, the composer went to "the trunk," his collection of scraps of song ideas. Digging out his notes for "God Bless America," he envisioned it as the patriotic song the country needed. "I'd like to write a great peace song, but it's hard to do," he told an interviewer. Peace, he said, was hard to dramatize. After false starts with songs with working titles such as "Thanks America" and "Let's Talk about Liberty," Berlin remembered his song for the army play.

He made a few changes. The line "Stand beside her, and guide her, through the night with a light from above," for instance, had been phrased originally as "... *to the right* with a light from above." Back in 1918, Berlin noted, the idea of a political "right" had not yet been adapted widely in America. By the 1930s, however, the lyricist felt compelled to avoid any suggestion of a political "right," or, for that matter, a left.

The singer Kate Smith first sang Berlin's "new," twenty-year-old song in a radio broadcast on Armistice Day, 1938. The commemoration marked the twentieth anniversary of the treaty signed at the "eleventh hour of the eleventh day of the eleventh month" between the Allied nations and Germany, which brought about the cessation of hostilities along the Western Front and the beginning of the end of the Great War. (The Treaty of Versailles, which ended the state of war between Germany and the Allied powers, was not in fact signed until June 28, 1919.)

Smith already had been hosting her annual Armistice Day tribute for nearly a decade. But with reports from Europe growing more ominous by the day, in 1938 she was looking for something that would distinguish that year's program. She wanted to sing "a new hymn of praise and love and allegiance to America." The song Berlin came up with was "his masterpiece," she told her radio audience. "When I first tried it over, I felt, here is a song that will be timeless—it will never die—others will thrill to its beauty long after we are gone."[19]

Known as the "First Lady of Radio," the zaftig singer was already an American sweetheart, having hosted a series of nationally syndicated radio programs. Her rendition of Berlin's patriotic song—and it was her rendition; though he'd conceived it as a love song, a ballad, she made it a march—was an instant sensation. Both political parties quickly adopted "God Bless America" as a theme song. Organizers of sporting events, both professional and amateur, soon began featuring the song in a tradition that endures today. A call arose (though both Berlin and Smith were opposed to it) to replace "The Star-Spangled Banner" as the official national anthem. And, as part of the country's growing anti-German sentiment, the Hay Fever Sufferers' Society of America suggested a change of another sort, dismissing the traditional wish for good health offered to someone who sneezes—"Gesundheit!"—in favor of saying "God bless."[20]

But Berlin's anthem was not without its denigrators. Woody Guthrie, for one, was repulsed by what he felt was the song's simplistic jingoism. The itinerant Oklahoman had known poverty, joblessness, and despair during the Great Depression, and he resented the song's blind devotion to a nation in desperate need, he felt, of reforms.

After finding his bearings in the entertainment world as a Los Angeles radio personality in the late 1930s, Guthrie was squeezed off the air for his socialist leanings. In 1940 he traveled to New York City to reunite with his friend, the actor Will Geer, who was then performing on Broadway in the long-running theatrical version of Erskine Caldwell's tenant-farming novel

Tobacco Road. While staying in a hotel at 43rd Street and Sixth Avenue, Guthrie wrote an acerbic rejoinder to Berlin's song. He borrowed the melody outright from "When the World's on Fire," an apocalyptic tune from the Carter Family, the first family of country music. They in turn had adapted the song from "Rock of Ages," a traditional hymn reworked as a folk-blues gospel song by the elusive recording artist Blind Willie Davis. Eventually known as "This Land Is Your Land," Guthrie's song bore a working title that was intended as heavy sarcasm: "God Blessed America for Me."

Guthrie did not record his song until 1944, in an unreleased version during a recording session with Moe Asch, the legendary proprietor of the heritage label that would become Folkways. Guthrie's original lyrics included verses that have long been overlooked. Taking a contrarian's position against capitalism ("Was a high wall there that tried to stop me/A sign was painted, said 'Private Property'") and organized religion, the sullen "lost" verses remain unfamiliar to many listeners.

> *One bright sunny morning in the shadow of the steeple*
> *By the Relief Office, I saw my people*
> *As they stood hungry, I stood there wondering if*
> *This land was made for you and me*

Berlin, who wrote "God Bless America" from his own personal experience as a successful American immigrant, wrote not long after the song was popularized that "no political party has the exclusive rights" to the song. It has been sung by workers on strike and citizens demonstrating for their civil rights. But it also took on a conservative tone during the counterculture years of the Vietnam War. At a peace rally at New York's Town Hall in 1966, a police detective was roundly booed when he seized a microphone and attempted to drown out the proceedings by singing the song. Richard Nixon often quoted from the song during his presidency, and he occasionally performed it in public, accompanying himself on the piano. Pro-military construction workers facing off against protesters flashing peace signs used the song as a "sonic weapon" against the hippies, writes Sheryl Kaskowitz.[21]

"God Bless America" also played a key role in an early episode of the sitcom *All in the Family*, which satirized the culture clash between a World War II–generation traditionalist and his radical son-in-law. In a flashback during the second season of Norman Lear's classic show, the principal characters recall their introduction. In the Bunker family living room, the antiwar activist Michael Stivic (played by Rob Reiner) argues with his future father-in-law,

Archie Bunker (played by Carroll O'Connor), about a newspaper article detailing the arrest of two hundred Vietnam War protesters—"peaceniks," as Archie belittles them. When Mike attempts to defend the protesters, Archie calls him the derogatory name that would make the character famous.

"Oh, yeah, now I see what your idea of a free country is," Mike says. "You're free to say anything you want, but if anyone disagrees with you, they're either thrown into jail or called a 'meathead,' right?"

As Mike continues to argue, Archie begins to recite the lyrics to Berlin's anthem. He rises from his chair, drowning out his daughter's increasingly agitated boyfriend with the songwriter's patriotic words: "From the mountains, to the prairies, to the oceans white with foam." Though the program's themes were plucked from the headlines of its day, it remains a timeless television moment. In the unending debate about the morality of war, both sides have historically resorted to song. Whatever the answers, the question endures: "What are we fighting for?"

Industrial Workers of the World rally, Union Square, New York City, April 11, 1914.
Credit: Library of Congress, Prints & Photographs Division, George Grantham Bain Collection.
http://www.loc.gov/pictures/resource/ggbain.15713/

2 WORKERS UNITE

Which Side Are You On – Joe Hill – The Preacher and the Slave – Bread and Roses – I Am a Girl of Constant Sorrow – I Don't Want Your Millions, Mister – I Hate the Capitalist System – Dark as a Dungeon – Sixteen Tons – They'll Never Keep Us Down

The Nobel laureate Desmond Tutu once remarked that neutrality favors only the powerful. "If an elephant has its tail on the foot of a mouse, and you say that you are neutral, the mouse will not appreciate your neutrality."[1]

The long tradition of the protest song in America has some of its deepest roots in the fight for the rights of the working class. Better pay and shorter workdays, medical and retirement benefits, safeguards against workplace injuries, the abolition of child labor: all these ideals were seen as moral imperatives for the collective good. Throughout most of the country's history, workers have organized to persuade the elephant to lift its foot. And the labor songs they sang were often the only way to get the beast's attention.

There was no "neutral" in Harlan County, Kentucky, a region modest in population but rich in coal. By the beginning of the Great Depression, a surplus of coal, competition from other fuel sources, and the nation's economic woes combined to throttle the coal industry. When mine operators reduced the already dismal salaries of their employees in Harlan, the workers, as had so many before them, went out on strike. The company enforcers sent to rough up the strikers weren't prepared for their tenacity, and the county soon became known as "Bloody Harlan."

Sam Reece was one of the strike leaders targeted by the company men. When they came looking for him, he was not at home, leaving his wife, Florence, and their seven children to stand by helplessly as the raiders looted their house. Incensed, Mrs. Reece tore a calendar off the wall and wrote the song **"Which Side Are You On?"** She called out the sheriff hired by the mining company, J. H.

Blair, by name: "You go to Harlan County/There is no neutral there/You'll either be a union man or a thug for J. H. Blair."

For the people of Harlan County, choosing sides was no playground game. With the arrival of the National Miners Union, an offshoot of the American Communist Party, many locals were reluctant to join the union cause. But Reece's song—set to the tune of the Baptist hymn "Lay the Lily Low" and the traditional British folk song, "Jack Monroe," which borrows from the hymn—made it emphatically clear that any miner's family attempting to stay out of the fray was in fact aiding the men who owned the coal companies. More than forty years after the Harlan County Wars, when a new generation of miners was fighting the Eastover Mining Company's Brookside Mine and Prep Plant, an elderly Florence Reece sang her song in support of another strike.

Nearly a century after Reece dashed off her song, its simple demand has become a common refrain during disputes of all sorts. In a letter to the *Boston Globe* in late 2016, one reader took issue with the call for unity after a divisive presidential election. Two articles about conflict resolution "say we need to listen and pay attention to each other," the writer noted.

"I have a different response, which poses another question: 'Which side are you on?'

"Are you on the side of those whose actions threaten the future of our planet by denying the science of climate change?

"Are you on the side of those who normalize and trivialize sexual assault?

"Are you on the side of those who encourage bigotry toward Muslims or Jews?

"Are you on the side of those who refuse to accept that Black Lives Matter?

"Are you on the side of those who don't believe in public education or a living wage or a woman's right to choose?

"Are you one of those who excuses everything above because you 'want change' or 'feel forgotten'?

"I don't want to listen to these excuses. My heart is not open to them.

"A line needs to be drawn, and people have to decide which side they are on."[2]

Earl Robinson was an aspiring young composer from Seattle when he took a job on a cruise ship in 1934, performing popular songs for the passengers. On a voyage to several Asian cities, he found politics during a visit to the American consulate in Shanghai, "located behind a wall twenty feet high," as he wrote in his 1997 autobiography. "There, in this city of eight million Chinese, I actually saw a sign posted: 'No Chinamen or dogs allowed.'"[3]

For Robinson, this was an epiphany. Once he was back in the United States, he joined the socialist cause. Growing since the end of the first World War, and as the Great Depression slogged on, socialism was considered by some members of both the intellectual and working classes to be a viable alternative to capitalism.

Over the summer of 1936, Robinson served as musical coordinator at Camp Unity, an interracial summer retreat in Wingdale, New York, about sixty miles from Manhattan. The left-leaning camp featured political discussions by day and nightly performances that included such rising figures as the singer Paul Robeson and the jazz trumpeter Dizzy Gillespie. Though Robinson was classically trained, he had a knack for arranging simple folk songs that all the campers could sing together. One of the songs he produced that summer was inspired by a poem that had been published in the *New Masses*, then the preeminent magazine of the political left. Written by the screenwriter Alfred Hayes, **"Joe Hill"** recalled the narrator's dream of an encounter with the late labor activist of that name:

> *I dreamed I saw Joe Hill last night, alive as you and me*
> *Says I, "But Joe, you're ten years dead."*
> *"I never died," says he.*
> *"I never died," says he.*

Robinson's musical setting of the poem soon became a phenomenon. By the 1930s, the real Joe Hill was a martyred icon of the labor movement. The activist, a songwriter for the Industrial Workers of the World (IWW), had been shot to death in 1915 by a firing squad in Utah for his conviction in the shooting death of a storekeeper and his son. To this day, many supporters believe that Hill was an innocent victim of the state's vindictive reaction to a strike by copper miners, which Hill helped organize.

Born Joel Hagglund in Sweden in 1879, in America the immigrant adopted the name Joe Hill. He moved to the United States at age twenty-two, following the death of his mother; his father had been killed in an industrial accident when the boy was eight. Making his way as an itinerant worker to Spokane, Washington, Hill began writing parodies of Salvation Army hymns for his fellow "Wobblies," as the members of the IWW were known. There was no work to be found in the aftermath of the Bankers' Panic of 1907, when the financial markets collapsed, so Hill and his colleagues commiserated in the union offices. While relying on the union network to find work elsewhere, along the shorelines of San Pedro and San Diego, Hill recalled his youthful obsession with the violin and began writing songs on acoustic guitar. Within a matter of months, he would become the labor movement's favorite songwriter.

Hill earned some of his earliest recognition for **"The Preacher and the Slave,"** a repudiation of the "long-haired preachers" who promised an afterlife for starving workers with "pie in the sky." (It was Hill who coined the phrase.) The 1912 edition of the IWW's *Little Red Songbook*, the annual guide to the protest songs unionized workers were encouraged to sing in solidarity during demonstrations, featured four songs by Hill, including "Casey Jones—the Union Scab" and "Coffee An'." The latter song, set to the tune of a familiar gospel hymn, bitterly condemned the meager meals available to unemployed workers, sometimes no more than coffee and donuts. Hill's songs made up ten of the twelve in the 1913 *Songbook*, including "There Is Power in a Union"; "Mr. Block," a satire of a "common worker" who was no more than a disposable tool of production, set to the tune of a popular 1908 hit; and "The Tramp," which imagined an unemployed wanderer who is unwelcome not only on the job sites, but in church, in heaven, and even in Hell.[4] "If I catch you 'round again, you will wear that ball and chain," Hill's tramp is warned.

Nearly a century after Hill's execution, author William M. Adler expertly recreated his trial and uncovered new evidence supporting a long-held theory about Hill's conviction, in his book *The Man Who Never Died*. Hill had been shot on the night of the assault in the grocery store; though he refused to testify about his bullet wound in court, Adler makes a convincing case that it was the result of a dispute with a friend over a young woman with whom both were romantically involved.

As he awaited his appointment with the firing squad, Hill did what he could to prepare his own legacy as a martyr to the workingman's cause. In a famous telegram he sent to labor leader "Big Bill" Haywood in Chicago, Hill sent a clear-eyed farewell: "I will die like a true-blue rebel. Don't waste any time in mourning—organize."[5]

For Adler, Hill's legacy is comparable to that of the ill-fated abolitionist John Brown. Both inspired anthemic songs—the marching band standard "John Brown's Body" and Hayes and Robinson's "Joe Hill." Both "seem to float with Paul Bunyan and John Henry and Johnny Appleseed in a celestial realm somewhere between fiction and legend," Adler writes.[6] The memorable words to Hayes and Robinson's song—"I dreamed I saw Joe Hill last night"— have helped immortalize the gaunt Swedish immigrant as a guiding light for unionization.

The labor movement in America stretches at least as far back as the Revolutionary War era, when printers in Philadelphia conducted a successful strike in their demand for better wages. A few years later, in 1791, carpenters in the same city struck to have their hours on the job reduced to ten per day. The Industrial Revolution first took hold in the young nation in Massachusetts cities such as Waltham, along the Charles River, and Lowell and Lawrence, where textile mills were built along the Merrimack River. Young women seeking steady pay and a path out of the claustrophobic existence of small-town life flooded these cities in search of mill jobs in the 1820s and 1830s.

In short stories she wrote for a literary journal produced by the women of the mills, a young woman named Sarah Bagley ascribed to her heroines a condition she called "Lowell fever"—a desperate desire for opportunities other than the typical livelihoods available to Yankee farm girls as teachers or domestic help.[7] The factories offered boardinghouse residency, which meant that single young women did not have to live alone. Many of the millworkers moved to the cities in part to take advantage of the educational opportunities that abounded in night classes and lending libraries.

The city of Lowell grew out of the tiny village of East Chelmsford, which had two hundred residents in 1820, to claim a population of eighteen thousand just sixteen years later. More than half of its residents toiled in one of its ten mill complexes. Women made up the vast majority of the rank and file, with as many as eighty filling a workroom, operating looms or "carding" cotton onto cylinders. Men worked as supervisors. The pay discrepancy was significant, with women earning between $2.25 and $4 per week, while the men took home $4 to $12.

Distinctly aware of the perception that young, single women who'd come to the big city were susceptible to corruption, the women of the mills held themselves to high standards. Theirs was "a moral atmosphere as clear and bracing as that of the mountains from whose breezy slopes" they had arrived, as the poet Lucy Larcom, who had gone to Lowell seeking work at the age of eleven, would recall years later in the *Atlantic Monthly*.

But the exemplary model of the "Lowell Miracle" could not disguise the fact that there were working conditions the employees found increasingly unacceptable. The workday was based on that of life on the farm, dawn to dusk, meaning the women were on the job as many as fourteen hours each day. The drudgery of answering the bell in the morning and awaiting its recurrence at the end of the day made the women feel like "living machines," wrote one millworker in the *Lowell Offering*, the community's literary journal: "I won't stay here and be a white slave."[8] With the system designed to maximize productivity, workers soon found themselves burdened with mounting demands. Each woman would be responsible for the output of multiple machines, an expansion of duty known as the "stretch-out." The quickened pace of operations was called the "speedup." Atmospheric conditions, too, were inferior. Respiratory problems attributed to the unfiltered cotton lint in the air became commonplace, and various contagious illnesses were blamed on the generic, ubiquitous "mill fever."

Following an episode of labor unrest in a textile mill in Paterson, New Jersey, in 1828, isolated cases of workforce complaints in Lowell were dismissed as "New Jersey feelings." In fact, the workers of Lowell were developing a sense of solidarity. When word spread about a potential wage reduction during a recession in 1834, one woman, fired for speaking to her colleagues about the wage proposal, led a walkout of more than eight hundred workers, who marched to the Lowell Common, attracting many more women from other mills along the way.

"No one could recall a woman ever giving a public speech before in Lowell," according to one account.[9] But there had been a few previous examples of factory walkouts in other cities. One of those took place in Pawtucket, Rhode Island, where women went out on strike in 1824 to oppose increased hours and a wage reduction imposed by owner Samuel Slater. He was the British-born entrepreneur often credited as the "father of the American factory system." (In England, he was better known as "Slater the Traitor," for absconding to the New World with the plans for the water-powered spinning machine.) Another walkout had been conducted by hundreds of female workers in 1828 in Dover, New Hampshire. Hearing of the action, one Philadelphia newspaper warned that local officials might be compelled to call up a militia to put down the impending "gynecocracy."[10]

In Lowell, the brief strike of 1834 ended within a matter of days, with a few of the most vocal organizers losing their jobs and the others quietly returning to the factory floor. But the event laid the groundwork for another work stoppage two years later, when local workers protested a proposed rent hike at the boarding houses. This time, the walkout drew an estimated two thousand participants, and an abundance of community support. The mill owners were eventually persuaded to reconsider the rent hike.

Such sentiment about the rights of the new class of workers was already stoking a national debate. The wage earners' bosses, they felt, didn't care for them as people, only for the profits they could help deliver. As this notion took hold, some workers began comparing themselves to the slaves of the American South. In the pages of the *Liberator*, William Lloyd Garrison's abolitionist newspaper, the editor faced off against a representative of one fledgling labor organization, the New England Association of Farmers, Mechanics, and Other Workingmen. While Garrison expressed outrage that the working class would have the audacity to compare their own plight to those in actual bondage, William West argued that factory workers were deliberately kept, like slaves, in a state of dependence, solely for the financial benefit of the wealthiest capitalists. Charles Sumner, the Massachusetts lawyer, statesman, future senator, and staunch abolitionist, bolstered the comparison between the "lords of the loom and the lords of the lash."[11]

The demonstrations in Lowell helped encourage other American workers to unite in opposition to unfavorable working conditions. In Philadelphia in 1835, more than twenty thousand workers in various industries went out on a general strike, demanding a ten-hour workday. "We have rights and duties to perform as American citizens and members of society," the protesters wrote in a pamphlet outlining their demands, "which forbid us to dispose of more than ten hours for a day's work." When city employees joined the coalition of printers, carpenters, bakers, and other tradesmen on strike, the city government quickly adopted the ten-hour system. The Philadelphia general strike inspired others around the country, eventually resulting in a standardized ten-hour workday.

It would be decades, however, before the labor movement would successfully organize into unions. The American court system had long held that any form of workers' solidarity was a conspiracy (typically labeled a "combination"), and as such unlawful in its obstruction of commerce. A group of bootmakers in Philadelphia had attempted to organize themselves against unjust wages as far back as 1806. Their indictment set a long-standing precedent against the formation of labor unions. But unionization advocates such as Sarah Bagley and Seth Luther, who wrote and distributed an influential pamphlet known as the "Ten Hour Circular," led the rebuttal. "Men of property find no fault with combinations to extinguish fires and to protect their precious persons from danger," Luther noted. "But if poor men ask justice, it is a most horrible combination."

The National Labor Union (NLU)—the first of its kind, established in 1866—successfully promoted the drive to further reduce the workday from ten to eight hours, a standard that received Congressional approval in 1868. But the NLU would soon dissolve, forced into irrelevance by its dismal attempts to affect electoral politics and the financial Panic of 1873.

In its wake rose the Knights of Labor. Operating under the slogan "That Is the Most Perfect Government in Which an Injury to One Is the Concern of All," the Knights of Labor began as a secret organization of Philadelphia tailors in 1869. During the economic downturn that began a few years later, the union caught on among the miners of the coal region of northeastern Pennsylvania. Under the leadership of Terence Powderly, a lawyer and later three-term mayor of Scranton, the KOL, as it was known, experienced rapid nationalization. The organization welcomed to its ranks unskilled as well as skilled workers (the tradesmen who had historically constituted the local union shops), advocated the social and educational betterment of its members, and downplayed the efficacy of strikes, as had the NLU. But the Knights of Labor also worked to thwart the immigration of Chinese immigrants, who were coming to the United States in droves to lay track for the swiftly expanding railroads. The immigrants were taking jobs that might have gone to American citizens, the union argued, and their willingness to work for reduced wages was having widespread implications. The union's support helped usher the passage of the 1882 Chinese Exclusion Act, the first time in US history that a specific immigrant group had been restricted entry to the country.

The Knights of Labor reached its pinnacle in the mid-1880s, when an estimated one in five of all American workers could claim membership. The group's decline was steep: poor organization and another financial crisis, this one beginning in 1893, effectively put it out of operation, with another new national labor association, the American Federation of Labor (AFL), stepping in to fill the void. But the KOL had a lasting effect on the labor movement and American culture beyond its efforts to shorten the workday, eliminate child labor, and support worker cooperatives: the union was the first to emphasize the use of labor songs to express its ideals and build morale among its members.

The song that may have been most associated with the KOL had its origins in the Civil War. Five years after the war ended, Major Daniel Whittle relayed a story from his service in the Union Army to a Sunday school meeting in Rockford, Illinois. Outside of Atlanta, at Altoona Pass, Union troops charged with protecting a stock of food had come under heavy fire. "Hold the fort," read the message that was relayed to them as the fighting raged. "I am coming." The message was signed W. T. Sherman. The story inspired a well-known evangelist to write a popular hymn called "Hold the Fort." That song, in turn, was adapted by the Knights of Labor as "Storm the Fort"[12]:

Storm the fort, ye Knights of Labor
Battle for your cause
Equal rights for every neighbor
Down with tyrant laws

From the earliest examples of labor songs, fair pay was a major theme. So too was the desire to expel the corrupting influence of certain captains of industry, as personified by the "robber barons," the tycoons with names that still ring familiar today—Vanderbilt, Carnegie, Gould, Rockefeller, J. P. Morgan. Their consolidation of the country's biggest businesses, such as steel, oil, and the railroads, helped create the critical imbalance of wealth between the working stiffs whose daily labor enabled those industries to thrive and the ownership class that would be characterized (more than a century later, during the Occupy movement of 2010) as "the 1 percent."

But the union singers were concerned with far bigger issues than the dollar amount in their pay packets. They were singing for the dignity of the working man, for compassion, common sense, and morality. It was, writes Clark D. "Bucky" Halker, a folk singer and scholar of historic labor songs, "a battle for liberty, justice, and equality; a battle for Christian morality; a battle for the rights of all Americans. Citizen-soldiers in a struggle of universal proportions, workers enlisted in nothing less than a battle over the meaning of America itself."[13]

For Halker, one unsung songwriter by the name of Rees E. Lewis epitomized the thousands of unheralded contributors to the canon of folk songs for the labor movement during the so-called Gilded Age of the robber barons. (It was Mark Twain who gave the era its derogatory nickname; Twain, too, is often credited, however mistakenly, as the originator of the popular aphorism "When the rich rob the poor it's called business. When the poor fight back it's called violence.") Lewis, an employee in the Pittsburgh steel industry, wrote an inspirational verse that he set to the tune of an old folk song, sending it to the *National Labor Tribune*:

Rouse, ye noble sons of Labor,
And protect your country's honor,
Who with bone, and brain, and fiber
Make the nation's wealth.[14]

Labor songs, often set to familiar folk melodies, were typically crafted to encourage group participation. Singing in unison created camaraderie, and the songs were often underscored with ample wit and sarcasm:

My country, 'tis of thee,
Once land of liberty,
Of thee I sing.
Land of the Millionaire,
Farmers with pockets bare,
Cause by the cursed snare—
The Money Ring.

Thomas Nicol's bitter verse was published in the *Alliance and Labor Songster* as "A New National Anthem." The songbook was distributed as a rallying tool for the People's Party, an agrarian political organization of the early 1890s that emphasized opposition to the consolidation of power in the banks and railroads. (The People's Party, also known as the Populists, would be absorbed into the Democratic Party by the last years of the century.)

Poets and ministers were too often held in thrall to the powerful, wrote Leopold Vincent, the songbook's compiler, in the preface to the collection's third edition. The aim of the *Songster* was to provide some comfort and humor to the "single-handed farmer, mechanic, and day-laborer" who hoped to return from a satisfying day's work "with a song on his lips, and be met by the sweet sound of wife singing 'Home, Sweet Home'"—on the doorstep of the family's stand-alone home, not in the stairwell of a tenement. The sheer power of song lay at the heart of the *Songster*'s existence: as the publisher wrote, "May the harmonizing influence of music have the effect of sealing the sympathies of our people till political strife shall be of the past." Songs in Vincent's fourth edition included "To the Polls," the Knights of Labor's "Storm the Forts," and "The March of Labor," sung to the tune of the "Battle Song [*sic*] of the Republic"[15]:

Come and see the Sons of Labor rising in their might and main
Come and join in the procession, come and follow in the train
Let us haste the day Monopoly shall cease his tyrant reign
As we go marching on

Earning enough money to put food on the table was a daily concern for the working class in America, but there was a spiritual hunger to be fed, too. What was a life if it was consumed by back-breaking toil, with no joy, no beauty, no music?

Worse, many factory workers imperiled their own lives every day on the job. In 1911, New York City was appalled by the worst industrial disaster in the city's history. When a fire broke out in the Triangle Shirtwaist Factory on the upper floors of the ten-story Asch Building in Greenwich Village, hundreds of young workers, mostly women, were trapped inside. They were unable to escape because the exit doors had been locked to prevent employees from stealing or taking unauthorized breaks. One hundred forty-six workers died, many of them burned alive, others by jumping to their deaths.

The horrific incident spurred the call for increased workplace safety measures. A week after the fire the union activist Rose Schneiderman called for stronger working-class solidarity in a blistering speech to the Women's Trade Union League. "Every year thousands of us are maimed," she said. "The life of men and women is so cheap and property is so sacred.... The strong hand of the law beats us back, when we rise, into the conditions that make life unbearable."

In a speech she made the following year, Schneiderman spoke on behalf of her fellow workers' faith that there had to be more to life than wage slavery. The laborer, she said, wants "the right to live, not simply exist—the right to life as the rich woman has the right to life, and the sun and music and art. You have nothing that the humblest worker has not a right to have also. The worker must have bread, but she must have roses, too."[16] Her words were inspired by a recent poem that celebrated the women's rights movement, **"Bread and Roses,"** written by James Oppenheim, a Whitmanesque poet, novelist, and literary magazine editor.

The phrase would soon become synonymous with a strike of textile workers in Lawrence, Massachusetts, where a pay cut led more than twenty thousand workers across the city to respond to the call of union organizers: "Short pay! All out!" Often called the "Bread and Roses" strike because women reportedly held signs that read "We want bread, and roses, too," the unrest carried on for more than two winter months. Drawing "Big Bill" Haywood, Elizabeth Gurley Flynn, and other nationally recognized union figures to Lawrence, and supplying dramatic images of the demonstrators in their overcoats and bonnets facing armed militias, the textile strike would become one of the most iconic work stoppages in American history. After years of neglect, Oppenheim's poem was reprinted in a 1952 issue of *Sing Out!*. It has since inspired several songwriters, most famously Mimi Farina, younger sister of Joan Baez. Married at a young age to the novelist and folk singer Richard Farina, with whom she cut two albums, Farina was widowed on her twenty-first birthday when her husband died in a motorcycle accident.

A few years later, she attended a concert at the Sing Sing Correctional Facility in New York State featuring the blues singer B. B. King, and soon after, she performed at a halfway house. These experiences inspired Farina to found Bread and Roses, a not-for-profit organization to "bring the joy of live entertainment to people shut away from society," in prisons, hospitals, retirement homes, and other institutions.[17] She set Oppenheim's poem to a new melody, and the song would become the title track of a Judy Collins album. "Our days shall not be sweated from birth until life close," as Oppenheim had written. "Hearts starve as well as bodies, give us bread, but give us roses."

At a time when worker strikes are largely considered a thing of the past, coal mining provides a lasting impression of labor strife in America. Lewis Hine's stark photographic portraits for the National Child Labor Committee, for instance, which featured scores of haunting images of grimy, grim-faced "breaker" boys (who sorted coal by hand), "tipple" boys (who unloaded freight cars), and "trapper" boys (who took on the dangerous task of operating the mines' trap doors), were instrumental in the groundswell of support for the abolition of child labor.

Miners' wages plummeted in the years after the Civil War. The typical miner worked in "abominable" conditions, writes Philip Foner: "Knee deep in water, his head and body drenched by seepage, his vision obscured by thick clouds of powder smoke and coal dust, the miner toiled in the most dangerous occupation in the nation, constantly risking bodily injury or death."[18] In Schuylkill County, Pennsylvania, 566 men and boys were killed and 1,655 more seriously injured over a seven-year period in the years after the Civil War.[19]

On September 6, 1869, more than one hundred men were killed by a fire that started in the wooden encasement at the face of the Avondale Mine in northeast Pennsylvania. The fire ignited the processing plant overhead, trapping the miners underground. This tragedy proved an immediate recruiting opportunity for the Workingmen's Benevolent Association, a miners' union organized just the year before. As the bodies were being recovered from the mineshaft, union president John Siney mounted a platform and implored the surviving mineworkers to renounce the coal barons: "Men, if you must die with your boots on, die for your families, your homes, your country," he bellowed, "but do not longer consent to die like rats in a trap for those who have no more interest in you than in the pick you dig with." His union reported gaining thousands of new members in the immediate aftermath of the incident.[20]

The nation's densest coal mining regions, along the Appalachian range across Pennsylvania and West Virginia and into Kentucky, were home to deeply impoverished villages where families lived with the daily knowledge that the father of the house might not return that night. Children recited a familiar rhyme: "Oh Daddy, don't work in the mines today, for dreams have so often come true; Oh Daddy, dear Daddy, please don't go away, I never could live without you."

One of the earliest and most influential of the many songs that emerged to address the rough plight of the coal miner originated in 1872 in England. "Down in a Coal Mine," written by J. B. Geoghegan, a music hall manager and promoter, was intended as a celebration of the men toiling in an unheralded occupation—"down in a coal mine underneath the ground/Where a gleam of sunshine never can be found."

Decades after the disaster at Avondale, the job of the coal miner was still poor-paying and fraught with danger. Periodic walkouts had earned only incremental concessions from the coal barons, whose government backers and hired enforcers outlasted the striking workers as often as not. The United Mine Workers' (UMW) general strike of 1894, which came in response to wage cuts prompted by the economic downturn of the Panic of 1893, ended unsuccessfully after eight weeks. The failure hobbled the UMW, which would need another twenty-five years before it could regroup under a new president, John L. Lewis.

A ferocious advocate for the working man, Lewis helped establish the Congress of Industrial Organizations (CIO), the powerful union that would have a long rivalry, and a recurring alliance, with the American Federation of Labor. By the time of Lewis's ascent, coal mining was supplanting frontier farming in southeastern Kentucky. One local resident named Oliver Perry Garland had begun his young working life as a farmer and minister, but soon turned to the mines. He trusted in the union, paying dues with the Knights of Labor before joining the UMW. He had four children with his first wife, and after her death he had eleven more with his second. Three of Garland's children—Molly Jackson, Jim Garland, and Sarah Ogan Gunning—would take to folk singing, and they would each contribute notably to the modern notion of coal mining songs.

The trouble in Harlan County began in June 1917, when a UMW organizer named William Turnblazer addressed a rally of mine workers in the courthouse square. The speech drew a reported 2,500 miners, three-fifths of whom were said to join the union that day. Two months later, after lobbying unsuccessfully for an audience with the local operators to express their grievances, the men went out on strike. When violence erupted, one strike leader was killed by a bullet to the head. The strike, which lasted two months, earned a range of concessions from the operators, including a pay hike and shorter hours, as well as the formation of a grievance committee. The union had predicted, correctly, that a strike would be won: with the war on and the demand for coal high, ownership would be eager to settle and maintain production.

The UMW called a short-lived national strike two years later, in November 1919. Though it ended after ten days, when President Wilson obtained an injunction ordering the miners back to work, the two sides in Harlan County fought on. The operators refused to accept terms that included increased wages and shorter workdays, and so the strike continued. At the time, the striking miners were not demonstrating; they simply stayed off the job and congregated to play cards or pitch horseshoes. But as a local man named Tillman Cadle would recall, the standoff became vengeful when the guards gunned down a one-legged miner as he talked with a neighbor. "These gunmen, if they couldn't get some trouble started, they wouldn't have a job, you see," said Cadle. "Their job depended on trouble." The guard who was charged with the murder was given a life sentence, but was immediately pardoned, according to Cadle: "See, I began to see then what justice was like."[21]

One UMW organizer who went to Harlan County in 1922 at Lewis's request was shocked at the hostility. "When I got there I saw we could do nothing," he said. "They killed anyone who talked union." One night at the house he was renting, a window smashed; someone had shattered it with a rock attached with a stick of dynamite. The union man and his wife left town the next morning.[22]

By the time the Depression hit, the miners in Harlan County were in desperate shape. The union had been broken. With their profits dwindling due to decreasing demand and competition from other coal regions, the mine owners had imposed a series of wage cuts and were in many cases reduced to operating their facilities part-time. Without the financial aid of a union, the miners who weren't already blacklisted for organizing had little choice but to take the low-paying work. Many families were shoeless; mobs of men resorted to looting the local grocery stores to feed their families. Faced with another 10 percent wage cut in 1931, the miners of Harlan County were moved to organize once again. Many who were forced out of the company towns settled in Evarts, one of the only independent communities in the region. In the fierce Harlan County conflict that would be characterized as a "ten-year war," the town would become the site of a deadly standoff known as the Battle of Evarts. "If you struck you starved; if you worked, you starved," recalled Tillman Cadle. "It had come down to just a matter of starvation and war against starvation. It got to the point where I didn't consider it a strike, I considered it a war against starvation."[23]

In fact, the county did resemble a war zone. Of the 169 men Sheriff Blair deputized to help guard the owners' interests, sixty-four had been charged with felonies, and more than half of those had been convicted. The Kentucky National Guard was called in to respond to the Battle of Evarts, to guard against violence directed at the scab workers. Meanwhile, Blair's men tear-gassed union meetings and attacked the striking miners when they congregated. The visiting writer Malcolm Cowley reported that he saw more weapons in Harlan County—"rifles, high-powered shotguns, and automatic revolvers and machine guns"—than he had since he'd served as a journalist on the Western Front during World War I.[24]

"They wasn't deputy sheriffs, they was thugs, because they'd kill the men anytime the wanted to," Florence Reece, the songwriter behind "Which Side Are You On?," would recall years later. Because her husband was a union organizer, Blair's men ransacked the family's house several times while he was away at meetings, looking for any kind of incriminating evidence. She channeled her feelings of helplessness into the words of her timeless song.

"They still sing that song at all the rallies," as another local told the oral historian Alessandro Portelli in 1988. "Sometimes it's not union or scab. Sometimes it's the black people singing about what's happening to them. Sometimes it's women. You're choosing a side when there's an issue out there."[25]

From her youngest years, Sarah Ogan Gunning could remember her father, Oliver Perry Garland, hosting union meetings in the family home. At fifteen she married a young man from Tennessee named Andrew Ogan, who had moved to Bell County, Kentucky, to work in the Fox Ridge Mine. Sarah Ogan was politicized by the union activism of her husband and her brother Jim Garland. For a few years in the mid-1930s, she and her husband and their children lived in New York City, where Sarah developed her talent as a songwriter in the company of many of the key figures of the folk music scene of the Depression years, including Woody Guthrie, Pete Seeger, the composer Earl Robinson, and Huddie Ledbetter, who recorded as Lead Belly. A year before her husband's death from tuberculosis in 1938, she recorded several songs for the musicologist Alan Lomax. She also recorded a batch of duets with her brother, which were deposited in the Library of Congress.

The widow remarried in 1941, and she and her second husband, Joseph Gunning, eventually settled in Michigan, where he was lured by the prospect of employment with the automobile manufacturers. Though Guthrie, among others, had sung Sarah's praises as a singer and songwriter—her thin, high voice was "dry as my own," he wrote, "with the old outdoors and down the mountain sound to it"—she effectively stopped pursuing any kind of recognition for her music, restricting her performances to church.[26] In 1953, though, one of her songs, "I Am a Girl of Constant Sorrow," was included in John Greenway's *American Folksongs of Protest*. That song was a variation on the traditional mountain song "Man of Constant Sorrow." In it, the singer explained that she had to leave Kentucky to feed her children, because the miners were forced to exist on "bulldog gravy" (water, flour, and grease) for breakfast and beans and bread for supper.

"Aunt" Molly Jackson, thirty years older than her sister Sarah, lost her first husband in a mining accident in 1917. She was an outspoken member of the communist-affiliated National Miners Union, writing protest songs including "I Am a Union Woman" and "Poor Miner's Farewell." Legend has it that her second husband divorced her in order to keep his job with the mining company. It was the discovery of Jackson in 1931 that led to her family's introduction to the folk music community in New York City. The journalist and novelist Theodore Dreiser, best known for *Sister Carrie* and *An American Tragedy*, responded to reports of harassment in Harlan County, where miners disputing wage cuts were accused of communist collusion. Dreiser, a committed socialist, enlisted the help of several fellow writers, including John Dos Passos and Sherwood Anderson, to document the miners' stories in a collection that would be called *Harlan Miners Speak: Report on Terrorism in the Kentucky Coal Fields*.

Molly Jackson became a midwife at the age of twelve. Though midwives in the mountains were typically known as "Granny," she was instead called Aunt Molly Jackson due to her youth at the time. "According to Molly's own estimate," wrote her brother, Jim Garland, in his memoir, *Welcome the Traveler Home*, "she attended over 5000 births,"[27] but she told the Dreiser Committee that she'd delivered sixty-five children. Jackson's legend was built largely on another story impossible to verify: it was said she once pulled a gun on a company store clerk, demanding food for her neighbors' malnourished children. Her brother also claimed that, during a skirmish on a picket line, four women pinned down a company guard while Aunt Molly took his pistol and threatened to shoot him in the hindquarters. "Never did this particular gun thug show his face there again," Garland wrote.[28]

Whatever the truth of these incidents, Jackson had a reputation as a fear-less woman who was clearly not averse to violence. A decade after she left Harlan County, when the early honky-tonk star Al Dexter scored his biggest hit with "Pistol Packin' Mama"—incidentally the first number one hit on the Juke Box Folk Records chart, which would later become *Billboard* magazine's country music chart—Aunt Molly claimed the song was about her.[29]

In the late 1950s, the folklorist Archie Green tracked down Jackson in California for a series of interviews, conducted not long before she died. Frustrated by her cagey answers to his questions, he sought out her siblings for corroboration. That led to the family's reintroduction in the music business.

Jim Garland, who operated a broom factory for much of his adult life after leaving Kentucky, was invited to sing at the Newport Folk Festival in 1963. Two of his songs, **"I Don't Want Your Millions, Mister"** and **"The Ballad of Harry Simms,"** appeared on the album *Newport Broadside: Topical Songs at the Newport Folk Festival*, in 1963, alongside performances by Pete Seeger, Joan Baez, Tom Paxton, Phil Ochs, the singer and activist Peter La Farge, and the newcomer Bob Dylan. "I Don't Want Your Millions, Mister" had been recorded first in 1941 by the Almanac Singers, the New York City–based folk quartet that featured Pete Seeger and Woody Guthrie.

We worked to build this country, Mister,
While you enjoyed a life of ease
You've stolen all that we built, Mister,
Now our children starve and freeze

"The Ballad of Harry Simms," sometimes called "The Death of Harry Simms," or "The Murder of Harry Simms," or, in Seeger's 1964 version, simply "Harry Simms," was a mournful ode to a young union organizer from Springfield, Massachusetts, who was sent to Harlan County to recruit for the National Miners Union. Garland befriended Simms, who was twenty years old when he died of a gunshot wound in nearby Knox County. The murderer was a guard for one of the local coal companies, a gun thug deputized by the sheriff's department to put down the miners' strike. ("They Ask for Bread, the Coal Barons Answer with Bullets," as one union report charged.)

Sarah Ogan Gunning performed briefly at Newport the year after her brother did, and in Detroit she soon recorded an album of her songs, which was released in 1965. As she would tell researchers in her later years, her material was drawn directly from her own life experience. She'd lost two of her four children to starvation. Her song titles and lyrics tell the story of her despair and bitterness, and her search for someone to blame for her misfortune—"Dreadful Memories," "I Hate the Company Bosses," and "**I Hate the Capitalist System.**" Most of the songs were written after she arrived in New York and began learning about socialist theory. Late in life, she told a group of students that she had to look up the meaning of the word "capitalist": "I found out it was the people who had all the money," she said, smiling ruefully.

In Archie Green's notes for Gunning's first album, *Girl of Constant Sorrow*, he proposed several reasons to appreciate her unsung talent. "We can hear her as an excellent exponent of mountain style, we can seek out her rare song variants for comparative purposes, we can be moved by the beauty of her ballads," he wrote. Or "we can turn her message into bellows to fan the flames of social action."[30] Though her recorded legacy was modest, Green once told an interviewer, each song was "a gem, and each stood for the tension in Appalachia in the Thirties."[31]

From a peak of nearly 900,000 coal miners in the United States during the 1920s, in 2017 there were only an estimated 77,000 miners left making a living underground. The introduction of blasting machines and other forms of mechanization vastly improved efficiency, but it also decimated the rank and file of men hauling picks and axes down into the mineshafts.

Coal mining as a concept, however, remained a fertile source of material for popular songs well into the twentieth century. The visual imagery of grimy, exhausted men in coveralls, the clear dangers of the occupation, and the familiar reports of violent clashes between company men and unionized miners all gave the coal industry a disproportionate role in telling the story of the working class struggle in popular culture. In 1946 the Kentucky native Merle Travis, having moved to Hollywood for work in Western swing bands and the movies, was approached to record a collection of traditional folk music. *Folk Songs of the Hills*, originally issued as a box set of four 78 rpm discs, featured a mix of traditional ballads, such as the railroad work songs "Nine Pound Hammer" and "John Henry," and Travis originals, two of which drew on his family's experience working the mines of Muhlenberg County.

"**Dark as a Dungeon**" is a cautionary tale, in which the narrator warns his listeners against seeking their livelihood in "the dark, dreary mines." In a spoken introduction, Travis recalls crossing paths with an old family friend who tells him never to forget how lucky he is that he doesn't "have to dig out a living from under these old hills and hollers, like me and your pappy used to." After Travis recorded it, the song went on to a long life of renditions by other performers, perhaps most notably by Johnny Cash on his live *At Folsom Prison* album.

> *O midnight, or the morning, or the middle of the day*
> *It's the same to the miner who labors away*
> *Where the demons of death often come by surprise*
> *One fall of the slate and you're buried alive*

Where "Dark as a Dungeon" was sobering and contemplative, Travis's song **"Sixteen Tons"** would become a massive, unexpected hit in the hands of country crooner Tennessee Ernie Ford, reaching the top spot on the *Billboard* pop chart in 1955. The coal industry had long set quotas for miners, which rose dramatically over the years. A miner who was required to extract two tons of coal per day in the 1860s was expected to produce sixteen tons each shift by the 1920s. "You load sixteen tons, and what do you get/Another day older and deeper in debt," Travis wrote, crediting the line to his brother John, who worked in the mines. Though a folk song-writer named George S. Davis would claim in the 1960s that he was the song's true author, Travis maintained that it was his father who provided the song's memorably rousing final line: "I owe my soul to the company store."

Merle Travis was among the estimable artists gathered onstage at the Smithsonian Folklife Festival in 1969—others included Maybelle Carter and Dock Boggs—when Hazel Dickens debuted her own song about the perils of mining. The West Virginia native wrote the wrenching, hymnlike "Black Lung" for her brother, who died the same way so many of his fellow miners have died, of prolonged exposure to coal dust. She wrote it, Dickens once said, so that her brother "would have some kind of a voice in this world."[32] Dickens had plenty of firsthand experience with the hardships of mining. "When my sisters said goodbye to their husbands, they never knew if they would come back," she once said. "All of them married coal miners."[33]

A few years later, Dickens was asked to contribute a closing song for Barbara Kopple's *Harlan County U.S.A.*, the Academy Award–winning 1976 documentary that showed how little progress had been made in the industry. When Kopple asked her to write an original tune, Dickens agonized over the assignment. "It was real important that it be strong and that it speak to a lot of people," she recalled. Rising to the occasion, she called her new song **"They'll Never Keep Us Down."** Performing it with a band as a lively bluegrass tune, she left no doubt about her conviction: in Dickens's delivery, the repeated line "They'll never shoot that union out of me" comes across as a cause for celebration.

Today, labor unions are far less influential than they were at their peak, post World War II, when one-third of the nation's working adults were said to pay dues. By some accounts, that figure has fallen to 10 percent. But the union ideal remains the same as it was nearly two hundred years ago in America: it was essential, as Dickens said, that it be strong, and that it speak to a lot of people.

Demonstrators at the March on Washington for Jobs and Freedom, August 28, 1963.
Credit: Library of Congress, Prints & Photographs Division, photograph by Marion S. Trikosko.
http://www.loc.gov/pictures/resource/ds.04000/

3 CIVIL RIGHTS

Oh Freedom – The House I Live In – Strange Fruit – Black and White – We Shall Overcome – Keep On Pushing – Blowin' in the Wind – A Change Is Gonna Come – Why (Am I Treated So Bad) – Mississippi Goddam

The night before the March on Washington for Jobs and Freedom, vandals sabotaged the sound system. It took an emergency intervention by the Army Signal Corps of Engineers to ensure that a spontaneous sermon by the Reverend Dr. Martin Luther King, Jr., would be heard on that hot, humid day in late August 1963. When an estimated 250,000 people gathered along the Reflecting Pool at the foot of the Lincoln Memorial to rally for human rights—the largest such assembly that had ever gathered in the United States to date—Dr. King delivered a speech that would be immortalized by its most celebrated line, "I have a dream."

The day was filled with memorable moments. The contralto Marian Anderson, who'd performed in 1939 at the foot of the massive monument to the man who signed the Emancipation Proclamation, made a return appearance with the spiritual "He's Got the Whole World in His Hands." Odetta, the classically trained vocalist who became a critical messenger of the American folk tradition in the 1950s, sang her "Spiritual Trilogy," and two of her young protégés took their own turns at the microphone. Joan Baez—a pure-voiced soprano, a converted Quaker who preferred to perform barefoot—sang **"Oh Freedom"** and "We Shall Overcome." Bob Dylan sang "When the Ship Comes In" with Baez, his girlfriend at the time, and a solo version of "Only a Pawn in Their Game," a new song he'd written in response to the murder of the voting-rights organizer Medgar Evers.

The audience was predominantly black—by some counts, more than 80 percent so. Though Dylan would later suggest he was uncomfortable in his new role as a civil rights mouthpiece,

Baez (whose father was born in Mexico) had been cultivating a mixed-race audience for some time. On a tour of Southern states in 1961, she recalled, the venues she played had been designated for whites only. Returning on tour a year later, she stipulated that promoters make tickets available to black and white alike. Just beginning to parlay her fame, she felt compelled to contact regional NAACP offices to urge their associates to help integrate concerts "for someone they'd never heard of."[1] By the time of the March on Washington, Baez knew how to move a crowd, regardless of creed or color. When Dr. King, at the urging of the gospel singer Mahalia Jackson,[2] strayed from his prepared remarks to tell the throngs of demonstrators about his dream, Baez was enthralled. The eloquent minister "let the breath of God thunder through him," she remembered, "and up over my head I saw freedom, and all around me I heard it ring."[3]

The song "Oh Freedom" was likely nearly a century old by the time the crowd at the historic March on Washington sang along with Baez to its simple, repetitive refrain, not once but twice on that summer day: "And before I'd be a slave, I'll be buried in my grave/And go home to my Lord and be free." The bright hymn was an enduring example of the "freedom songs," the traditional sing-alongs handed down by anonymous Americans from slavery days and the Reconstruction era. The song was noted in William Eleazar Barton's *Old Plantation Hymns*, an 1899 collection of the "quaint, weird" jubilee songs sung by generations of slaves and their ancestors. The author, a Congregationalist minister who wrote several books about Lincoln, spent considerable time in Tennessee, where he asked some of his African-American neighbors to help him document their musical heritage.

Taking notes at an ironing board, Barton listened as two women he referred to as Aunt Dinah and Sister Bemaugh sang in unison all the lyrics they could retrieve from memory. He marveled at the way the narrators' dejections were eclipsed, time and again, by their faith and consolation: "I'm in no ways weary," they sang.

"Oh Freedom," Barton noted, "speaks the freedman's joy in his new manhood."[4] He recalled an old acquaintance named Uncle Joe Williams, a former slave who'd apparently been treated with uncommon decency. "He always hired his time from his master and made money enough to pay for his labor, and had a good start toward buying his wife and children when freedom came. But this is the hymn he loved to sing, sitting before his door in the twilight." For Pastor Barton, it was a revelation that even a well-respected slave would have preferred to be "buried in [his] grave" than remain in human bondage.

The Thirteenth Amendment, adopted on December 18, 1865, abolished slavery and involuntary servitude. Yet more than one hundred fifty years later, the true meaning of freedom is still debated. "You are either free or you are a slave," said H. Rap Brown, a national figure during the radicalized years of the civil rights era. "There's no such thing as second-class citizenship."

What is America to me? That was the question twenty-nine-year-old Frank Sinatra asked in a short film that premiered as a public service announcement in movie theaters in late 1945, just months after the official end of World War ll. Written as a patriotic ode to the ideals of freedom, tradition, democracy, and diversity, the song Sinatra sang, "**The House I Live In**," celebrated the American melting pot: "The church, the school, the clubhouse, a million lights I see/But especially the people, that's America to me."

In the film the singer—then an impossibly slender young man with high cheekbones and a velvet voice, the dream beau of a generation of "bobby soxer" schoolgirls—takes a break from a recording session to have a smoke in an alley behind the studio. There he encounters an unruly gang of boys chasing a Jewish kid because he's different. Sinatra takes the opportunity to teach them a lesson. "Your blood's the same as mine. Mine's the same as his," he says. The country they all share is composed of "a hundred different kinds of people, and a hundred different ways of talking. And a hundred different ways of going to church. But they're all American ways." Then the pop star bursts into song, crooning "The House I Live In," which had debuted three years earlier in a short-lived Broadway revue called *Let Freedom Sing*.

But in the film (which would earn an honorary Academy Award), Sinatra's version of the song skips certain lyrics—in particular, a verse that alludes to a fully integrated community: "The house I live in, my neighbors white and black/The people who just came here, or from generations back." The typically mild-mannered man who wrote those lyrics, Abel Meeropol, was infuriated by their absence.

Abel Meeropol taught English at his high school alma mater, DeWitt Clinton, in the Bronx. He was also a poet and lyricist publishing under the pen name Lewis Allan. (The pen name was adopted from the names of Meeropol's two stillborn babies.) In 1937, he published **"Strange Fruit,"** a haunting song inspired by a photograph of a notorious lynching:

> *Southern trees bear strange fruit*
> *Blood on the leaves and blood at the root*
> *Black bodies swinging in the southern breeze*
> *Strange fruit hanging from the poplar trees*

Seven years earlier, two black men, Thomas Shipp and Abram Smith, had been lynched in Marion, Indiana, after their arrest as suspects in the murder of a local factory worker and the alleged rape of his wife. A huge mob of vigilantes, thousands of them, amassed as the suspects were hauled from their jail cell, beaten with sledgehammers, and hanged from a tree. A local photographer who captured the photo claimed he sold hundreds of copies of the picture in the days after the lynching. (A third suspect, James Cameron, was rescued from his own hanging. Years later, he founded an institution called America's Black Holocaust Museum in Wisconsin.)

An occasional composer, Meeropol chose to write the music for "Strange Fruit" himself. He and his wife, Anne, a singer, introduced the song to some friends in the labor movement, which was an early breeding ground for civil liberties action. "Strange Fruit" was presented to the jazz singer Billie Holiday, who made the powerful song her customary encore at her running engagement at Café Society, the first integrated nightclub in Manhattan. When Holiday's label, Columbia Records, balked at the provocative lyrics of the song, she was granted a temporary release from her contract so she could cut a version for the politically engaged producer Milt Gabler on his Commodore label. The recording went on to sell more than a million copies, becoming the biggest hit of Holiday's career, and it was distributed to members of the US Senate with a letter urging passage of an anti-lynching bill. In the words of the jazz critic Leonard Feather, "Strange Fruit" was "the first significant protest in words and music" against Jim Crow segregation—"the first unmuted cry against racism."[5] In 1999, *Time* magazine named "Strange Fruit" the "song of the century."

"Strange Fruit" is the most influential work of a man fiercely committed to racial equality throughout his life. In five simple lines, a short poem written by Meeropol lays bare his empathy for the African-American condition from his perspective as a Jew:

> *I am a Jew.*
> *How can I tell?*
> *The Negro lynched*
> *Reminds me well.*
> *I am a Jew.*[6]

His strong stance against racism was intertwined with possible Communist Party affiliation and activity. In 1940, as part of the government's dogged pursuit of political activists with communist ties, Meeropol was called before the Rapp-Coudert Committee, a New York state version of the House Un-American Activities Committee investigating suspected communist school teachers. His inquisitors on that committee demanded to know whether he had been paid to write his best-known song by the Communist Party. He flatly denied it.

Over a decade later, the Meeropols adopted the orphaned sons of Julius and Ethel Rosenberg, the Jewish-American couple infamously executed as spies for the Soviet Union in 1953. The two young boys, Michael and Robert, were pushed into the limelight during the affair, and continued for decades to pursue proof of their parents' innocence.

Meeropol's objection to the editing of "The House I Live In" to leave out the lines about racial equality is indicative of the decade of the 1940s, when Jim Crow laws remained commonplace and many Americans still considered African-Americans second-class citizens. Yet the American public received Sinatra's version as a welcome expression of national pride at the close of the World War, when the country was eager to rebuild itself. Meeropol's words were set to music by Earl Robinson, the songwriter who had written "Joe Hill."

Like Meeropol, Robinson was deeply committed to racial progress. In 1954, responding to the landmark Supreme Court decision in *Brown v. Board of Education*, which ruled unconstitutional the racial segregation of public schools, Robinson co-wrote **"Black and White."** The song, which celebrated the notion of education for all, would be recorded by Pete Seeger and Sammy Davis, Jr., among others, before topping the Billboard singles chart in 1972 in a joyful version by Three Dog Night.

The prolific Robinson also composed a cantata called "Ballad for Americans," an elaborate precursor of sorts to "The House I Live In." Written in 1939 (with the working title "Ballad for Uncle Sam"), the showy ten-minute epic traced the history of the Republic from the American Revolution to the eve of the Second World War, embracing every job description, religious affiliation, and immigrant group ("I'm just an Irish, Negro, Jewish, Italian, French and English . . . Greek and Turk and Czech and double-Czech American") that the lyricist for the work, John La Touche, could imagine. Written for a theatrical production by the performance initiative of the Works Progress Administration, FDR's job-creating New Deal agency, "Ballad for Americans" was popularized by the singer, actor, and activist Paul Robeson, who performed it multiple times on the CBS radio network in his unmistakable deep bass voice.

Robeson had been a noted scholar and an All-American collegiate athlete at Rutgers University in New Jersey, the third African American to enroll at the institution, graduating as class valedictorian in 1919. Three years later he had a law degree from Columbia University and an illustrious start to a professional singing career. He became a household name during the Roaring Twenties, when he appeared in the London production of *Show Boat* and as the title character in Shakespeare's *Othello*. It was his duty, he felt, to represent the cultural sophistication of African Americans through his art, and he dedicated his life to principle: "The artist must take sides," he said. "He must elect to fight for freedom or slavery."[7]

Following the lynching of four African Americans in 1946, Robeson met with President Truman to advocate legislation that would condemn lynching. Truman quickly shut down the meeting, saying that the time was not right for such a measure. Robeson stepped up his efforts to use his celebrity on behalf of civil rights, founding the American Crusade against Lynching that same year. In the era of patriotic "Red-baiting," however, any form of progressive activism led to increased scrutiny. Called before a US Senate committee, Robeson was asked about his affiliation with the Communist Party. "Some of the most brilliant and distinguished Americans are about to go to jail for the failure to answer that question," he replied, "and I am going to join them, if necessary." By the early 1950s, Robeson had achieved a cultural eminence that included, among many other prominent roles, a speaking engagement at the opening of the United Nations. Yet because of this suspicion of communist allegiance, he was effectively blacklisted from the entertainment world, and the US government denied him a passport to travel overseas.

Through the work of the American Negro Theater, a "Negro Unit" of the WPA's Federal Theatre Project, Robeson met a young New Yorker named Harry Belafonte, the son of mixed-race Jamaican immigrants. After a performance of *Juno and the Paycock* by the Irish playwright Seán O'Casey, Belafonte and Robeson were introduced backstage. Robeson's commitment to justice inspired Belafonte's careful integration of his own creative expression with his political concerns.[8]

To support his young family and pay for his acting classes, Belafonte took up nightclub singing around New York City. He had an auspicious beginning, taking the stage to sing for the first time at the Royal Roost, a hub of the bebop scene. He was backed by Charlie Parker's jazz band, which at the time featured Max Roach and Miles Davis. Quickly attracting a following for his genial style, Belafonte released his first single, "Matilda," in 1953. His 1956 album, *Calypso*, launched a wave of middle-class American enthusiasm for the syncopated Afro-Caribbean folk music of the same name, holding the number one position on the Billboard album chart for thirty-one weeks. (The album is sometimes noted as the first to achieve sales of one million copies within a year of release.)

Belafonte's commercial success led to prestigious gigs across the country, and the entertainer took many of those opportunities to press for wider social acceptance of African Americans, both his fellow performers and their audiences. He was the first black headliner at the Cocoanut Grove Lounge in Los Angeles and the Empire Room at the Waldorf-Astoria in New York, among other venues. When he signed a contract to perform at Miami's Eden Roc Hotel, he demanded and received access to all of the hotel's amenities, breaking the city's color line in the process.[9] He also helped integrate the TV airwaves, appearing on Ed Sullivan's variety program *Toast of the Town* several times during the mid-1950s.

Soon Belafonte was enough of a ratings attraction that he could begin to dictate his own terms. "It is not enough for a singer like [Nat] 'King' Cole to just appear occasionally and sing some pretty tunes," he told the press: top black stars deserved the same creative control their white counterparts enjoyed.[10]

Cole got his own show in 1957, on which Belafonte agreed to appear as a guest. Two years later Belafonte negotiated a deal to host his own TV special, *Tonight with Belafonte*, sponsored by the cosmetics company Revlon. He envisioned the show as something more ambitious than straight entertainment—"a portrait of Negro life in America, told in song."[11] With guests including the veteran bluesmen Sonny Terry and Brownie McGhee and the rising, classically trained folk singer billed by the single name Odetta, Belafonte's hour-long program showcased songs with elements that subtly protested black America's second-class citizenship, while inviting white audiences to consider their roles in the making of the status quo. Chain gang chants, blues laments, and spirituals that promised redemption were all acted out by the modern dancers Mary Hinkson and Arthur Mitchell, the first black dancer for the New York City Ballet. The show was a major success with critics and viewers alike, making Belafonte the first black performer to win an Emmy Award. The integrated chorus presented on *Tonight with Belafonte* and the show's direct appeal to Americans of all backgrounds helped recast the cause of civil rights not as a radical gesture but "as natural as a morning's sunrise," as a writer for the *Chicago Defender* suggested.[12]

Belafonte met Martin Luther King, Jr., during King's first fundraising trip to New York City, in 1956. The singer was as yet uncommitted to what he considered the mainstream civil rights movement, which had distanced itself from the leftist activism that included Robeson. But King seemed different to Belafonte: he was "doing things that were on the one hand so radical, and on the other hand, coming in under the name of the Church."[13] By 1960, Belafonte was touting the work of King and his Southern Christian Leadership Conference to the presidential candidate John F. Kennedy, who had asked the singer for his endorsement. In May of that year, Belafonte headlined a "freedom rally" at the 369th Armory in Harlem, appearing alongside his old acting friend Sidney Poitier, jazz singer Sarah Vaughan, the Nigerian drummer Babatunde Olatunji, and Odetta. The event, which marked the anniversary of the decision in *Brown v. Board of Education*, began with a ceremony at the Statue of Liberty. Belafonte sang "The Star-Spangled Banner," and Odetta sang "Oh Freedom." The day, wrote a reporter for the *Amsterdam News*, marked Belafonte's graduation from "amateur status" to a role of real leadership in the civil rights movement.

As an emerging voice of the movement, Belafonte had a female counterpart in Odetta. Odetta Holmes was groomed by her mother to be the next Marian Anderson, the classical singer who had been representing black culture to America and the world since the 1930s. Born in Birmingham, Alabama, in 1930, Odetta was brought up in Los Angeles, where, at a young age, she took up musical theater. While traveling with a national touring company performing the Irish-immigrant musical *Finian's Rainbow*, she began performing folk songs on the nightclub scene in San Francisco's North Beach neighborhood. Her solo debut, *Odetta Sings Ballads and Blues* (1956), would have a major impact on the generation of folk revivalists that would provide the soundtrack to the growing activism of the early 1960s. Belafonte, Bob Dylan, and many others would cite the album as a formative influence on their work; Joan Baez called Odetta "a goddess" with "a massive voice."

Odetta Sings Ballads and Blues included songs associated with country music pioneer Jimmie Rodgers and the folk-blues guitarist Lead Belly, as well as several traditional hymns, prison and work songs, and stark, unaccompanied laments. The original album closed with a "spiritual trilogy"—"Oh Freedom," "Come and Go with Me," and "I'm on My Way." Each of those songs, as well as several others on Odetta's early albums, would become familiar strains on the demonstration marches of the 1960s, and she was frequently introduced as "the voice of the civil rights movement." When the activist Rosa Parks was asked which songs associated with the civil rights movement meant the most to her, she replied, "All of the songs Odetta sings."[14]

"Oh Freedom" is one of the core songs of the civil rights repertoire, some of which had their origins in the spirituals associated with slavery, the Underground Railroad, and the Reconstruction era of the nineteenth century. The writer James Baldwin borrowed the title of his book *The Fire Next Time* from a line in the Negro spiritual "Mary Don't You Weep": "God gave Noah the rainbow sign/No more water but fire next time." Though the freedom songs sometimes conveyed dire sentiments, when sung in unison by dozens (or hundreds) of unfettered voices, they expressed collective exuberance. Frederick Douglass, who was born into slavery in Maryland, noted that overseers often required their slaves to "make a noise," to keep track of their whereabouts in the fields and preclude any hushed conversation. In response, the slave songs and spirituals they sang often carried secret messages.

Among the oldest and most familiar of the "freedom songs" were "No More Auction Block," "I Shall Not Be Moved," "Glory, Glory," "'Buked and Scorned," "Come Go with Me" (as credited in the landmark 1867 collection *Slave Songs of the United States*, compiled by the abolitionists William Francis Allen, Lucy McKim Garrison, and Charles Pickard Ware), and "Keep Your Eyes on the Prize." The last-named song would lend its title to *Eyes on the Prize*, the colossal, fourteen-hour Public Broadcasting documentary series on the history of the civil rights movement that debuted in 1987.

In his book *True South* (2017) about the making of *Eyes on the Prize*, series producer Jon Else recalled an experience he'd had while working with the Student Nonviolent Coordinating Committee in Selma, Alabama, in 1965. Else was on hand as Amelia Boynton, a local activist then in her fifties, worked the line of demonstrators outside a registrar's office, encouraging African-American citizens who were hoping in vain to register to vote. When Sheriff Jim Clark ordered her away from the line, she refused. Incensed, he grabbed her by the back of the neck and began shoving the "striking, statuesque" black woman in high heels down the sidewalk to a waiting squad car—in full view of the network television cameras that had converged on the city to cover the demonstrations. "Clark had delivered the goods, the gaudy media goods," Else writes, "exactly as movement strategists hoped, exactly as Selma's few moderate whites feared."[15]

Members of the movement had been advised to alter the lyrics to the freedom songs as they saw fit, to incorporate the details of the circumstances at hand. "Ain't gonna let Jim Clark turn me around!" sang dozens of Boynton's fellow demonstrators as they were loaded into a prison bus. That night an energetic crowd overflowed Brown Chapel Church, and Else was there. Before Dr. King took the pulpit to call for "a veritable *symphony* of *justice* in Selma," the congregation raised its collective voice in a thundering rendition of "Oh Freedom." "I could feel the floor shake," Else wrote.[16]

Amelia Boynton was beaten unconscious by police during the "Bloody Sunday" crossing of the Edmund Pettus Bridge. Undaunted, she would go on to become an elected official in Selma. In 2015, Mrs. Boynton crossed the bridge once again to mark the fiftieth anniversary of the Selma marches. Then 103 years old and in a wheelchair, she was front and center among a large surge of commemorators, holding the hand of Barack Obama, the first black president of the United States.

On the first day of February 1960, four college freshmen in Greensboro, North Carolina, did something seemingly unremarkable: they sat down at a lunch counter and asked to be served. The four young men—Joseph McNeil, Franklin McCain, David Richmond, and Ezell Blair, Jr.—were all students at North Carolina Agricultural and Technical State University, and they were all black. At the time, the lunch counter at the Woolworth department store in Greensboro did not serve people of color.

There had been other "sit-ins" to demonstrate against Jim Crow racial segregation in businesses and institutions open to the public. In 1939, a Virginia lawyer named Samuel Wilbert Tucker organized a sit-in at a public library in Alexandria, where African Americans were denied borrowing privileges. Three years later, an integrated group of young adults, some of them students at the University of Chicago, requested and were refused service at the Jack Spratt Diner. As a result of that protest, management there soon did away with their "no service" policy for black customers.

Other peaceful demonstrations followed in cities across the United States, but the Greensboro sit-in catalyzed a new movement across the segregated South. The students were already well versed in the power of demonstration. Ezell Blair was familiar with the tradition of nonviolent protest advocated by Mohandas Gandhi, the spiritual leader who organized India's resistance to British rule in the years between the World Wars. Joseph McNeil had recently attended a concert at which some African Americans had been unruly; at the lunch counter, he instructed his fellow protesters to maintain decorum, no matter what kind of injustice they might face.

Denied service, the "Greensboro Four" returned the following day with reinforcements, twenty-nine students in all. Their peaceful protest soon spread to include students from neighboring schools, not all of them black, and to additional stores that had counter service. By the weekend, well over one thousand demonstrators were on hand at the five-and-dime on South Elm Street, crowding the cafeteria and forming a picket line outside. The sit-in movement quickly came to symbolize the ongoing degradation of

African-Americans in a society that pledged allegiance every day to a republic "with liberty and justice for all."

Two months after the Greensboro Four staged that first sit-in, the inaugural conference of the Student Nonviolent Coordinating Committee took place in Raleigh. Convened at Shaw University, a historically black college (HBC), the meeting was organized by Ella Baker, an alumnus who had been working with civil rights organizations since her hiring as a secretary with the National Association for the Advancement of Colored People in 1938. Through her affiliation with the Southern Christian Leadership Conference, she invited sit-in leaders and student coordinators from a dozen states, including a Howard University student named Stokely Carmichael, Fisk University student John Lewis, and several others who would go on to assume prominent roles in the civil rights movement. Baker persuaded Dr. King, the SCLC president, to pledge $800 toward the conference, which would lay the groundwork for one of the key organizing bodies of the civil rights era.[17]

At that formative meeting was a young folk singer named Guy Carawan. Born in 1927 in Santa Monica, California, Carawan had moved to New York City in the early 1950s to soak up the folk revival there. He soon hit the road with two fellow folk singers, Frank Hamilton (who would go on to help found Chicago's Old Town School of Folk Music) and Jack Elliott (who would become a legend as Ramblin' Jack, a direct link between Woody Guthrie and Bob Dylan). Along their travels the threesome stopped at the Highlander Folk School in Monteagle, Tennessee, a progressive labor college established in the 1930s. Carawan liked it there so much, he chose to stay.

Zilphia Horton, wife of the school's founder, Myles Horton, knew the power of song. She had been raised in a coal settlement in the Ozarks, and at Highlander she served as music director, collecting and teaching traditional labor songs and other folk music until her death in 1956.[18] Carawan succeeded her as the school's music director.

By the mid-1950s, Highlander was a hive of activity for Southern antisegregationists, with a staff deeply versed in the labor movement's tradition of activism and poised to apply those lessons to the demand for civil rights. One of the songs Carawan introduced to those early organizers of SNCC was one he'd learned at Highlander known as **"We Shall Overcome."** Like many other songs born out of scraps of melody in the public domain, the song had a long, complicated history.

In 1935 the Reverend Thomas Dorsey, the "father of gospel music," attended the National Convention of Gospel Choirs and Choruses, held that year in Cincinnati. There he met a promising young hymn writer named

Louise Shropshire, who was living in the city with her family after they moved north to escape the sharecropper's life. Shropshire, who would marry a prominent bail bondsman and become part of her adopted city's "black royalty," had one hymn in particular that she'd written for the congregation in her Baptist church. "I will overcome, I will overcome, I will overcome someday," her lyrics went. "If my Jesus wills, I do believe, I will overcome someday." Calling her song "If My Jesus Wills," each year Shropshire distributed hundreds of copies of the sheet music to choir directors from across the country at the gospel convention. Eventually, in 1954, she was granted a copyright.

Her song had striking similarities to lyrics that were apparently sung as a labor song in the 1940s. Both may have originated, at least lyrically, with a hymn credited to the Methodist minister and gospel composer Charles Albert Tindley, sometimes known as the "Prince of Preachers." Born in 1851 to an enslaved father and a free mother, he was the longtime pastor of a Philadelphia church that was renamed, after his death in 1933, Tindley Temple. Among his compositions were the hymns "What Are They Doing in Heaven?," "(Take Your Burden to the Lord and) Leave It There," and "I'll Overcome Someday." According to Carawan's obituary in the *New York Times* in 2015, a variation on Tindley's lyrics, set to a different melody, was sung on picket lines, including one involving striking tobacco workers in Charleston, South Carolina, in 1945: "We will overcome/And we will win our rights someday." Those workers, most of whom were female and most African American, were members of the Food, Tobacco, Agricultural, and Allied Workers union (FTA-CIO). They sang the song at the end of each day of picketing under the leadership of Lucille Simmons. Simmons would teach the song to Zilphia Horton at the Highlander Folk School. Horton, in turn, made it a school favorite, teaching it to her students up until her death.

Shropshire's name went unmentioned when, in 1960, the song was registered for copyright. The registrants included Carawan, Frank Hamilton, and Pete Seeger, who claimed to have learned the song from Zilphia Horton in 1947. Seeger made subtle amendments to the song, changing, for instance, the phrase "We will" to "We shall." His wife, Toshi, "kids me that it was my Harvard grammar," Seeger once said, "but I think I liked a more open sound. 'We will' has an alliteration to it, but 'We shall' opens the mouth wider."[19] Carawan's work in teaching the song to the SNCC demonstrators would have an incalculable impact on the civil rights movement. As he and his wife, Candie, would point out in their 1963 collection *Sing for Freedom*, commissioned by SNCC, the freedom songs helped develop "a singing spirit that moves the hearts of all who hear," sung "at mass meetings, prayer vigils, demonstrations, before freedom rides and sit-ins, in paddy wagons and jails, at conferences, workshops and informal gatherings. They are sung to bolster spirits, to gain new courage and to increase the sense of unity."[20] Few if any songs were as ubiquitous in the movement as "We Shall Overcome."

In the hands of the student protesters, the song was often performed with "more soul" than the folk singers had given it, as one organizer for SNCC would recall—"a sort of rocking quality, to stir one's inner feeling. When you got through singing it, you could walk over a bed of hot coals."[21]

The birth of rock 'n' roll is often credited to an unholy marriage of country music and rhythm and blues. But gospel music had a profound effect on the new music, too. The so-called Golden Age of Gospel, typically assigned to the 1940s and 1950s, made stars of church-based groups including the Swan Silvertones, the Dixie Hummingbirds, and the Soul Stirrers, who would produce a future pop phenom named Sam Cooke. Ray Charles soon secularized the ecstatic sound of "hard" gospel in hit songs such as "This Little Girl of Mine," "What'd I Say," and "I Got a Woman," a scarcely disguised reworking of a 1954 gospel number called "It Must Be Jesus." "I'd always thought that the blues and spirituals were close—close musically, close emotionally—and I was happy to hook 'em up," as Charles wrote in his autobiography.[22]

In 1963 the balladeer Al Hibbler, a veteran of Duke Ellington's big band, took a stand on behalf of civil rights in a manner that many of his peers, concerned for their careers, were reluctant to make. In Birmingham, Alabama, when protesters faced the notorious police chief Bull Connor and his department's aggressive German Shepherds and high-pressure fire hoses, Hibbler joined the picketers. Hibbler's career had peaked in the mid-1950s, when his version of "Unchained Melody" (preceding the Righteous Brothers by a decade) rose to number three on the *Billboard* pop chart. Like Ray Charles, Hibbler was sightless. "Though I'm blind, I can see the injustice here," he said of the clashes in Birmingham. He tried on more than one occasion to get arrested, but was detained by Bull Connor himself, who quietly returned Hibbler to his motel room. Instead, Hibbler performed a benefit concert for Dr. King's Southern Christian Leadership Conference, which had organized the Birmingham protests.

Four months after Bull Connor's fire hoses made the evening news, sharply influencing public perception about the civil rights protests, the historically black Miles College hosted an all-star concert called Salute to Freedom 1963. Raising money for the March on Washington for Jobs and Freedom were Ray

Charles, Nina Simone, the Shirelles, and the comedian Dick Gregory, among others. The event was an early example of the rallies that would increasingly feature well-known entertainers, both black and white, who were ready to risk their livelihoods in favor of the movement.

At a time of agonizing uncertainty, one popular singer who'd come up in a church choir began making popular music characterized by an unwavering faith in humanity. Curtis Mayfield was a young product of the Chicago housing projects, a musical prodigy and remarkably prolific songwriter who formed a series of his own record labels beginning in the early 1960s. With his early group the Impressions, he scored a handful of hits ("Gypsy Woman," "It's All Right") before releasing **"Keep On Pushing,"** an explicit call to action, at the outset of the "Freedom Summer" of 1964. With a swelling horn arrangement and a rhythm like the steady surge of a crowd, the song imagined "a great big stone wall" standing in the narrator's way. "But I've got my pride, and I'll move it all aside," Mayfield sang in his familiar falsetto, "and I'll keep on pushing."

Fueled by King's nomination for the Nobel Peace Prize and the impending passage of the Civil Rights Act of 1964, Mayfield sat down in a hotel room on the road and began scrawling the lyrics to his new topical song. According to Mayfield's son, Todd, in *Traveling Soul*, his 2016 biography of his father, the singer knocked on band mate Fred Cash's door in his pajamas to play him the new song. "Where did you come up with all these words?" Cash asked when Mayfield finished.

"I'm living," came the reply.[23]

Though Curtis Mayfield never wanted to be a preacher, writes his son, "he'd just written his first sermon."[24] Curtis Mayfield had a pet phrase for his chosen medium, passing along spiritual encouragement over the pop music airwaves, often to folks who'd never seen the inside of a church: "Painless preaching," he called it.

"Keep On Pushing" kicked off a series of socially conscious releases for Mayfield: a martial version of the gospel classic "Amen," the organization anthem "Meeting over Yonder," and the Impressions' best-known Movement hymn, "People Get Ready." That song in particular would have a long shelf life, covered by a wide range of artists, from Bob Dylan to Bruce Springsteen and Bob Marley; the song would become one of the twenty-five culturally significant songs added to the National Recording Registry in 2016.

With its open invitation for all concerned to board "the train to Jordan," "People Get Ready" invoked the righteous hymns of the Underground Railroad. Mayfield's lyrics "brought the coded messages of old Negro spirituals into the turbulent '60s," writes his son. "When he sang about a train to Jordan, everyone fighting for their rights in Mississippi, Alabama, Florida, and Georgia knew what he meant."[25] Two years later, the Impressions released another song that explicitly addressed the civil rights movement, this one called "We're a Winner." The lyric came to Mayfield in a dream, he would recall: "We needed to come from crying the blues to standing tall." For him, the song's heavy funk epitomized the shift from King's church gospel to the inner-city street smarts of leaders such as Stokely Carmichael and H. Rap Brown. The song "spoke to Black Power in a way pop music had never done,"[26] as his son writes. Perhaps unsurprisingly, it was banned by several radio stations, including WLS in Chicago, Mayfield's hometown, for being too "militant."

In the aftermath of the assassinations of Dr. King and Robert F. Kennedy in 1968, Mayfield struggled to maintain his usual optimism. "Too many have died in protecting my pride/For me to go second class," he wrote for another anthemic song, "This Is My Country." Still, he denied that any of his music was intended as anything more than "interpretations of how the majority of people around me feel. . . . I'm not singing protest. I'm only singing happenings—the actual reality of what's going on around us, whether we'll admit it or not—it's there."[27]

Many of the black performers who came of age during the civil rights era were products of churchgoing homes. A good number of them were in fact the sons and daughters of men of the cloth. Nina Simone, a preacher's daughter from North Carolina, once explained that she and her peers saw no real distinction between gospel music and the blues, unlike their parents, who felt the two styles should not intersect. "Negro music has always crossed all those lines," she said, "and I'm kind of glad of it. Now they're just calling it soul music."[28]

In other cases, though, the transition was not made lightly. Sam Cooke, himself the son of a Holiness minister, was wary enough of losing his gospel audience that he released his first single, "Loveable" (1957), under a pseudonym. By the time of the March on Washington six years later, Cooke was firmly established as a pop star, with an impressive run of crossover hits—"You Send Me," "Wonderful World," "Cupid." But he was chagrined when he first heard Dylan's **"Blowin' in the Wind,"** which borrowed its melody in part from the old spiritual "No More Auction Block." The song asked a barbed question: "How many roads must a man walk down/Before you call him a man?" Cooke, marveling that it took a white boy to write it, vowed to write his own song for the progressive movement. It was an incident in which the singer, his wife, and his band mates were denied accommodations at a Holiday Inn in Shreveport, Louisiana—Cooke, incensed, was arrested for disturbing the peace—that compelled him to compose his song.[29] Shortly after Christmas 1963, he summoned his friend and fellow musician J. W. Alexander to his home, where he ran through the somber ballad he called "**A Change Is Gonna Come**." He recorded the song in late January 1964, at RCA Studios in Hollywood, with a full orchestral arrangement, and performed it a week later on *The Tonight Show Starring Johnny Carson*.

That would turn out to be the one and only time Cooke sang the song in public. Cooke was unsettled by the song's grave tone, and his friend Bobby Womack agreed, admitting that he thought the song sounded "like death." In the brief time he had left, Cooke declined to sing it again. He was killed on December 11, 1964, in a bizarre shooting incident at a Los Angeles motel.

"A Change Is Gonna Come," which had first been issued on an album called *Ain't That Good News* back in March, was released as a single less than two weeks after Cooke's murder, as the B-side of the posthumous hit "Shake." The version of the song released to radio stations omitted the verse that most clearly referred to racism: "I go to the movie and I go downtown/Somebody keep telling me, don't hang around." Despite its muted release, "A Change Is Gonna Come" has been handed down as Cooke's best and most significant song. It was added to the National Recording Registry in 2007.

Regrettably, the tape of Cooke's *Tonight Show* performance does not survive. But if the singer was reluctant to revisit the song onstage, he was emboldened in his last months to speak his mind in other ways. In July 1964, he returned to headline the Copacabana, the swank New York City nightclub where he'd bombed shortly after launching his pop career several years earlier. This time he commanded the stage, adding to the set list a version of one of the songs most associated with the civil rights movement, "This Little Light of Mine," which Cooke interpolated with the traditional gospel "Amen." He also reportedly pledged to contribute "A Change Is Gonna Come" to an album called *The Stars Salute Dr. Martin Luther King*, compiled as a fundraiser for the SCLC. The completed album featured tracks by Belafonte, Lena Horne, Louis Armstrong, Nat King Cole, Sammy Davis, Jr., and others, but it didn't include Cooke's.

As the Sixties marched on, many more popular artists began wading into the civil rights conversation through music. In "The Love You Save (May Be Your Own)," Joe Tex assigned some of the blame for the black community's high rate of broken homes to the ongoing psychic toll of segregation:

I been pushed around, I been lost and found
I been given to sundown to get out of town
I been taken outside and brutalized
And I had to always be the one
To smile and apologize

James Brown used his fame as the "Hardest Working Man in Show Business" to promote a message of black dignity in his funky anthem, "Say It Loud—I'm Black and I'm Proud." Sly and the Family Stone celebrated "Everyday People" and urged those folks to "Stand!"

In 1971 the Staple Singers began a steady run of conscious, deeply soulful hit singles with "Respect Yourself." Written by Stax Records songwriters Luther Ingram and Mack Rice, the song grew out of a frustrated comment attributed to Ingram: "Black folk need to learn to respect themselves." The Staple Singers—patriarch Roebuck "Pops" Staples, a veteran gospel blues guitarist, his son Pervis, and his daughters Mavis, Yvonne, and Cleotha—were already closely associated with the call for racial harmony, having recorded many of the traditional spirituals and written a song called "Freedom Highway" to commemorate the Selma march. After appearing on a 1963 TV special called *Folk Songs and More Folk Songs*, which also featured the newcomer Bob Dylan, the Staple Singers became one of the first groups to record a cover version of the enigmatic young folk singer's "Blowin' in the Wind." They also recorded gospelized versions of Dylan's "A Hard Rain's a-Gonna Fall" and "Masters of War."

Throughout the decade, the group consistently addressed the civil rights movement in song, both with versions of key traditional and contemporary anthems and with their own originals. For an album called *Amen!* they recorded "As an Eagle Stirreth Her Nest," a song credited to the Reverend W. H. Brewster, the Memphis gospel composer who wrote one of the first gospel sides purported to sell a million copies, Mahalia Jackson's "Move On Up a Little Higher" (1948). The significance of the biblical imagery on the "Eagle" song to the civil rights struggle was unmistakable:

But as an eagle stirreth her nest
So that her young ones will have no rest
God in His own mysterious way
Stirs up His people to watch and pray

In 1965, Pops Staples wrote **"Why (Am I Treated So Bad)."** In a half-spoken intro, the patriarch mentioned witnessing a group of little children denied access to a school bus because they were a different "nationality," as Staples put it. "My friend, you know this old world is in a bad condition," he said. The song, as he once explained, was inspired by the Little Rock Nine, the teenage students barred from integrating their local high school by order of the segregationist governor Orval Faubus in 1957.

With their arrival at Stax, the home of Otis Redding, the Staples family moved squarely into the mainstream of commercial radio, securing the airplay that had largely eluded their promised-land pop-gospel. The rhythmic production of songs such as "I'll Take You There," "Be What You Are," and "If You're Ready (Come Go with Me)," often augmented by the punch of the Memphis Horns, gave the group newfound appeal beyond the church. On "I See It" (1968), the family expressed their stubborn belief in the eventual triumph of justice—they saw blue skies on the horizon, "people living side by side/A nation repairing its damaged pride." The album version of the song nodded to the psychedelic spirit of the day with an instrumental coda, a droning, slightly out-of-tune string rendition of "The Star-Spangled Banner."

"You got to stay true to yourself," said Mavis Staples in a 2010 interview, not long after releasing a solo album that revisited the songs of the civil rights era—"Eyes on the Prize," "We Shall Not Be Moved." "From the time we recorded 'Uncloudy Day' (in 1956), people were trying to get me to sing R&B, offering big money. Pops would tell me and I'd say, 'I want to sing with the family.' It just didn't seem right to me." Eventually, however, she grew comfortable inhabiting both the spiritual and secular worlds.

Nina Simone aspired not to pop stardom but the conservatory. Born Eunice Waymon, she hoped to become the first black woman to have a recital at Carnegie Hall. Denied admission to the Curtis Institute of Music in Philadelphia despite her talent as a pianist, she took work playing nightly from midnight until seven A.M. in an Atlantic City bar. There she was required to sing, and a unique entertainer—not quite cabaret or jazz or R&B, but an unprecedented fusion of the three—was born.

By 1963, five years into her recording career, Simone had already achieved her goal of headlining Carnegie Hall. It was around that time that she uncovered the righteous fury that would signify the rest of her career. Appalled by the June murder of NAACP field secretary Medgar Evers in the driveway of his home in Jackson, Mississippi, and distraught over the bombing in September of the 16th Street Baptist Church in Birmingham, Alabama, Simone let her inhibitions go in the song **"Mississippi Goddam."** It was an acid "show tune," she declared, for which "the show hasn't been written . . . yet."

Lord, have mercy on this land of mine
We all gonna get it in due time
I don't belong here
I don't belong there
I've even stopped believing in prayer

In an era of sanctimony and self-censorship, the singer made little effort to tamp down her rage. As the comedian and activist Dick Gregory would recall, "not one black man would dare sing 'Mississippi Goddam'" at the time (*What Happened, Miss Simone?*). Radio stations wanted no part of her frank repudiation. According to Simone's daughter, program directors returned copies of the single by the boxload, each of the records broken in two. "Mississippi Goddam" "came as a rush of fury, hatred, and determination," Simone would write in her autobiography. "In church language, the Truth entered me and I 'came through.'"

Her political dedication was no momentary phase. "Four Women" (1966) demanded dignity for black women, united, whatever the circumstances of their births and upbringing, by being "strong enough to take the pain." Two days after the assassination of Dr. King, Simone debuted a despondent ode to "the King of Love." ("They're shooting us down, one by one," she said from the stage.) And she paid tribute to another friend who died young, the playwright Lorraine Hansberry (*A Raisin in the Sun*), the first black woman to have a play produced on Broadway, with the 1969 song that introduced another popular phrase to the movement: "To Be Young, Gifted, and Black." Simone was "the singer of the black revolution," SNCC chairman H. Rap Brown declared, "because there is no other singer who sings real protest songs about the race situation." In the end, Nina Simone's association with the civil rights movement was inevitable. "When every day is a matter of survival," she once said, "I don't think you can help but be involved."

Protesting an anti-abortion candidate at the Democratic National Convention, New York City, July 14, 1976.

Credit: Library of Congress, Prints & Photographs Division, photograph by Warren K. Leffler.

http://www.loc.gov/pictures/resource/ppmsca.09733/

4 THE RIGHTS OF WOMEN

*You Don't Own Me – Don't Make Me Over – Chains – Wild Women Don't Have
the Blues – Tain't Nobody's Biz-ness If I Do – Mal Hombre – It Wasn't God Who
Made Honky-Tonk Angels – Respect – Just Because I'm a Woman – The Pill*

It was an unlikely setting for social reform: an auditorium full of screaming, swooning young girls in plaid skirts and and boys in chinos. The project was designed as a celebration of "teenage" music, with fans at the live event at the Santa Monica Civic Auditorium (and, later, screening the footage in movie theaters) punching ballots for their favorite performers. The Teenage Awards Music International would kick off an ongoing series of shows to be broadcast on one of the major television networks; proceeds would benefit music scholarships for young people around the world.

While those plans never materialized, the one-time concert event known as the T.A.M.I. Show would set the bar for rock 'n' roll spectacles to come. The idea was wildly ambitious. Using a new high-resolution camera system called Electronovision, the producers would film some of the most recognizable pop stars of the moment. A live color edit from four camera angles would be transferred to 35mm film, then presented as a concert event on movie screens across the country. At the time—1964, still televised largely in black and white—the concept was revolutionary.

Though the film was officially out of print for decades, the T.A.M.I. Show nevertheless inspired an outsize legend. Seven of the show's dozen acts, including Chuck Berry, Marvin Gaye, and the Beach Boys, would be elected to the Rock and Roll Hall of Fame. The show, filmed shortly after the contentious passage of the Civil Rights Act of 1964, featured an integrated bill, with almost as many black acts as white. Most famously, a young British group called the Rolling Stones were scheduled to take the stage after the soul singer James Brown, who established his crossover appeal to white audiences with an astonishing performance that, as the T.A.M.I. Show mythology has it, left Stones singer Mick Jagger dumbstruck with awe.

At the time, however, there was one name on the program that eclipsed all the others. The biggest star on American radio at the time was a young singer—still a teenager herself—with a Jackie Kennedy–style coiffure and a bedroom in her parents' suburban home in Tenafly, New Jersey. "She was the biggest name on the bill," director Steve Binder would recall.[1] Her name was Lesley Gore.

Introduced by show hosts Jan and Dean, who wore matching sweatshirts stamped with her surname, the prim young lady in heels and a wool skirt stepped to the microphone in front of the house band—the redoubtable session musicians known as the Wrecking Crew—and began her brief set with her latest hit single, "Maybe I Know." The bouncy song admitted the singer's suspicion that her boyfriend has been unfaithful, "but what can I do?"

Then she removed the microphone from its stand and strode to the lip of the stage, where the central camera captured her close-up in a gauzy filter. To an ominous, minor-key arrangement in 3/4 time, Gore began to sing: "You don't own me/I'm not just one of your many toys." When the song abruptly shifted to an exultant major key—"don't tell me what to do/don't tell me what to say"—she lifted her gaze to the ceiling and permitted herself a satisfied smile.

I'm young and I love to be young
I'm free and I love to be free
To live my life the way I want
To say and do whatever I please

"You Don't Own Me" was, at the time, a complete surprise. In an era of preordained roles for young men and women—Gore's own album titles presented her singing *For Mixed-Up Hearts* and about *Boys, Boys, Boys*—female pop singers had rarely been so bold about declaring their independence. In the early years of rock 'n' roll, the subject of the music was often rock 'n' roll itself. Chuck Berry's "Roll Over, Beethoven" imagined the great classical composers turning in their graves over the rowdy new music. Everybody in the old cell block, as Elvis sang, was dancing to the "Jailhouse Rock."

By 1957, the music was settling in for the long haul. In Philadelphia, the disc jockey Dick Clark was about to bring the television program he hosted to a national audience. With a simple format—groups of teenagers dancing in a television studio to the latest pop hits—the show's name was changed to reflect its vastly broadened audience, from *Bandstand* to *American Bandstand*. One of the songs that helped establish the show's popularity was written by two Philly kids, John Madara and David White. They crafted their lyrics around a West Coast "dance sensation that is sweeping the nation," the Bop. According to Clark, he urged White's group, Danny and the Juniors, to make the lyric less specific to a fad that would soon fade. (Voice instructor Artie Singer, who had a co-songwriting credit, claimed it was his idea.) In any case, "let's all do the bop" became "let's go to the hop." The song, "At the Hop," reached the number one spot on the national charts in the first week of 1958 and stayed there for seven weeks.

White and Madara continued to write songs together. They co-wrote "Rock and Roll Is Here to Stay," a second national hit for Danny and the Juniors, and they began working with an African-American schoolgirl from Philadelphia named Maureen Gray. Madara owned a record shop in a black neighborhood in the city—"jazz, gospel, and R&B music, that was it"[2]—with a piano in the back room. The two composers were impressed with the work of the songwriting team of Burt Bacharach and Hal David, who'd engineered hits for Gene Pitney and a dramatic young singer from Chicago named Timi Yuro. Bacharach and David had another young protégée named Dionne Warwick, who sang on their demo version of a new song called "Make It Easy on Yourself." She'd hoped the song would launch her own career; instead, it went to Jerry Butler, Curtis Mayfield's cofounder in the Impressions, who had moved on to a solo career.

Warwick, not yet twenty-two years old, was distraught, feeling the songwriters had betrayed a promise to help establish her as a recording artist in her own right. "Don't make me over, man!" she is said to have shouted at Bacharach and David. "Accept me for what I am." Those words would soon be heard on radio stations across the country: **"Don't Make Me Over,"** the exquisitely orchestrated R&B ballad that Bacharach and David crafted out of the singer's admonishment, became the first in a steady stream of Top 40 hits that would last through the decade for the three collaborators. The song "displays a protofeminist sense of control," wrote Dave Marsh in his book on the greatest singles of all time, *The Heart of Rock & Soul*.[3]

Madara and White soon composed a similar song with Maureen Gray in mind. "You Don't Own Me" was a "sideways" variation on "Don't Make Me Over," as Gray once described it. But the songwriters never got around to recording it with her. Instead, they showcased it for Quincy Jones, who urged them to play it for Lesley Gore. At a record company retreat in the Catskills, the two Philly songwriters approached Gore at poolside and sang "You Don't

Own Me" for her, with Madara strumming a baritone ukulele. Inside the resort, they played it again, this time at a piano. With Gore eager to record the song, White and Madara were invited to sit in on a New York studio session. The simple idea behind the song, Madara said, was to write a song "about a woman telling a guy off. We always hear about guys saying things about girls, and girls pleading their cases. How about a song about a girl coming from her point of view?"

The song was certainly an anomaly at a time when "girl groups"—the Shirelles, the Shangri-Las, Martha & the Vandellas—and showy pop singers like Yuro, Patsy Cline, Brenda Lee, and Connie Francis ("Where the Boys Are") dominated the commercial airwaves. Almost every song of the era written for female voices was lyrically subservient, playing into traditional notions of demure young women hopelessly devoted to their dreamy, overprotective sweethearts. "He's so fine," cooed the Chiffons, from the Bronx. "He is my destiny," crooned Little Peggy March, a product of suburban Philadelphia who was just fifteen when her song "I Will Follow Him" topped the pop chart in early 1963. "My boyfriend's back and you're gonna be in trouble," as the Angels—like Gore, teenaged girls from New Jersey—taunted an unwanted suitor.

The girl group phenomenon of the early 1960s, an answer of sorts to the mostly male-voiced doo-wop format of the previous decade, projected a collective image of puppy love, with boys typically acting as they pleased, and their doe-eyed girlfriends perpetually ready to forgive them. The trend was a product of the music-business hit machine, in which producers, executives, and talent managers—almost all of them men—"shaped" their artists into prescriptive molds based on the industry's most recent commercial successes. Al Kooper, who worked in the legendary songwriting mill known as the Brill Building in Midtown Manhattan, once explained the process: "I'd come into work and I'd go into this little cubicle that had a little upright piano . . . and every day from ten to six we'd go in there and pretend that we were thirteen-year-old girls and write these songs. That was the gig."[4]

Many of the girl groups were black, adding another hurdle to any notions they may have had of autonomy or self-determination. Rare was a song like **"Chains,"** a buoyant regret by the Cookies, a veteran R&B vocal group originally formed in Brooklyn, in which a lover laments the invisible "chains of love" that impede her attraction to another guy. There was a reason that song (written by the husband-and-wife team of Gerry Goffin and Carole King) gave the girls as much independence as the guys: first recorded (though not released) by the Everly Brothers, later covered by the Beatles, it was written from a male perspective.

Some critics were dismissive of the "girl groups" and the narrow scope of their apparent interests. Al Aronowitz, who would make his name as the journalist who introduced Bob Dylan to the Beatles, wrote a piece for the *Saturday Evening Post* in 1963 headlined "The Dumb Sound." The Brill Building formula, he wrote, amounted to a modern version of Tin Pan Alley "packed with so many kids, they've started calling it Teen Pan Alley." A writer for a Christian newspaper neatly summarized the plot of a typical girl group record: "Things happen to me. I have no control over them and no responsibility for them."[5] Yet regardless of who wrote the songs (and to some degree in spite of their vapid content), the "girl group" period helped a generation of young women discover their own voices, by singing along with their pop-star stand-ins.

At the conclusion of Gore's recording session, Quincy Jones passed around a hat, asking those in attendance to write down the name of the song they felt should be the lead single from the singer's next album. They all wrote down "You Don't Own Me." "It was just a powerful record," Madara said. "Over the years it became more of a women's anthem. It's taken on a life of its own." Ironically, though Gore claimed not to harbor any bitterness about it, she never received a gold record for "You Don't Own Me"—but Madara and White, the two male co-writers, did.[6]

When Gore first heard the demo version of "You Don't Own Me," she thought it had "an important humanist quality," she said a few years before her death in 2015.[7] "As I got older, feminism became more a part of my life and more a part of our whole awareness, and I could see why people would use it as a feminist anthem. I don't care what age you are—whether you're sixteen or 116—there's nothing more wonderful than standing on the stage and shaking your finger and singing, 'Don't tell me what to do.'" Later in life, Gore hosted episodes of the long-running PBS series *In the Life*, a newsmagazine devoted to lesbian, gay, bisexual, and transgender issues. While she officially came out of the closet in 2005, it wasn't due to some internal pressure to do so, she said at the time. Hosting the PBS series "was just kind of my way of saying, here I am and this is what I feel I should be doing now, and it was sort of a natural evolution for me as opposed to, you know, this great gong in the head."[8]

It was not until the 1960s that the term *feminist* began to take on a positive connotation in the United States, though the rights of women have been demanded and debated since the country's founding. One very early example of a popular American protest song was, in fact, called "Rights of Woman." With lyrics published anonymously (credited to "A Lady") in a Philadelphia women's magazine in 1795, the song was inspired by Mary Wollstonecraft's 1792 treatise *A Vindication of the Rights of Woman*, in which the author called for proper education for women and equal standing with their spouses. The song, set to the tune of "God Save the King," exhorts the women of America to demand their rights alongside their revolutionary male counterparts:

> *O Let the sacred fire*
> *Of Freedom's voice inspire*
> *A Female too,—*
> *Man makes his cause his own,*
> *And Fame his acts renown,—*
> *Woman thy fears disown,*
> *Assert thy due.*[9]

At the first women's rights convention, held in Seneca Falls, New York, in 1848, Elizabeth Cady Stanton read aloud the Declaration of Sentiments, a document that echoed the Declaration of Independence. The statement called for the right to vote (the "elective franchise"), property rights, religious freedom, and the abolition of "an absolute tyranny" of man over woman. "We hold these truths to be self-evident: that all men and women are created equal," reads the document's preamble.

An amendment establishing women's right to vote was first introduced in the Congress in 1878. More than thirty years later, women were still fighting for the vote. Inspired by the suffragette movement in the United Kingdom, the Congressional Union for Women Suffrage staged a major demonstration on the steps of the US Capitol in May 1914. The crowd sang "The March of the Women," the official anthem of the Women's Social and Political Union, the organization leading the campaign for suffrage in the United Kingdom. By the 1910s, with the rise of the music industry through sheet-music sales and the new phonograph technology, a few songwriters were trying their hands at writing topical songs that addressed the suffragettes. One of the more successful of these was a tune called "She's Good Enough to Be Your Baby's Mother, and She's Good Enough to Vote with You." Set to music by Herman Paley, the lyricist was Alfred Bryan—the same songwriter responsible for the antiwar song "I Didn't Raise My Boy to Be a Soldier."

Women made their voices heard in the Roaring Twenties, accompanied by the emergence of the archetypical independent-minded "flapper." Bessie

Smith, the "Empress of the Blues," led a detachment of female blues and jazz singers with big, brassy voices and unapologetic songs. As promoted by Smith, "Ma" Rainey, Ida Cox, Victoria Spivey, Sippie Wallace, and others, "[b]lues-style love was no idealized realm where dreams for future happiness were stored. Rather, blues songs were often linked with possibilities for greater social freedom."[10] For these singers, the longing was not for romantic love, as in traditional popular songs, but sexual liberation. That kind of freedom was usually couched in metaphor: a woman wanted some sugar in her bowl. And men are like streetcars, sang Rosetta Howard: "If you miss this one here, you'll get another one right away."

Cox, sometimes billed as the "Uncrowned Queen of the Blues," was one of the first women in the music business to manage her own touring company. With her third husband, Jesse "Tiny" Crump, she mounted a traveling revue called *Raisin' Cain*, which ran for several years into the 1930s. In 1939 the producer John Hammond featured Cox on the landmark "From Spirituals to Swing" concert series he booked into Carnegie Hall. Years later, after the singer quit performing, Hammond placed an ad in the show-business trade magazine *Variety* seeking her whereabouts. The comeback album she recorded in 1961 featured a new version of one of her signature songs, **"Wild Women Don't Have the Blues."**

You never get nothin' by being an angel child
You better change your ways and get real wild
I wanna tell you something, I wouldn't tell you a lie
Wild women are the only kind that really get by

Cox was a particular inspiration for Victoria Spivey, a singer and piano player who broke through in 1926 with two defiantly bawdy songs she co-wrote with Lonnie Johnson, "Black Snake Blues" and "Dirty Woman Blues." Like Cox, Spivey was rediscovered in the early 1960s, one of the many elder beneficiaries of the folk revival of the period. She soon formed her own record label, Spivey Records; one of the company's early releases, a joint effort with Big Joe Williams, featured harmonica playing and backing vocals by the folk-scene newcomer Bob Dylan. A few years later Spivey's label helped revive the career of another strong Southern blueswoman, Sippie Wallace.

The feminist strains that united the work of the classic blueswomen who emerged during the 1920s often alluded to an open secret many of them kept: their fluid sexuality. Alberta Hunter may have sung songs such as "Aggravatin' Papa" and "If You Want to Keep Your Daddy Home," but she shared her private life for years with a girlfriend, Lottie Taylor, the niece of the black vaudeville star Bert Williams. Hunter was one of the first to record one of the classic liberation songs, **"Tain't Nobody's Biz-ness If I Do,"** as did Sara Martin ("The Famous Moanin' Mama") and Bessie Smith. The song, often credited as "Ain't Nobody's Business," is one of the most enduring examples of vaudeville-style blues. Though it was written by two men, pianists Porter Grainger and Everett "Happy" Robbins, and has been covered many times by male performers (Sam Cooke, B. B. King, Willie Nelson), it was originally conceived as an expression of female autonomy.

> *There ain't nothin' I can do nor nothin I can say*
> *That folks don't criticize me*
> *But I'm gonna do just as I want to anyway*
> *And don't care if they all despise me*

The scholar and activist Angela Davis, in her book *Blues Legacies and Black Feminism*, took on the common criticism that one particular verse in "Tain't Nobody's Biz-ness" seems to condone domestic violence ("Well, I'd rather my man would hit me than to jump right up and quit me"). Such an attitude, Davis writes, is "extremely painful" to hear, expressed so matter-of-factly. But the song's apparent tolerance of male domination "occurs within a larger affirmation of women's rights as individuals to conduct themselves however they wish," regardless of the consequences. The simple fact that Alberta Hunter and Bessie Smith (and Billie Holiday, among others, after them) named the existence of domestic violence "may itself have made misogynist violence available for criticism," Davis argues.[11]

The allusion to violence, in fact, often cut both ways. In Ma Rainey's "See See Rider Blues," she vows upon learning of her lover's infidelity that she will "kill my man and catch the Cannonball." In Smith's "Hateful Blues," the singer threatens to take her "weddin' butcher" knife to her unfaithful man and "cut him two and two."

The blues was not the only song form in which women made themselves heard. Released as the Tejano singer Lydia Mendoza's first solo recording on the Bluebird Records label in 1934, the Spanish-language **"Mal Hombre"** found an immediate and enthusiastic audience among the growing Mexican-American population for its frank, defiant tone. It has been claimed that the "Lark of the Border," as she was known, discovered the lyrics on a gum wrapper.[12] In translation:

You treated me like all men
Who are like you treat women
So don't be surprised that now
I say it to you face what you are
Bad man
Your soul is so wicked it has no name
You are a pig, you are evil
You are a bad man

"It's her most famous song and it's pretty fierce," said the contemporary song interpreter Rhiannon Giddens when she revived Mendoza's song in recent years. After a former lover abandons the narrator, "she's going to tell him to his face what she thinks of him and what he is."[13]

Frank discussion of human behavior in the risqué blues of the 1920s and 1930s was a product of post-emancipation culture in black America. The collective concerns of slavery days had given way to the individual needs and desires of a free people, and the shift in African-American culture—from spirituals to swing, as it were—reflected that adjustment in consciousness. Just as sexual choices were one manifestation of personal freedom, so too was the right to travel freely, which helps explain the parallel tradition of "road" songs and the prevalence of songs about cars in the commercial music industry.

Though the songs of the queens and empresses of the blues were undoubtedly a form of protest, they have not always been recognized as such. As Davis points out, the late historian Samuel Charters maintained that "there is little social protest in the blues." Anger, frustration, complaint—yes, of course, those emotions are represented in the blues. But Davis hears Charters's failure to consider "the interpretive audience to which the blues is addressed" as a form of paternalism.[14]

The Nineteenth Amendment to the Constitution was finally ratified in August 1920, ensuring a woman's right to vote nationwide. Three years later, the Equal Rights Amendment would be introduced for the first time in Congress. These and other advances triggered an unfavorable response to the women's movement. Recalling an attempt to quell the ambitions of women during the second half of the nineteenth century, when one Harvard professor wrote a popular book claiming an infertility epidemic among educated women (the so-called brain-womb conflict), male authoritarian figures renewed the outcry against women who put their own intellectual fulfillment ahead of child-rearing. Such women were "criminals against the race," thundered Theodore Roosevelt.[15] Feminists were blamed for rising divorce rates, and—for the first time in US history—abortion was outlawed in a majority of states. A decade after the term "feminist" entered widespread usage (the silent film star Theda Bara proudly identified as one), by the 1920s membership in women's organizations was in steep decline, and "ex-feminists" submitting their *mea culpas* were common fodder for the newspapers. While some of those reversals were credited to an assumption that the women's movement had secured many of its demands, feminist leaders worried that many of their gains were being lost. "All about us we see attempts being made, buttressed by governmental authority, to throw women back into the morass of unlovely dependence from which they were just beginning to emerge," wrote one correspondent for the official publication of the National Women's Party.[16]

The 1940s brought a new wave of progress on women's issues, spurred in part by the wartime emergence of female factory workers and their patriotic "Rosie the Riveter" ideal. Congress passed dozens of bills concerning women's issues, and the Senate Judiciary Committee voted the Equal Rights Amendment to the floor of the legislature three times, though it did not pass. Upon the end of the war, however, at least two million women were let go from their industrial jobs, and elected officials sided with returning veterans in the scramble for career jobs. "Motherhood cannot be amended and we are glad the Senate didn't try," editorialized the *New York Times* when the ERA was defeated.[17]

Despite the loss of those industrial jobs following the war, by the 1950s more women were going to work in America than ever before. While the cultural imagery of the 1950s was flooded with "happy housewives," notes Susan Faludi, in fact, many mothers with children were working—but they were typically relegated to positions as "poorly paid secretaries."[18] In early 1963, the year Lesley Gore first heard the words of "You Don't Own Me," a Smith College alumna named Betty Friedan published a book based on a survey of her classmates on the occasion of their fifteenth reunion. *The Feminine Mystique* described a widespread "problem that has no name," in which a generation of women raising seemingly thriving families in an affluent society nevertheless shared deep-seated feelings of unhappiness. The "feminine mystique" of her title was the product of a patriarchy that, through the media, television, and advertising, had created the false impression that women were more fulfilled by homemaking than achieving career goals. "We can no longer ignore that voice within women that says: 'I want something more,'" Friedan wrote.

For Friedan, the long-held supposition that feminism was rooted in man-hating and penis envy was a "strangely unquestioned perversion of history." In fact, she noted, Mary Wollstonecraft, Margaret Fuller, Elizabeth Cady Stanton, and Margaret Sanger, the founder of Planned Parenthood, all had loving relationships with men. Did women want the right to vote, the leadership roles that shaped our society, and the ability to decide between right and wrong "because they wanted to be men? Or did they want them because they also were human?"[19] The "second wave" feminism that Friedan's book helped launch sought to dismantle the false dichotomy of women's choices—on one side, the "man-eating" feminist and career woman, "loveless, alone"; on the other, the doting mother and housewife, protected by her husband, adored by her children.[20]

Even in a "liberated" song such as "I'm a Woman," the assertive vamp recorded by Peggy Lee in 1963, the familiar tropes of the mid-century housewife were pronounced. Once again, a song perceived as quintessentially "female" had been written by a man—in this case, two men, the hip rock 'n' roll songwriting team of Jerry Leiber and Mike Stoller, who broke through with "Hound Dog" for Big Mama Thornton in 1953 and went on to write for Elvis Presley, the Coasters, the Drifters, and many more. Written as an answer to Muddy Waters's "Mannish Boy" and Bo Diddley's "I'm a Man," the song was conceived as a feminist anthem, written not for the teenagers supporting the "girl group" phenomenon, but for grown, self-sufficient women, as Leiber would note.[21] The song, with its distinctive spelling lesson—"'Cause I'm a woman, W-O-M-A-N, I'll say it again"—is a cheeky boast: the narrator ticks off a litany of chores she can do "before you can count from one to nine," not to mention her ability to get dressed up and "swing til four A.M.," then rise at six and do it all over again. She can make the sick well, she can break your spell: "I can make a dress out of a feedbag and I can make a man out of you."

Lee was already a stage veteran of two decades when she uncovered the song in a stack of demo recordings. She'd arrived as a singer with Benny Goodman's big band in the early 1940s; one of her early hits was a version of the well-traveled "woman's blues" "Why Don't You Do Right." Briefly retiring after her first marriage, she returned to resume a long career on the nightclub circuit punctuated by the occasional chart hit, such as her atmospheric, catlike version of "Fever" (1958). Though Leiber and Stoller were well established by the time they learned that Lee was performing their song and planning to record it ("I'm a Woman" was first recorded by Christine Kittrell, a veteran R&B singer from Nashville who reflected the kind of artist the songwriters typically wrote for), they were a bit awed: she was "the funkiest white woman alive," as Leiber recalled. He wasn't thrilled with her approach to the song. "She didn't play with the rhythm in the manner of Billie Holiday, one of her heroines," he said. "She simply sat on the beat." Yet he had to admit that she presented as a strong woman, just as the song imagined. "You could only push this gal so far," he remembered.[22] Lee's version of the song would be revived in 1978 as the basis for a long-running television commercial for a women's cologne.

As the "women's lib" movement gained momentum in the latter half of the 1960s, some of the most specific lyrics about women hoping to enlighten the opposite sex came from quarters that may have seemed unlikely. The Nashville music business had been dominated by men—male artists, male songwriters, and of course male executives—from its earliest years. When Tammy Wynette's "Stand by Your Man" came out in 1968, Epic Records took out a full-page ad in *Billboard* magazine proclaiming that the new single was "Tammy Wynette's Answer to Women's Lib." "Stand by Your Man" would become one of the best-selling country singles of all time, but it would also provoke a backlash that would far outlast its run on the charts. Critics claimed the song, co-written by Wynette and producer Billy Sherrill, encouraged women to remain subservient to their husbands. It was written, *Newsweek* concluded, "for the beleaguered housewife who grits her teeth as destiny dumps its slop on her head."

But Wynette defended the song, insisting its message was more complicated than its detractors believed. A licensed beautician who had three children by the time she was twenty-two, she'd left her first husband in part over their disagreement about her yearning to become a country singer. Years later, when her ex-husband attended a show and asked for an autograph, she signed it with the same comment he'd made when she moved out: "Dream on, baby."

Wynette was no shrinking violet. Among her first hits were "Your Good Girl's Gonna Go Bad" and "D-I-V-O-R-C-E." The song that was her most familiar and most controversial, she often said, wasn't about women putting their husbands' needs ahead of their own, but a call for forgiveness. ("After all, he's just a man.") "I don't see anything in that song that implies a woman is supposed to sit home and raise babies while a man goes out and raises hell," she wrote in her 1979 autobiography.[23] She had created her own financial independence, raised children as a single mother, and run a business. "I consider myself a lot more liberated than many of the 'sisters' who criticized the song," she wrote.

Sixteen years before Wynette released "Stand by Your Man," one of her predecessors, a journeywoman named Kitty Wells, happened upon a demo that she would shape into another of the genre's most irrepressible songs. Wells, like Wynette at the time of her own breakthrough, was raising three children at the time. Frustrated by her inability to score much radio play with her music, she was preparing to give up the music industry in favor of full-time motherhood. But when her husband, who was also a performer, suggested she listen to a new song called **"It Wasn't God Who Made Honky-Tonk Angels,"** she agreed to record it for the union-scale payment she would receive for the session: $125.

Hank Thompson was then enjoying a long run at the top of the country charts with his maudlin song "The Wild Side of Life," in which the singer laments the unfaithful urges of his woman. "I didn't know God made honky-tonk angels/I might have known you'd never make a wife," he moans, speaking on behalf of a generation of men who were collectively fretting over their female counterparts' growing sense of independence. Wells brought a sober, maternal reading to the "answer" song written by Jay Miller, which turned the tables on men. If some women were inclined to cheat, the song suggested, well, it's married men who "think they're single" that will lead women astray. "It's a shame that all the blame is on us women," Wells sang over a traditionally spare guitar-and-fiddles arrangement. If it was socially acceptable for men to walk into bars alone, why weren't women allowed the same freedom?[24]

In the hands of one of Wells's "saucier" contemporaries, as one country historian has written, the song could have come across like "an endorsement of loose living."[25] The fact that the song shared a familiar, old-fashioned tune not just with "The Wild Side of Life," but with country music standards by founding figures Roy Acuff and the Carter Family, helped soften the blow "of what was then a fairly radical lyric." In practical terms, the success of Wells's song led directly to opportunities for dozens of female country singers to come, in an industry that had previously taken as conventional wisdom their lack of commercial appeal. Wells, soon crowned the Queen of Country Music, went on to earn top honors from the country-music trade publications each year for more than a decade, well into the 1960s.

The Equal Employment Opportunity Commission (EEOC) engendered controversy as soon as it was established, in 1965. Newspapers, the commissioners agreed, could no longer permit job listings that specified a preferred race. But the panel's four male appointees (among five seats) chose to ignore complaints about help wanted ads that distinguished between male and female applicants. The provision in the Civil Rights Act of 1964 that assured job-seeking women equal protection under the law had been the subject of widespread ridicule; even in the country's most august publications, editorials mocked it as the "bunny law"—one that would, it was suggested, require the Playboy Club to allow men to apply as waitresses. And the commissioners seemed to hold the provision in similar regard.[26]

But Dr. Pauli Murray, a Yale Law School professor who had served on the President's Commission on the Status of Women, formed by John F. Kennedy in 1961, led the criticism of the ruling, and she soon entered discussions with Betty Friedan that would help revive the feminist movement. At a conference in Washington, DC, in June 1966, Friedan convened a group of delegates frustrated by the EEOC's inability to enforce Title VII, the section of the Civil Rights Act that prohibited employer discrimination by sex. The breakaway group agreed to create an organization that would "take action to bring women into full participation in the mainstream of American society now." As indicated by the three letters Friedan jotted on a napkin—"N O W"—the group would be called the National Organization for Women.

The group's initial officers included Friedan as president and Aileen Hernandez—one of two EEOC commissioners on the losing side of the 3–2 vote to permit gender-specific wording in employment ads—as executive vice president, pending her resignation from the EEOC. Echoing the Declaration of Sentiments written at Seneca Falls more than a century earlier, NOW's Statement of Purpose vowed to protest the "false image of women" that was still rampant in the mass media and the country's social institutions. With women's life expectancy having increased to nearly seventy-five years, the organizers wrote, the old excuse that women should be disqualified from certain career jobs because of the duties of child-rearing was irrelevant. Though more women were working, NOW argued, they were increasingly concentrated on the lower rungs of the job ladder—in clerical, cleaning, or assistants' positions or other menial labor. To make matters worse, as Friedan wrote in her statement draft, "[t]oo many women have been restrained by the fear of being called 'feminist.' There is no civil rights movement to speak for women, as there has been for Negroes and other victims of discrimination. The National Organization for Women must therefore begin to speak."[27]

At its second national conference, in 1967, NOW prepared a Bill of Rights for Women. The document advocated passage of the long-dormant Equal Rights Amendment, the establishment of publicly funded child care, and, for the first time in the history of the women's movement on a national scale, the legalization of abortion. NOW's publicity campaigns drew immediate attention, as well as some notable results. By the end of 1967, the *New York Times* led a coalition of newspapers that were among the first to remove gender specificity from their employment ads. The following year, NOW member Shirley Chisholm became the first African-American woman elected to the US House of Representatives. (She would go on, in 1972, to become the first black candidate of either sex to run for the presidential nomination of a major political party.) On Mother's Day 1969, NOW launched its "Freedom for Women Week," conducting demonstrations at the White House, where participants demanded "Rights, Not Roses."

In an era of sustained debate about civil rights, women's issues were in fact permeating "the mainstream of American society." From the beginning of the decade, skirt hemlines crept up from just above the knee to mid-thigh, progressing from the miniskirts ubiquitous in Swinging London to the "micro mini," and precipitating a clamor about women's fashion choices. On network television, sitcoms such as *Bewitched* and *That Girl* began to show that women could be the stars of their own lives, not dependent on male counterparts to forge their identities. Demonstrations were growing more dramatic, too. During a women's antiwar conference in the nation's capital in 1968, hundreds of participants marched by torchlight to the Arlington National Cemetery, where they symbolically declared the "Burial of Traditional Womanhood." Later that year a group calling themselves Radical Women protested the Miss America pageant, awarding the title to a sheep and stuffing a "Freedom Trash Can" with bras, wigs, and more "women's garbage."[28] On the most basic level, women were appealing for a simple concession: respect.

Amid all this activity, on Valentine's Day 1967, a young woman entered Atlantic Studios at 60th and Broadway in New York City, hoping to translate her enormous singing talent into her first real commercial success. Aretha Franklin was a daughter of the Baptist minister C. L. Franklin, reared alongside musical sisters Carolyn and Erma. Raised as a gospel singer, Franklin had struggled to gain traction after being signed in 1960 to Columbia Records. She abandoned her gospel roots in favor of a lush vocal-jazz approach, like that of Sarah Vaughan and Ella Fitzgerald. Despite landing a few minor hits on the R&B and Easy Listening charts, she was frustrated. After six years with the world's most prestigious record label, she elected not to re-sign, instead joining the roster at Atlantic Records. The decision was difficult, recalled her sister Carolyn. But Aretha understood the contemporary pop marketplace, and she decided that Columbia, the home of Billie Holiday, Johnny Mathis, and Bob Dylan, did not.[29]

She'd had an unfortunate introduction to her new label, Atlantic. While she was recording with a multiracial group of musicians in Muscle Shoals, Alabama, Aretha's husband had gotten into a racially charged, alcohol-fueled altercation with studio owner Rick Hall. After taking some time off in Detroit, Franklin and her sisters headed to New York to fulfill her obligation for her first album with Atlantic. It felt like they were on a mission, as Carolyn Franklin would recall. "We realized that our sister was on the brink of letting the world know what we had always known—that she was hands-down the scariest singer in the world. When she was in her element, no one could touch her."[30]

The key song Franklin recorded during those sessions was **"Respect,"** which had been a modest hit in 1965, written and recorded by Otis Redding. Franklin had been performing the song onstage for some time, and she'd changed it significantly. Franklin and her sisters transformed Redding's down-on-my-knees pleading into a hip, soulful celebration, a rollicking testament to the power of a woman. It was time, she sang, that she got her "propers." To underscore the demand, she spelled out the title word—"R-E-S-P-E-C-T, find out what it means to me." The Franklin sisters' responsive backing vocals were contrived spontaneously, in the studio, according to producer Jerry Wexler. "They gave the song a strong sexual flavor," he told Franklin's biographer. "The call for respect went from a request to a demand. And then, given the civil rights and feminist fervor that was building in the Sixties, respect—especially as Aretha articulated it with such force—took on new meaning. 'Respect' started off as a soul song and ended up as a kind of national anthem."[31]

For Carolyn Franklin, whether listeners heard the song through the filter of feminism or the civil rights movement made little difference. "All those interpretations are correct," she said, "because everyone needs respect on every level." Otis Redding joked onstage at the Monterey Pop Festival in the summer 1967 that a "girl" had taken his song away. In fact, according to Wexler, Redding was delighted with Franklin's version. Wexler apparently played Aretha's single for its songwriter before it was released, and Redding asked him to pay it twice more. "The smile never left his face."[32]

"After Black Power, Women's Liberation." That was the headline on a *New York* magazine article published in 1969. The piece marked the emergence of the journalist Gloria Steinem as a leading voice of the women's movement. In fact, Steinem had been writing about women's issues since the early 1960s; her 1962 piece for *Esquire* about contraception and the family obligations of working women was published a year before *The Feminine Mystique*. Opportunities for women, as Steinem wrote for *New York*, grew rapidly after the passage of the Nineteenth Amendment in 1920. But, she noted, like the brief period of improving fortunes for black Americans during Reconstruction, the social order soon devolved. Much as the rise of Jim Crow segregation proved to be a long-term setback, a half-century after women won the vote they were still struggling to gain a sense of worth outside the home. The second-wave feminism of the women's movement, according to Steinem, was rooted in the experiences of educated young women in the larger "Movement," "from the Southern sit-ins of nine years ago to the current attacks on the military-industrial-educational complex." Even after demonstrating against reactionary politics, military leaders, and authoritarian college administrations, the women of Steinem's generation still found themselves relegated to the old, dutiful roles in organizations such as Students for a Democratic Society, "typing and making coffee." The eventual liberation of women would benefit not just half the population, she wrote: "The idea is, in the long run, that women's liberation will be men's liberation, too."[33]

One atypical women's libber was a bleach-blonde young singer from Tennessee who has voluntarily played to stereotypes throughout her long career. Dolly Parton was a twenty-year-old new arrival to Nashville in 1966 when she seized her first chance at recording. Though the first song on her first album was called "Dumb Blonde," it wasn't quite what the title implied. The lyrics, written by industry veteran Curly Putman, made it instantly apparent that Parton would refuse to be confined by the assumptions men might make about her appearance. "Just because I'm blonde don't think I'm dumb/'Cause this dumb blonde ain't nobody's fool," she sang on a pop arrangement gone Nashville with the singer's Smoky Mountains drawl, accompanied by pedal steel guitar.

The second song on her debut album, which Parton wrote herself, set to a go-go beat her complaint about a husband who expected the singer to perform not just the traditionally "female" chores, but the male ones as well—cutting the grass, washing the car, taking out the trash. "Your woman's gettin' tired of being your ole handy man," she growled.

But it was Parton's second album that confirmed her standing as a feminist paragon. The album's title track, **"Just Because I'm a Woman,"** called out a double standard: when the singer's future husband asks about her past relationships, she answers that they're no different from his: "My mistakes are no worse than yours, just because I'm a woman." Over the years Parton has declined to call herself a feminist, but her music has often suggested otherwise. At the height of her fame, she starred in the 1980 feature film *9 to 5*, an office comedy in which three women plot to overthrow a sexist boss. "If you don't like the road you're walking," she once said, "start paving another one."

In retrospect, the country music establishment was as good a place as any in the entertainment world for women and the men who supported them to push for the liberation movement. By the 1960s, country music was entrenched in the public mind, whether fairly or not, as the music of uncultured, uneducated "hillbillies." The variety show *Hee Haw*, which debuted in 1969, played the clichés about rural America for hokey laughs. But the Nashville recording industry was also eager for crossover success, adding strings, choral accompaniment, and trendy rhythms to its songs—the production techniques collectively known as "countrypolitan"—in a frank bid for pop acceptance. At the same time, much like the television industry, its writers were newly responsive to social change.

As a contract songwriter, the Kentucky native Tom T. Hall was known as "The Storyteller." A few years after arriving in Nashville, he wrote a song about a widow whose suggestive dress and affinity for the nightlife draws the attention of the local Parent-Teacher Association. He drew that particular story from an incident he recalled from his youth. The woman walks into the next PTA meeting and shames each of the committee members for their hypocrisy: they all drink and flirt, and the married ones are unfaithful to their spouses, or secretly hope to be: "And then you have the nerve to tell me, you think that as a mother I'm not fit."

The singer entrusted with the song was a relative unknown named Jeannie C. Riley, a young woman from small-town Texas who'd endured a rude awakening upon her arrival in Nashville. Exploited and degraded by unscrupulous men in the business, she "felt like a cheap floozy" by the time she was called in to record Hall's new song.[34] Whether or not her personal circumstances fed the bitterness that infused it, "Harper Valley PTA" rang a clear bell for millions of women in America. It hit number one on both the *Billboard* country and pop charts, a rare feat, selling nearly six million copies in the process. Riley became an overnight sensation, adopting an image in short skirts and go-go boots like a backwoods counterpart to Nancy Sinatra, whose hit song "These Boots Are Made for Walking" was a similar declaration of defiance. Though she never again approached the blockbuster success of her breakout hit, Riley played along gamely, releasing follow-up singles such as "The Girl Most Likely" (another song about those who would judge "by the way I look, not the way I am") and "The Rib" (which called for true equality, "not lesser than").

Some in the women's movement saw the body as the first battleground. They sought to empower women with the kind of knowledge about their own personal health needs that had long been considered taboo in a male-dominated society. One group that came together at a women's conference at Emmanuel College in Boston took it upon themselves to do just that, compiling a 193-page course booklet called *Women and Their Bodies*. In 1971, they changed the title to *Our Bodies, Ourselves* and had the book republished by a small press. An underground phenomenon, the book sold more than 250,000 copies at forty cents apiece, leading to a major commercial arrangement with Simon & Schuster.[35]

Our Bodies, Ourselves included a wealth of information about women's issues, from anatomy, sexuality, and pregnancy to self-defense, sexually transmitted disease, abortion, and birth control. "For women throughout the centuries, ignorance about our bodies has had one major consequence: pregnancy," wrote the group, the Boston Women's Health Book Collective, in the preface to the Simon & Schuster edition:

> Until very recently pregnancies were all but inevitable, and biology was our destiny: because our bodies are designed to get pregnant and give birth and lactate, that is what all or most of us did. The courageous and dedicated work begun by people like Margaret Sanger to spread and make available birth control methods that women could use freed us from the traditional lifetime of pregnancies. But the societal expectation that a woman above all else will have babies does not die easily. . . . [This knowledge] has given us a sense of a larger life space to work in, an invigorating and challenging sense of time and room to discover the energies and talents that are in us, to do the work we want to do. And one of the things we most want to do is to help make this freedom of choice, this life span, available to every woman.

The women's movement chalked up a genuine pop hit around this time with "I Am Woman," an anthem co-written by the Australian-American singer Helen Reddy. Belatedly recognized from her 1971 debut album, the song, with its famous opening lines—"I am woman, hear me roar, in numbers too big to ignore"—became the top song in America at the end of 1972, winning a Grammy as the year's best song. Reddy was a relative newcomer to the feminist movement after coming to America, she admitted. "I was looking for songs that would reflect the change in my consciousness. And there weren't any. . . . I realized that I was going to have to write the song." When a male interviewer asked her to explain just when a woman would know she'd been liberated, she replied, "When is a *person* liberated? When they are no longer discriminated against by the society."

The debate over women's reproductive rights spilled uncomfortably into the country music world when Loretta Lynn recorded a song called "The

Pill." Lynn had delivered four of her six children by the time she was twenty-one. A Kentucky native, she'd spent most of her teen years in Washington State, where her husband moved to find employment as a farm worker and logger. Working together to promote her singing career before she had a record deal, Lynn and her husband, O. V. "Doolittle" Lynn, quickly achieved a goal that took most country performers years, if not decades: membership on the Grand Ole Opry. As Lynn's fame grew in the mid-1960s, she earned a reputation with no-nonsense songs that alternately stood up to wayward men—such as "Don't Come Home a-Drinkin' (with Lovin' on Your Mind)"—and the women who would steal them away ("Fist City"). In 1972 she recorded a song dedicated to the life-changing wonders of a recent medical breakthrough: "The Pill."

Though the first oral contraceptive received Federal Drug Administration approval in 1960, it wasn't until 1965 that the Supreme Court struck down a Connecticut law prohibiting married couples from using it to plan childbirth. Seven years later, the high court granted unmarried couples the same freedom to use the pill. Yet despite its timeliness the song, co-credited to three contract writers, was deemed too controversial for Lynn's record company, MCA. They kept it on the shelf for three years before finally releasing it in 1975. Like many of Lynn's songs, the lyrics seemed to speak to her own life. Tired of enduring repeated pregnancies while her man stays out carousing, she vows to have some fun of her own: "There's gonna be some changes made/ Right here on nursery hill."

In an interview with *Playgirl* magazine, Lynn claimed she'd been prepared to quit the Opry over their threat to forbid her to sing the song onstage. Though dozens of radio stations did ban the song, its impact was profound. One rural doctor reportedly told the singer that her advocacy did "more than all the government programs put together" for raising awareness about the availability of contraceptives. Had they been accessible when she was getting pregnant, Lynn would have "taken 'em like popcorn," she told *People* magazine. "I wouldn't trade my kids for anyone's. But I wouldn't necessarily have had six, and I sure would have spaced 'em better."

The year 1975 marked the beginning of the Decade for Women, as designated by the United Nations. That year, President Gerald Ford announced the appointment of an independent commission to recommend ways the United States could form "a more perfect union" between men and women. Meanwhile, Congress voted to fund a series of state-level meetings on women's issues, where participants voted for delegates to attend a National Women's Conference. The event was held in Houston in November 1977. Though the convention drew an estimated twenty thousand visitors and received plenty of media coverage at the time, Gloria Steinem has called it "the most important event nobody knows about."[36]

While just six of the two thousand elected delegates were men, reporters noted that the conference was "far more diverse than any political gathering in American history in terms of race, ethnicity, class, age, occupation, and level of political experience," writes Marjorie J. Spruill in *Divided We Stand*.[37] First Lady Rosalynn Carter addressed the conference alongside former First Ladies Betty Ford and Lady Bird Johnson, the first time the three women had appeared together. The tennis star Billie Jean King, a few years removed from her defeat of Bobby Riggs in the so-called Battle of the Sexes, was part of a relay team that carried a symbolic torch from Seneca Falls, home of the first women's rights convention in 1848, to Houston.

The goal of the conference was to design a National Plan of Action on women's issues. There were also plenty of diversions: seminars, films, self-defense workshops, and entertainment, including a concert by the all-women, African-American a cappella group Sweet Honey in the Rock. Also performing on the "Seneca Falls Stage" in another convention center across the street was the group Deadly Nightshade, in what the group billed at the time as their last-ever appearance. Formed under the name Ariel in the late 1960s while the three core members were students at Mount Holyoke and Smith colleges in western Massachusetts, Deadly Nightshade described themselves as one of the first all-female rock bands.

Predictably, their experience with the music industry had been often unpleasant. Record labels declined to listen to their demo tapes, claiming they'd already signed one "all-girl" band. One producer interrupted an A&R meeting to urge his colleague not to sign the group, warning that the company would "only have to pay for their abortions." For several years the band had been playing women's music festivals, which were modeled on the first National Women's Music Festival, held on the University of Illinois campus in the summer of 1974. Deadly Nightshade billed themselves as "female dynamite," and their music as "women's lib with a sense of humor."[38] Their song "High Flying Woman" was a crowd-pleaser at women's marches and rallies, and the band performed it on a network television special about second-wave feminism. They also showcased another original song, "Ain't I a Woman," based on a speech by the former slave and women's rights advocate Sojourner Truth.

In a report to Congress and the president titled "The Spirit of Houston," organizers at the National Women's Conference outlined more than two dozen planks adopted at the convention. These included recommendations to forge new opportunities for women in employment, education, and elected office; suggestions to combat sex-role stereotyping in schools and on television; preventative measures against domestic violence and rape; improved child care and pregnancy disability benefits; and more.[39] The conventioneers also called for a stronger voice for women in foreign policy. During the conference, a Minority Caucus coined the term "women of color." When the delegates voted to support the ratification of the Equal Rights Amendment, which had passed both houses of Congress in 1972, they chanted "Three more states!"—the number that was preventing adoption of the amendment. Then they sang "God Bless America" and, to the tune of "The Yellow Rose of Texas," "The ERA Was Passed Today."[40]

Despite their exuberance, however, the Equal Rights Amendment faced strong opposition from a coalition of conservative-minded women who were as fiercely committed as their feminist counterparts. While the National Women's Conference was taking place in Houston, another twenty thousand or so citizens—largely women, but many of their husbands, too—were gathering across town at the Astro Arena. This countermovement was led by Phyllis Schlafly, the constitutional lawyer who founded the anti-feminist Stop ERA organization (later renamed the Eagle Forum) in 1972. Schlafly was a routine presence in the national media, and she produced an influential newsletter that helped establish the "pro-family" movement that has had a substantial role in American politics in the decades since. Under Schlafly's leadership, a broad coalition of religious conservatives, pro-life groups, opponents of gay rights, advocates of small government, and others challenged the women's delegates for the right to speak on behalf of American women. Schlafly and her supporters' success in influencing public opinion has been often credited as a major factor in the ultimate defeat of the ERA, which failed to earn ratification by its final deadline in mid-1982.

First Earth Day, New York City, April 22, 1970.

Credit: Jean-Pierre Laffont.

http://jplaffont.photoshelter.com/gallery-image/FIRST-EARTH-DAY-NYC/
G0000DW7ziK0xybU/I0000OaGeVcqv1zo/C0000YXRAHXQRMbg

5 THE ENVIRONMENT

Don't Go Near the Water – Whose Garden Was This – Going Up the Country – Find the Cost of Freedom – Solo Whale – Big Yellow Taxi – Mercy Mercy Me (The Ecology) – Burn On – (Nothing but) Flowers – Earth Song

In 1962 California became the most populous state in the nation, surpassing New York. The country's westward tilt was more than a century in the making, beginning in earnest with the California Gold Rush of the late 1840s. By then, many believed it was the "manifest destiny" of the United States to continue expanding through the undeveloped territories of the Midwest all the way to the Pacific Ocean. Providence, wrote the newspaper editor John O'Sullivan in the *New York Morning News* in 1845, had bestowed upon the American people "the whole of the continent . . . for the development of the great experiment of liberty and federated self-government entrusted to us."

The lure of the West has been a defining part of the American culture ever since. Hollywood beckoned with its land of make-believe. For any young person with no more responsibility than to fill up the gas tank, the open road led to the West Coast. By the early 1960s, a group of teenage singers from the Los Angeles suburbs began singing about the sun and sand of their state's budding surf culture. Changing their name from the Pendletones to the Beach Boys, they would eventually become one of the world's best-selling bands, largely by cashing in on the "California myth" they helped invent. Hundreds of surf-rock bands emerged from practice spaces in suburban garages across the country, most of them landlocked. The California myth was an idler's dream.

Through the early 1960s, the Beach Boys promised "surfin' safaris" and endless days and nights by the waterfront. By 1971, however, as alarming reports accumulated about the critical threat of oil spills, toxic runoff, and other industrial pollution, they were warning their generation to stay away. On **"Don't Go Near the**

Water," the group reflected the environmental devastation that was fast becoming one of the country's most earnest causes:

> *Oceans, rivers, lakes and streams*
> *Have all been touched by man*
> *The poison floating out to sea*
> *Now threatens life on land*

The dubious distinction of the largest marine oil spill in world history cur-
rently belongs to the Deepwater Horizon disaster of 2010, when the offshore
drilling rig of the same name exploded in the Gulf of Mexico. The blowout at
the seabed left hundreds of thousands of gallons of crude oil gushing into the
ocean each day, a contamination that continued for nearly three months, until
emergency workers finally managed to cap the well. In all, the spill unleashed
nearly five million barrels of oil (more than 200,000,000 gallons), ravaging
marine life and creating a situation that one physician called "the biggest
public health crisis from a chemical poisoning in the history of this country."[1]

Prior to the Deepwater Horizon incident (sometimes called the BP oil
spill, after the petroleum company primarily implicated in the accident), for
most Americans, the benchmark oil-related disaster was the grounding of the
Exxon Valdez tanker in Prince William Sound, Alaska, in 1989. Before that
calamity, however, the oil spill that helped synthesize the public's despair over
the environmental hazards of drilling for oil occurred off the coast of Santa
Barbara, California, in 1969.

The Santa Barbara Channel has always been a rich repository of petroleum. For centuries the native Chumash people of central California drew
from the tar that seeped naturally from the ocean floor to waterproof their
canoes. During the 1890s, entrepreneurs sought to profit from the same resource, establishing the first offshore drilling rigs in the United States. More
than twenty companies built a series of piers that extended hundreds of feet
from the shoreline into the Pacific, each outfitted with virtual tree farms of
derricks.

By the mid-twentieth century, the piers had been abandoned in favor of
offshore platforms, many built several miles from the coast. Residents no
longer looked out upon a field of machinery. Many of them took up surfing.
In late January 1969, however, the beach community was buffeted by the
news of a manmade disaster: one of the offshore wells built by Union Oil
had failed, spewing millions of gallons of oil across eight hundred square
miles of ocean.

The blowout quickly became national news. For a few days, northwesterly winds seemed to spare the shoreline the impact of the spill, but an incoming storm system soon pushed the slick back into the Santa Barbara harbor. An inches-deep layer of crude oil blackened every surface in sight, muted the sound of the waves on the beaches, and filled the air with the stench of petroleum.

Though the spill killed thousands of seabirds and an untold number of fish, Union Oil Co. President Fred L. Hartley was reluctant to call the incident a "disaster." "There has been no loss of human life," he said. "I am amazed at the publicity for the loss of a few birds."[2] In short order, that kind of corporate insensitivity would ignite the ire of a broad coalition of scientists, legislators, and activists. The magnitude of the outcry about the damage to the environment led eventually to a visit from the newly inaugurated president, Richard Nixon, who noted that the situation had "frankly touched the conscience of the American people." In late 1969, Congress, spurred by the groundswell of outrage over the Santa Barbara oil spill and other environmental disasters, passed the bill known as the National Environmental Policy Act (NEPA). On January 1, 1970, Nixon signed it into law.

NEPA called for the submission of Environmental Impact Statements from all federal agencies planning projects that could impact the environment. The statute was a forerunner of the Nixon administration's establishment of the Environmental Protection Agency later in 1970. "The 1970s absolutely must be the years when America pays its debt to the past by reclaiming the purity of its air, its waters, and our living environment," Nixon said upon signing NEPA into effect. "It is literally now or never."[3]

The government's commitment was a welcome development for many young Americans, some of whom were involved in the "back to the land" movement, moving to rural areas and establishing self-sustained community living experiments. Over two days in late January, a university group in Evanston, Illinois, called Northwestern Students for a Better Environment hosted a multifaceted "teach-in" on the growing environmental crisis. More than ten thousand students and community members attended the event, which was named Project Survival. Study sessions and workshops focused on issues including water pollution, overpopulation, and the limited supply of natural resources. During a midnight "sing-in," the folk singer Tom Paxton debuted a disconsolate new song, **"Whose Garden Was This."**

Paxton was a Chicago native who grew up in Oklahoma, a decade after the dust storms of the 1930s. From a young age he was attracted to the unfussy voices of Burl Ives and the Oklahoma native Woody Guthrie. But it was the

Weavers' recording of their 1955 appearance at Carnegie Hall—a comeback of sorts, after their blacklisting over their alleged communist sympathies—that really moved him. *The Weavers at Carnegie Hall* mixed labor songs ("Pay Me My Money Down," Merle Travis's "Sixteen Tons"), ethnic folk songs ("Wimoweh"), and a few of the group's own compositions ("Kisses Sweeter Than Wine").

"Something in the spirit of that album said there are bullies in this world, and they won't go away until we stand up to them," Paxton once said. "And yet that album was so *musical*. Folk music had a dimension that pop didn't have, some true salt to it."[4] Paxton became a fixture on the Greenwich Village folk scene of the early 1960s, watching a succession of talented newcomers arrive after him: Bob Dylan in 1961, Phil Ochs the following year. "We had a lot of fun," he said. "We were rivals, you know, but rivals for excellence." Paxton was one of the first to express specific opposition to the escalating Vietnam War in song ("Lyndon Johnson Told the Nation"), and he could draw a discomforting vignette (as he did in another antiwar song, "My Son, John").

Paxton wrote "Whose Garden Was This" expressly for his appearance at Project Survival. To the listener, it's not apparent whether the bleak landscape described in the lyric is the result of environmental degradation or some sort of nuclear holocaust. For the children of Paxton's generation, those concerns would often feel practically interchangeable. The earth on which they would one day raise their own children was under siege, from the looming catastrophe of the Cold War arms race to the exhaust fumes, toxic runoff, and inadequate waste management of the industrialized world. The narrator of Paxton's near future longs to hear stories about all this natural beauty he's never experienced firsthand—the lush forests, the green meadows and blue oceans, the gentle nighttime breezes ("I've heard records of breezes"). "Can you swear that was true?" he begs to know.

> *Whose garden was this? It must have been lovely*
> *Did it have flowers? I've seen pictures of flowers*
> *And I'd love to have smelled one*

In a time defined by marches, sit-ins, and teach-ins, the symposium at Northwestern was a precursor to what would become one of the most successful ongoing demonstrations of public advocacy in the country's history. On April 22, 1970, an estimated twenty million people attended events across the nation for the first Earth Day. Planned as a celebration of the natural world, it was also a condemnation of human carelessness. In the years since, Earth Day has become an annual reminder of the fragility of the planet.

It was the sight of the blackened California beaches in the wake of the Santa Barbara oil spill that moved Wisconsin senator Gaylord Nelson to engineer the original Earth Day. Nelson, a Democrat, persuaded the Republican California congressman Pete McCloskey to serve as his cochair, emphasizing growing bipartisan concern about environmental protection. He enlisted a young activist named Denis Hayes, then studying at the Kennedy School of Government at Harvard University, to coordinate the effort.

Nelson's belief in the critical importance of environmental policy had not been an easy sell. He'd grown up in Wisconsin's North Woods, a region that had been laid low by the timber industry, which wiped out the forest "in an eyewink of history and left behind fifty years of heartbreak and economic ruin," as he once wrote.[5] As the highest elected official in Wisconsin, he earned national recognition as the "Conservation Governor," rehabilitating neglected state parks and fighting the exploitation of natural resources by private industry. He created a Youth Conservation Corps, providing jobs for more than one thousand young people, and he spearheaded the Outdoor Recreation Action Program (ORAP), a $50 million initiative to acquire land for public parks and wildernesses. Upon becoming a member of the US Senate in 1963, a seat he would hold for three terms, Nelson was instrumental in convincing President Kennedy to speak out on behalf of conservation. But in his efforts to introduce legislation that would ban the use of DDT—the controversial pesticide that Rachel Carson targeted in her best-selling 1962 book *Silent Spring*—not one member of the Congress supported him.

While returning from a fact-finding mission to the Santa Barbara coastline, Nelson read about the various teach-ins that were proliferating on college campuses. In 1965, students and faculty at the University of Michigan at Ann Arbor staged the first teach-in, an all-night protest and educational conference on the mounting opposition to the war in Vietnam. In October 1969 a committee at Columbia University organized a one-day National Teach-In on World Community. "The American university may now be assuming a central role in social change," read the introduction to the group's statement of purpose. Declaring their opposition to racism and militarism, the committee booked a Who's Who of contemporary activists, including Allen Ginsberg, Students for a Democratic Society leaders Mark Rudd and Tom Hayden, and the ecologist Barry Commoner, whose best-selling 1971 book *The Closing Circle* would help introduce the concept of sustainability to the general public. In a letter to Nelson sent in December, 1969, the committee behind the teach-in invited the senator to be a featured speaker at a follow-up event planned at Columbia for the new year, one that would address "the four interconnected threats to the planet—wars of mass destruction, overpopulation, pollution[,] and the depletion of resources."

These events convinced Nelson that the way to foster commitment to environmental protection among his fellow politicians was through direct appeal to their constituents. Elected officials may not have been ready to take a stand against big business, but huge numbers of the electorate were. *Silent Spring* had awakened the public to the perils of humanity's growing dependence on technology and chemicals. It was a remarkable act of persuasion.

Carson's working titles for her book included *Remembrance of Earth, Man against the Earth*, and *Man the Destroyer*. A marine biologist, she'd already published a well-received trilogy of books about sea life before turning her sights to the use of pesticides. In an age of accelerated progress, one that elevated lab-coated scientists to celebrity status, the Swiss chemist Paul Hermann Muller was awarded a Nobel Peace Prize in 1948 for his discovery of the insecticidal properties of dichlorodiphenyltrichloroethane, or DDT. During World War II, the compound was used liberally as a curb on insect-borne and parasitic diseases such as malaria and typhus. By midcentury, the product was in wide use in the agriculture industries, to eradicate fire ants and other insects that attack crops.

Carson was an ecologist, as one of her biographers notes, concerned with a holistic view of the natural world at a time "before that perspective was accorded scholarly literacy." She grew up in a village north of Pittsburgh, where she watched as nearby coal-fired power plants polluted the local air and waterways. "The experience made her forever suspicious of promises of 'better living through chemistry' and of claims that technology would create a progressively brighter future."[6] Human beings are an element of the ecological system, not its master, she argued. To a generation that grew up terrified of the prospect of radioactive fallout from nuclear weapons, her dire warning of chemical contamination suddenly seemed like plain common sense.

To the chemical industry, however, Carson was a nuisance at best, or, more dramatically, an enemy to be neutralized. Not an academic—she had no Ph.D. or professorship, having worked as editor in chief of publications for the US Fish and Wildlife Service before setting out on her own—she was an outsider. She was also a woman. To the scientific community of the time, that may have been the most damning charge of all. Her detractors attempted to dismiss her as a "bird and bunny lover."[7] But Carson, who was dying of a metastasized breast cancer by the time of publication, ignored the criticism.

She was too busy ensuring that her plea on behalf of the sanctity of the natural world would be heard. "Wonder and humility are wholesome emotions," she wrote, "and they do not exist side by side with a lust for destruction." In the opening chapter of *Silent Spring*, she envisioned a once-verdant landscape overtaken by a "strange blight," marked by withered vegetation, mysterious illness, and the sudden absence of the songbirds—a silent spring.

Until the 1960s, the federal government considered the great outdoors primarily in terms of the preservation of public lands and the conservation of resources. Theodore Roosevelt, the "conservation president," helped establish twenty-three of the thirty-five national parks that were in existence by the time the National Park Service was created in 1916.

By mid-century, however, calls were increasing to regulate pollution and acknowledge the destructive relationship between human endeavor and the environment. Some called it the New Environmentalism. Congress passed the Federal Water Pollution Control Act in 1948 and, seven years later, the Air Pollution Control Act. Carson's *Silent Spring* was soon followed by another best seller, *The Quiet Crisis*, written by former Arizona senator Stewart Udall, who served as secretary of the interior under Presidents Kennedy and Johnson. "Plans to protect air and water, wilderness and wildlife are in fact plans to protect man," he said. In 1966, Congress passed the first comprehensive legislation protecting endangered species; when the first list of animals headed for extinction was issued a year later, it included among several dozen creatures the timber wolf, the Florida manatee, and the American bald eagle—the nation's symbol.

Two more publications, both issued in 1968, had their own profound impact on the public attitude toward the planet. Stanford professor Paul R. Ehrlich's *The Population Bomb* examined the global population "explosion" of recent decades and the crisis of its consequences on the natural world; the book predicted widespread food shortages and prescribed family planning and legalized abortion. That year Stewart Brand, a Stanford-trained biologist, began publishing his *Whole Earth Catalog*, a do-it-yourself guide to sustainable living. Brand's guidebook was packed with tutorials that emphasized the mastery of tools and skills. The idea was to develop "the power of the individual to conduct his own education, find his own inspiration, shape his own environment, and share his adventure" with anyone who might be interested. "We are as gods," Brand declared, "and might as well get good at it."

By the end of the decade, the generation increasingly known, for better or worse, as the hippies—the long-haired, eccentrically clothed, self-expressive young people committed to equal rights and, increasingly, against the war in Vietnam—was developing a "whole earth" ideology. Brand's catalog took its name from the ATS-3 satellite photo of our globe, the first of its kind. He'd petitioned NASA to release the photo; when they did, he used it on the cover of his first issue. Using tools ordered and ideas gleaned from the catalogs and other resources, many people who were coming of age at the time renounced urban development, industrialization, and the institutions of "straight" society and went back to the land.

Songwriters found the imagery of the back-to-the-land movement irresistible. At Woodstock, the band Canned Heat helped create the festival's aesthetic with a performance of their song **"Going Up the Country,"** based on an obscure 1920s tune by Texan Henry Thomas called "Bull-Doze Blues": "I'm gonna leave this city, got to get away/All this fussin' and fightin', man, you know I sure can't stay." As the title track of the subsequent *Woodstock* documentary, the song became a worldwide hit.

The new environmentalists trusted that Mother Earth had her own voice, and she was letting her inhabitants know that they were abusing their stewardship. "It's nature's way of telling you something's wrong," as the West Coast band Spirit put it. Young songwriters who had grown up in Brooklyn or the Bronx or some Midwestern suburb began subscribing to Native American notions of the Earth Goddess and the Greek deity Gaia. "Mother Earth will swallow you, lay your body down," sang Crosby, Stills, Nash & Young on their simple spiritual lament, **"Find the Cost of Freedom."**

The natural world was itself a song, and its invocation could be tendered as a form of protest. One especially unusual "protest" record came about in 1970, after a group of scientists confirmed their theory that whales communicate by song. Roger and Katy Payne were biologists with shared interest in sound and music; in his early career Roger Payne studied the echolocation of bats, while Katharine Payne, herself a researcher in acoustic biology, had been a music major in college. Roger Payne was working at Tufts University in Boston in the mid-1960s when he heard about a dead porpoise that had washed ashore on a nearby beach. He drove out to have a look; by the time he arrived, the carcass had been mutilated by vandals. There were initials carved in the creature's flank, and someone had plugged its blowhole with a cigar butt.

"I removed the cigar and stood there for a long time with feelings I cannot describe," as Payne would later write. Taking the incident as a sign they needed to apply their research skills on behalf of the magnificent creatures of the sea, he and Katharine were determined to investigate when they heard a rumor through a colleague about the "songs" of humpback whales. They traveled to

Bermuda, where they met with a Navy engineer monitoring by hydrophone for indications of Russian submarines. In his fieldwork he had captured what appeared to be the sound of humpback whales, but the engineer was reluctant to make his discovery public: he was afraid that whalers would use the recordings to hunt the animals. The engineer played his recordings for the Paynes, who were moved to tears. "We were just completely transfixed and amazed because the sounds are so beautiful, so powerful—so variable," Katy Payne would recall years later. The engineer, Frank Watlington, gave the Paynes his recordings and told them, "Go save the whales."[8]

By graphing these sounds, the Paynes and a colleague, Scott McVay, proved that male humpbacks emit specific songs, from six to more than thirty minutes long, during mating season. They called them "songs" because they had structure: clearly repeated intervals that the scientists compared with rhyming language. Excited, the Paynes were eager to share their findings. On a trip to San Diego to deliver a lecture, Roger Payne struck up a conversation with the head of the publishing company that produced the popular magazine *Psychology Today*. On the spot, the publisher decided to produce an album of the Paynes' whale songs.

The company worked diligently to attract attention to the project, getting *Newsweek*, for instance, to commit to a full-page, pro bono ad. Payne, meanwhile, set about playing whale songs for every cultural influencer he could contact. "I wanted to build whale songs into human culture," he said in a 2010 interview. "I played the songs for writers, musicians, composers, artists, playwrights, people in all media, ministers, poets, dancers and performers of every stripe. I got onto every major talk show and serious radio show of the period. A Pacifica Radio disk jockey played whale songs non-stop for four hours on one occasion and for three hours on another." As a result of all this publicity, sales of the atmospheric album soared improbably, into the hundreds of thousands. Folk singer Judy Collins recorded a version of the traditional British whaling song "Farewell to Tarwathie" accompanied by the muted cry of the whales. Eventually, the major label Capitol Records cut a licensing deal to reissue *Songs of the Humpback Whale*, assuring its continued availability.

"**Sole Whale**" led directly to the "Save the Whales" conservation campaign, which would become one of the most prominent environmental causes of the 1970s. In 1975 members of Greenpeace confronted Soviet whaling fleets in the North Pacific, setting in motion the continuum of "eco-terrorist" demonstrations that have included tree-sitting, the liberation of captive animals, and other "direct action" protests. That year

Payne oversaw the release of a second album of whale song, *Deep Voices*. Two years later he contributed a track to the *Voyager* Golden Record, the set of phonograph records containing greetings in multiple languages, various song styles, and a selection of earth sounds, sent into interstellar space aboard the Voyager spacecraft. By the end of the decade, with the "Save the Whales" campaign in full swing, interest in whale song continued virtually unabated: *National Geographic* ordered 10.5 million "flexi discs," thin "sound sheets" of playable vinyl, that were included in the January 1979 issue of the magazine. In the accompanying article, Payne explained what the discovery of whale songs meant to researchers: "We have learned that all men are created equal, but the whales remind us that all species are created equal—that every organism on earth, whether large or small, has an inalienable right to life."[9]

That insistence on the "right to life"—the sanctity of all living things—had a recurring presence in the world of popular music through the first years of the 1970s. The young songwriter Joni Mitchell was known primarily for versions of her songs recorded by other folk artists (Tom Rush, Judy Collins) until she released her third album, in 1970. *Ladies of the Canyon* featured "Woodstock," Mitchell's ode to the previous year's hippie pilgrimage to Yasgur's Farm, and another song that would become a signature for her, **"Big Yellow Taxi."**

> *Don't it always seem to go*
> *That you don't know what you've got til it's gone*
> *They paved paradise, and put up a parking lot*

She wrote the song during a visit to Hawaii with then-boyfriend Graham Nash, as she once explained. From her hotel window, she had a breathtaking view of the distant mountains. "Then I looked down, and there was a parking lot as far as the eye could see, and it broke my heart . . . this blight on paradise." The song specifies more than one element of the environmental movement: one verse laments the trees' incarceration in a "tree museum," and another implores the farmer to "put away the DDT." Years later the publicity-shy Mitchell would agree that "Big Yellow Taxi" was "a powerful little song," having inspired more than one town to tear up an existing parking lot and replace it with a park.[10]

The number one song in America in August of 1971 took into account more of the environmentalists' worries—smog, oil spills, radiation, "fish full of mercury." **"Mercy Mercy Me (The Ecology)"** was the second single from

What's Going On, a complete protest album by the dashing, smooth-singing Motown hitmaker Marvin Gaye. Gaye had endured a series of hardships in the last years of the 1960s, from the collapse and premature death of his duet partner, Tammi Terrell, and his brother Frankie's deployment to Vietnam to a rocky marriage to the sister of Motown's founder, Berry Gordy. As the new decade neared, Gaye retreated from the spotlight. By the time he re-emerged, he did so armed with a new commitment to social justice.

The title song "What's Going On" was an elegy for the times—the demonstrations and assassinations, and the racial tensions that the civil rights movement, for all its gains, still could not repair. Its recording became a sort of protest in itself: when Gordy refused to release the song as a single—it was too political, too loose and dreamy, too *different* for Motown's "Hitsville" song factory—Gaye staged a one-man strike, refusing to record another note for the label. Belatedly released, the song vindicated its singer, climbing higher than all but one of the dozens of previous hits he'd logged in a decade as the "Prince of Motown." The album that Gaye and his colleagues created in the wake of that success combined unabashed spirituality with black consciousness. "Mercy Mercy Me" was heartbreaking in ways that pop songs rarely achieve, with evocative, wordless backing vocals and a rhythmic undertow that keeps pulling the singer—and the listener—back from the brink of despair. Elsewhere on the album, Gaye reprised the ecological theme. On the gospel-influenced "Save the Children," he imagined a coming world where "flowers won't grow, bells won't be ringing," and wondered aloud, "Who's willing to try to save a world/That's destined to die?"

A few years after he completed his masterpiece, Gaye explained his transformation from stage entertainer to the vocal conscience of a troubled era. "My idea of living is, I would love to become an impeccable warrior, one who has no need for earthly things such as the wine, the women, the clothes and the diamonds, and the fine things to wear," he said. "I'd love to develop a distaste for those things and become only interested in knowledge and power that this earth will give us, if we're only willing to put in the time and effort. . . . I would love to quit show business and go after that knowledge and that power that the truly gifted sorcerer has. The power's here—it's in the rocks, it's in the air, it's in the animals."[11]

The 1970s were troubled times for the industrial cities of the nation. Urban blight was rampant, a result of the "white flight" to the suburbs that began post–World War II. In a struggling economy, whole blocks were condemned in once-thriving cities across the country. Air pollution had become so problematic that Congress was compelled to pass the Clean Air Act of 1970, which significantly expanded earlier air pollution measures adopted beginning in 1955.[12]

The Santa Barbara oil spill of 1969 was not the only incident that fueled the new sense of urgency about the environment. That year, a consortium of oil companies formed the Trans-Alaska Pipeline System to formally request permission from the US Department of the Interior to begin researching a proposed Alaska pipeline. Also in 1969, the city of Los Angeles issued an alarming medical alert about smog conditions, instructing teachers and parents to forbid children "to run, skip, or jump inside or outside" on days when the air pollution was most dangerous.[13]

In June, in a bizarre manifestation of the hazards of chemical waste, the Cuyahoga River in Cleveland caught fire. In fact, the Cuyahoga had burned several times previously, perhaps most notably in 1952. (One photo featuring massive black billows of smoke, which ran as part of *Time* magazine's coverage of the 1969 fire, was mistakenly identified; it had been taken during the 1952 fire.) As early as the end of the Civil War, there were about twenty oil refineries in the greater Cleveland area, including one of the largest in US history, Standard Oil of Ohio, owned by the magnate John D. Rockefeller. Given the routine disposal of unusable crude oil in the region's waterways, disaster was inevitable.

From the 1880s until the colossal blaze of 1952, the river caught fire at least a dozen times. By the late 1960s, Cleveland voters approved a $100 million bond measure to upgrade the city's sewer systems. But while that work was being prepared, the latest fire engulfed the river. Cleveland mayor Carl Stokes pledged to file a formal complaint with the state. "We have no jurisdiction over what's dumped in there," he said.[14]

On the first Earth Day, in 1970, students from Cleveland State University staged their own protest, marching from the campus to the banks of the Cuyahoga to draw attention to its plight. "The lower Cuyahoga has no visible signs of life," reported the Federal Water Pollution Control Administration, "not even low forms such as leeches and sludge worms that usually thrive on wastes." Days after he was sworn in as the first leader of the newly created US Environmental Protection Agency in late 1970, William Ruckelshaus warned the mayor of Cleveland, and his counterparts in Atlanta and Detroit, that they had six months to begin cleaning their contaminated waterways before the government would take them to court.

The fire on the Cuyahoga struck one songwriter as an absurd commentary on the human race's assault on our habitat. How, exactly, does a river catch fire? Randy Newman was a journeyman performer with a handful of hits under his belt, as performed by others (including Gene Pitney, Dusty

Springfield, and the band Three Dog Night), when he booked time in a series of Los Angeles studios to record his third album, *Sail Away*. The album featured several songs that would come to define the idiosyncratic performer's unreliable narrator and the arch sarcasm of his lyrics. The title track, Newman has suggested, was written, like much of his work, as a heavy parody—a recruitment jingle for a slave trader. ("You'll just sing about Jesus and drink wine all day/It's great to be an American.") "Political Science" lampooned the country's military swagger ("They all hate us anyhow/Let's drop the big one now"), and "God's Song (That's Why I Love Mankind)" pulled off a nifty feat, questioning the Almighty's existence by expressing contempt in His voice for the stupidity of his greatest creation, mankind.

Another song on the album, **"Burn On,"** paid ironic homage to Cleveland, which Newman mocked as the "city of light, city of magic." He conceived the song while watching, dumbfounded, the television news footage of the blaze on the river. Once again, the preposterous failings of human beings are the singer's preoccupation, as he sings directly to the river, one especially tragic symbol of the desecrated planet:

> *Now the Lord can make you tumble*
> *And the Lord can make you turn*
> *And the Lord can make you overflow*
> *But the Lord can't make you burn*

The era was ripe for broad satire. From the moment the band Talking Heads debuted their preppy, art-school brand of new wave music on the grimy New York City punk scene of the mid-1970s, David Byrne proved himself another ironically detached observer of American culture. On the band's debut album, *Talking Heads: 77*, which introduced the band's first hit single, "Psycho Killer," Byrne sang a childlike tune called "Don't Worry about the Government." On the surface, at least, the singer seems to have unfailing faith in citizenship and the institutions that make modern life go.

> *I see the states across this big nation*
> *I see the laws made in Washington, DC*
> *I think of the ones I consider my favorites*
> *I think of the people that are working for me*

Byrne's dispassionate social engagement would be a recurring theme for the band, with songs that seem to celebrate religious bliss ("Heaven"), middle-class complacency ("Once in a Lifetime"), and oblivion in all its senses ("Road to Nowhere").

After a decade of unlikely popular success driven by the band's relentless pursuit of rhythm and melody and Byrne's quirky persona (well suited as it was to the candy-colored music video format that defined '80s music), Talking Heads cut their last studio album together in 1988. *Naked*, recorded with a large contingent of international musicians in Paris, married the band's most pointed set of lyrics to date to some paradoxically festive musical arrangements, which veered from hard funk and mambo to Afrobeat.

The album's most widely played track was "(**Nothing but**) **Flowers**," another upbeat slice of musical tourism (in this case, Caribbean carnival music). Over nimble electric guitars and tripping syncopation, Byrne turned the memorable lament of Joni Mitchell's "Big Yellow Taxi" on its head. In Byrne's version, they paved paradise, only to have the wilderness reclaim the land. Due to some unspecified calamity—nuclear war? an apocalyptic weather event?—the planet has reverted to an underdeveloped state: "There was a factory/Now there are mountains and rivers," he yelps, singing in exasperated exclamation points. "There was a shopping mall/Now it's all covered with flowers."

Byrne being Byrne, he's not sure what to make of this imaginary idyll. Of course Mother Nature is magnificent, but she's not so . . . convenient. "If this is paradise," he sings, "I wish I had a lawnmower." After admitting his longing for the "honky-tonks, Dairy Queens and 7-Elevens," the song ends on a comically ominous note:

> *Don't leave me stranded here*
> *I can't get used to this lifestyle*

In its own characteristically cockeyed way, "(Nothing but) Flowers" was Byrne's unique response to our "progress" as citizens of the planet and what we do to it in the process. The human race, wrote Anthony DeCurtis in his *Rolling Stone* review of the album, has "a very destructive monkey on its back. Human survival is not guaranteed. With humor and good-hearted-ness, hope and fear, Talking Heads contemplate a world on the eve of destruction on this important record—and leave wide open the question of what the dawn will bring."[15]

Interviewed in a subsequent issue of the same magazine, Byrne made an effort to explain the song: "On the surface, it's a pleasant kind of tongue-in-cheek thing of me talking about giving it all up, throwing everything away and going out to live in the forest or the woods or the jungle, whatever," he said. "I guess it's a very common wish—but for the moment not all that likely."[16]

Michael Jackson claimed he was gazing at some of mankind's most elegant achievements—the theaters, academies, and museums of old Vienna's Ring Road—when he was inspired to write his own environmental protest song. "It dropped into my lap," he would recall.[17] Though the pop superstar began writing **"Earth Song"** on a European tour in 1988, the song wouldn't appear until the 1995 release of his album *HIStory: Past, Present, and Future, Book 1*. Somewhat mysteriously unreleased as a single in America, the song was a major hit across Europe, scoring the coveted Christmas week number one spot in the United Kingdom and fending off the Beatles' "Free as a Bird"— the band's first single in twenty-five years—at the top spot on the chart.

"Earth Song" is a kind of all-purpose elegy for the planet, a lengthy (nearly seven minute) gospel set piece that asks the singer's God about various concerns: what about heavens falling down, kingdoms turned to dust, the elephants and whales? "Did you ever stop to notice/This crying Earth, these weeping shores?" Jackson croons before the modulation that signals the call-and-response finale. Trading lines with the thundering Andrae Crouch Choir, Jackson wails with emotion as he builds to a forceful final line: "Do we give a damn?"

The video for "Earth Song" was an extended public service announcement of sorts. It unfurls footage of lush forests and a thriving savanna before giving way to gruesome images—a seal hunter, an elephant slain for its tusks—and a re-enactment of a traumatized family trudging through the bombed-out rubble of wartime. Jackson spends his own time on camera on a set made to look like a charred woodland, with flames still licking the ashes around him.

"Earth Song" was a centerpiece of Jackson's HIStory World Tour, which would prove to be his last before the comeback residency he planned for London's O2 Arena in 2009. For that concert series, called This Is It, Jackson envisioned elaborate special effects, including a rainforest replica that would appear during "Earth Song," releasing butterflies into the audience.[18]

Even for Jackson, who co-wrote (with Lionel Richie) the 1985 all-star blockbuster "We Are the World" for African famine relief, "Earth Song" was an outsize gesture. It would turn out to be the last song he ever sang; after rehearsing it for the O2 Arena shows on June 25, 2009, he died of sudden cardiac arrest. At the Grammy Awards the following year, Jackson was honored with an all-star tribute version of "Earth Song" featuring

Smokey Robinson, Celine Dion, Jennifer Hudson, Carrie Underwood, and Usher.

World-famous in life and in death, Michael Jackson is remembered for his phenomenal talent and his increasing eccentricity. But had he foreseen his own death, he may well have chosen to encore with the song that best represented his social conscience. "Earth Song" combines Jackson's extreme empathy and his grandiosity—two tendencies that would seem to be similarly useful in the quixotic business of saving the planet.

Free Speech Movement sit-in, Sproul Plaza, University of California, Berkeley, December 2–3, 1964.

Credit: Tom Kuykendall, Free Speech Movement Archives.

http://www.fsm-a.org/Tom_Kuykendall_photos_Dec_2-3_1964/Webpages/detail.np/detail-117.html

6 FREEDOM OF SPEECH

*Little Boxes – Rumble – All My Trials – Maggie's Farm – No Hole in My Head –
Ohio – California uber Alles – Freedom of Choice – Clones (We're All) – Smells like
Teen Spirit*

When Joanna Eberhart first arrived in her new hometown in Connecticut, she was taken aback. A professional photographer who'd lived in New York City until starting a family, she couldn't believe how little her fellow housewives seemed to crave any kind of creative outlet. She tried to organize a women's group—this was, after all, the Women's Lib era of the early 1970s. But the women only sat around "discussing various detergents with the intensity of television creatures whose only interest in life is to rid the world of rings-around-the-collar."

Those were the words of Vincent Canby, longtime *New York Times* film critic, in a review of the 1975 film adaptation of the bestselling novel *The Stepford Wives*, by Ira Levin. The title of Levin's 1972 book gave the culture a shorthand term for the conformist hazards of suburbanization: homemakers who have been rendered emotionally and culturally numb, utterly (and apparently voluntarily) oblivious to the wider world beyond the cul-de-sac.

Malvina Reynolds was already thinking along those lines when she conceived an idea for a song while driving with her husband and daughter through the San Francisco Bay Area one day in the early 1960s. En route from their home in San Francisco to a Quaker meeting in San Mateo County, Reynolds was struck by the homogeneity of the vast grid of tract housing built along the southern edge of San Francisco. The developer Henry Doelger had designed San Francisco's westernmost Sunset District, out by the coastline, atop sand dunes beginning in the 1930s. Herb Caen, the longtime *San Francisco Chronicle* columnist who had a knack for coining phrases, dubbed the neighborhood the "white cliffs of Doelger."[1] Eventually, Doelger's stucco empire would engulf Daly

City, the fast-rising suburb built on the flanks of San Bruno Mountain. In the brochures, the nearly identical homes were called the "House of the Moment." "He wanted to build for the average working man," as one architectural historian told the *New York Times* in a story that declared the developer "San Francisco's Champion of Conformity."

Reynolds's song, **"Little Boxes,"** was a snapshot of social commentary in which the Doelger homes represent the sacrifice of singularity in favor of middle-class aspiration. It became a minor hit in 1963 for her friend Pete Seeger. "There's a pink one and a green one and a blue one and a yellow one," Reynolds sang in her untrained warble on her own version of the song, a few years later. "And they're all made out of ticky-tacky, and they all look just the same."

Born into a family of socialist immigrants in San Francisco in 1900, Reynolds married a labor organizer. Her career in music didn't begin until she was in her late forties, when she met fellow left-wing songwriters such as Earl Robinson while living in southern California. She'd been radicalized in part by a terrifying incident in which members of the Ku Klux Klan burned a cross on the lawn of the family's bungalow in Long Beach.[2]

Besides Seeger, Reynolds saw other, better-known artists cover her songs. Joan Baez, for instance, often sang her ballad about nuclear fallout, "What Have They Done to the Rain," which was also a Top 40 hit for the British group the Searchers. Reynolds's homey, plainspoken style was well suited for children, and in her later years she made guest appearances on *Sesame Street*. A year before her death in 1978, she conducted a radio interview, singing a newer song called "The Little Mouse," inspired by a news item about a gnawing rodent that wreaked havoc on a South American city's electrical supply. "I know it speaks to people's resentment of the mechanization of society, the computerization of their lives," she said.

To critics including Reynolds, Doelger's tract homes, like those in Levittown, New York, were an unfortunate byproduct of the postwar invention of the great American middle class. William J. Levitt perfected his assembly-line model of homebuilding on potato farmland on Long Island in the late 1940s, where demand among returning GIs was so high that more than 1,400 contracts were drawn up in a single day. Levitt's uniform homes— a basic Cape Cod–style design was priced at $7,990, a ranch for $9,500—were built on concrete slabs, without basements. Levitt and his brother, Alfred, looked to Henry Ford's factory model for inspiration. They determined that there were twenty-seven separate elements to a completed home, and then they put together twenty-seven crews to do the work. Once up and running, the Levitt teams were completing an average of thirty-six houses each day. To Alfred Levitt, who was more of an aesthete than his brother, the repetitive work was clearly dull, but it was lucrative: "the reward of the green stuff seems to alleviate the boredom of the work."[3]

Such readymade suburban neighborhoods represented the dawn of a major, countrywide shift away from city life. For decades beginning in 1950, most of the nation's largest cities experienced free-falling population numbers. Meanwhile, by 1980, the suburbs had gained sixty million people.[4] Within a few years, developments like those built by Doelger and Levitt were attracting not just eager prospective buyers, but routine criticism. The author of a 1956 book called *The Crack in the Picture Window* called such tracts the country's "fresh-air slums." They were "inhabited by people whose age, income, number of children, problems, habits conversations, dress, possessions, perhaps even blood types are almost precisely like yours," wrote John Keats, and they often drove to the brink of madness "myriads of housewives shut up in them." The social and architectural critic Lewis Mumford was particularly outspoken, implying that the new suburbs created "bland people in bland houses leading bland lives," as David Halberstam paraphrased him.[5] (In fact, Keats called his hypothetical suburban couple Mr. and Mrs. "John Drone.")

In response, a new generation of young people found an escape from suburban monotony in the garages of their family homes, where they plugged into amplifiers and taught themselves to play rock 'n' roll. In the decades since, complacency, complicity, and a lack of critical thinking have been ripe themes for topical songs across various genres. Rock 'n' roll itself has always represented a social movement of its own: an amplified strike against social norms and the expectations of "proper" behavior.

When older generations expressed alarm at the recklessness and sheer volume of many of the early rock 'n' rollers, some of those performers and their fans were quick to embrace the perception that they were juvenile delinquents. Three years into his recording career, Elvis Presley had a number one hit with Leiber and Stoller's "Jailhouse Rock," which included a line— "You're the cutest jailbird I ever did see"—that seemed to imply the homoeroticism of prison life. Transgressive songs glorified drag racing, street-corner posturing, and turf wars. A year after "Jailhouse Rock," several radio stations forbade their disc jockeys to play **"Rumble"** by the part-Shawnee electric guitar innovator Link Wray, fearing that the song would incite teen violence.

"'Rumble' represented gang fights, like in *West Side Story*," Wray said in a 1997 interview. "It was mean. They banned 'Rumble' in New York City and Boston, but it just made it sell more." The song, a measured stroll with a sinister guitar sound often cited as the precursor of the heavy metal power chord, had no lyrics to telegraph its intentions, only the amplified sound of the same kind of protest staged by the young Marlon Brando in the classic biker-gang movie *The Wild One*: asked what it is he's rebelling against, Brando pauses a moment, then blithely replies, "Whattaya got?" When the success of "Rumble" (in spite of the radio bans) forced Dick Clark's hand, the *American Bandstand* host agreed to feature Wray on the show, though he refused to introduce the song by name.

The future civic leaders of America, meanwhile, were being molded by the country's institutions of higher learning. Post–World War II, the middle class would be defined increasingly by its ability to send its offspring to college. While less than 5 percent of all adults age twenty-five and over could claim to have a bachelor's degree in 1940, that figure had risen to nearly 25 percent among twenty-five to twenty-nine-year-olds alone by the mid-1970s. For a high school education, the numbers were even more dramatic: just one-quarter of the population over the age of twenty-five had a high school diploma in 1940, but by 1980 that figure was well over 60 percent.[6]

By the early 1960s, many social scientists believed that the United States had reached "the end of ideology," with only technological adjustments to come to ensure the productivity and mutual benefits of industrial democracy. "A rationally organized, meritocratic society, with university education as the ladder to success, excluded such 'counterproductive' behavior as student demonstrations," wrote the philosopher John Searle in hindsight, in his 1971 book *The Campus War*.[7] During the 1960s, however, students discovered a seemingly bottomless well of opportunity to participate in the "counterproductive" behavior some of their elders had assumed obsolete. The reasons were manifold, as Searle noted, from the agonies of the Vietnam War and the civil rights struggle to a generalized contempt for the patriarchy; from the "Luddite's dying gasp . . . against the electronic computerized era now aborning" to "the feeling of being redundant in an advanced economy." The campus wars began in the form of the Free Speech Movement at Berkeley in 1964.

Students at Berkeley had begun organizing as early as 1958, when a group of them formed a coalition of student government candidates united in their support for a range of causes including free speech on campus, the campaign against racial discrimination, and the abolition of the school's mandatory ROTC policy. The following year, University of California chancellor Clark Kerr issued a series of "directives," prohibiting the debate of such "off-campus" issues as discrimination, capital punishment, and the continuing investigations of the House Un-American Activities Committee (HUAC), the long-standing panel charged with rooting out political "subversives." In 1960, several Berkeley students were arrested for protesting a HUAC hearing at San Francisco City Hall, and demonstrators were blasted with fire hoses. The Berkeley coalition, known as SLATE, was temporarily banned from campus as the Kerr administration responded to complaints from the local community and the state legislature. Meanwhile, student bodies at other universities across the country began to form similar alliances. For the next few years, SLATE (not an acronym) hosted a series of summer conferences, which ranged from a symposium on "The Negro in America" to a discussion of students' rights and academic freedom—growing concerns for the nation's burgeoning college population.

To test the administration's announcement that it would strictly enforce its existing rules against political canvassing, in the fall of 1964 a former graduate student named Jack Weinberg set up a table on Sproul Plaza, a newly dedicated common ground at the intersection of Bancroft Way and Telegraph Avenue, near a main gateway to the campus. The sidewalk itself was a disputed subject: though the Board of Regents had voted to transfer the property to the city, the exchange had not taken place. Technically, the ground on which the students held signs, handed out leaflets, and recruited their peers into political causes still belonged to the university. In September 1964, several student groups defied the administration's orders against solicitation on the plaza. When five students were ordered to the office of the Dean of Students, four hundred more filed into the Administration building on the plaza and staged an all-night vigil, a sit-in.

Weinberg, a Buffalo native who'd spent the summer of 1963 traveling through the American South to advocate for voters' rights and the end of segregation, was president of the Berkeley chapter of the Congress of Racial Equality (CORE). The day after the sit-in, he set up his table on Sproul Plaza, where campus police approached and asked to see his student identification. Refusing to give his name, he was arrested and placed in the back of a patrol car. Outraged students quickly began surrounding the car, preventing it from moving. At the height of the demonstration, several thousand students were gathered. Weinberg ultimately spent thirty-two hours in the back seat, as fellow activists climbed atop the hemmed-in police cruiser to deliver impromptu speeches.

Mario Savio was one of those student activists. A brilliant scholar who graduated at the top of his high school class in Queens, New York, he'd once planned to become a priest. Instead, he focused his intellectual energies on helping the less fortunate, spending the summer of 1963 volunteering with a Catholic relief organization in Mexico. The following year, Savio went south for the Freedom Summer, where he participated in voter registration drives and taught a classroom of black schoolchildren. When the Berkeley students reached a tentative agreement with the Kerr administration to end the standoff on Sproul Plaza, it was Savio who told his fellow students to go home peacefully.

In the aftermath of the incident, Berkeley students officially organized their free speech movement. They appointed an executive committee of about fifty, including all eight of the students who were suspended following the occupation of the Administration building (the initial five summoned to the Dean's office, plus three leaders of the sit-in). The committee also included several former members of the United Front, a confederation of representatives from various student groups. Savio became the group spokesman, Weinberg its chief strategist. To raise money for the cause, they sold Free Speech Movement buttons and satirical recordings, including a 45 rpm disc featuring seasonal "Free Speech Carols." One of those songs was a lampoon of their fellow students who were preparing to step onto the first rung of the corporate ladder. That song was called "O Come All Ye Mindless" ("conceptless and spineless"). "We of the FSM are serious," wrote the students behind the recording, "but we hope we are still able to laugh at ourselves, as well as those who would restrict our Constitutional freedoms."[8]

Negotiations with Kerr's administration continued for weeks. With various elements of the free speech movement—conservative, liberal, radical—unable to come to consensus on their aims, it took a retroactive disciplinary measure from the administration, charging Savio and three others for their roles in organizing the early October demonstrations, to spur the students to action. On December 2, 1964, a group of about two thousand students gathered on Sproul Plaza, many of them carrying sleeping bags for the latest proposed demonstration. From the steps of Sproul Hall, Savio was the last of several speakers to address the crowd. He questioned UC Berkeley's "arbitrary exercise of arbitrary power" and the position that the university—all universities—should be run as a business. If so, he argued, then the faculty were merely employees, and the students were "the raw material." Rising to the occasion, Savio asked his fellow students to engage in an act of civil disobedience against their own commodification.

There's a time when the operation of the machine becomes so odious, makes you so sick at heart that you can't take part! You can't even passively take part! And you've got to put your bodies upon the gears and upon the wheels, upon the levers, upon all the apparatus—and you've got to make it stop! And you've got to indicate to the people who run it, the people who own it—that unless you're free the machine will be prevented from working at all![9]

In its way, Savio's impromptu speech was cut from the same cloth as Malvina Reynolds's song about little boxes:

And the people in the houses
All went to the university
Where they were put in boxes
And they came out all the same

Having delivered the speech of his life—one of the key moments, as it would turn out, of the radicalized 1960s—Savio introduced Joan Baez, who had just arrived on campus.

Just as Savio had urged the students to remain nonviolent and refrain from vandalism, Baez asked the protesters to enter the building with "as much love as they could muster."[10] Before they did so, she sang a few songs, including Dylan's "The Times They Are a-Changin'" and **"All My Trials,"** a traditional Bahamian folk tune she'd recorded for her 1960 debut. At Carnegie Hall the year before that, Harry Belafonte had performed the song, which was written from the perspective of a dying mother who tells her child not to worry: "All my trials, Lord, soon be over."

I've got a little book with pages three
And every page spells liberty

The bittersweet melody was another prominent feature of the demonstrations of the 1960s, sung at countless rallies and recorded by Peter, Paul & Mary, Dave Van Ronk, and many others.

When Baez finished singing, a cheer erupted, and then the students once again climbed the steps from the plaza to the Administration building, singing "We Shall Overcome" as they went. They occupied the building and staged a sit-down strike in the halls and offices inside. They watched films, including *Operation Abolition*, a documentary on the 1960 HUAC protest in San Francisco. On the third floor, they heard from teaching assistants and others, including the poet Gary Snyder, who agreed to lead "freedom schools" on the importance of the First and Fourteenth Amendments. Baez served as co-instructor of a class on "Music and Non-Violence." Savio, meanwhile, delivered a speech in which he compared the civil rights movement and the fight for free speech. The two "battlefields" were not quite so different as they might appear, he argued. The two critical problems of the era, he said, were racial injustice and automation. Both groups wanted "the right to participate as citizens in democratic society and the right to due process of law." Both were confronting an "impersonal bureaucracy . . . in a 'Brave New World.'"

History had not "ended," he said, though the bureaucrats would have you believe that no substantial changes to American society were forthcoming. "A better society is possible," Savio concluded, and it "is worth dying for."[11]

At three o'clock in the morning, under orders from California governor Edmund G. "Pat" Brown, Sr., Berkeley police began the systematic process of arresting the protesters for trespassing. By three o'clock the following afternoon, 773 demonstrators, most of them students, had been removed to detention centers. These demonstrators became known as "the Eight Hundred."

The free speech movement would continue on the campus through the decade, in what has been called the "six-year war." The Board of Regents, while making certain concessions about what constituted permissible campus activism, continued to insist upon a "law and order" culture. In the spring of 1965 the activists drew unwanted national attention when one demonstrator carried a sign onto Sproul Plaza hand-lettered with a single word: "Fuck." Still forbidden at the time—the comedian Lenny Bruce was then spending his last days in court, fighting charges of obscenity in his stage act—the word on the sign helped create a public backlash to the student protesters. The regents once again increased their calls for more discipline; Ronald Reagan, then preparing to run for governor of California, would demand the activists' expulsion. "They are spoiled and don't deserve the education they are getting," he said. "They don't have a right to take advantage of our system of education."[12]

Kerr, caught between the students and the regents, became a scapegoat. He was dismissed as chancellor of the University of California system three weeks after Reagan's election. The new governor would go on to wage a protracted battle against the Berkeley activists, who by the late 1960s had shifted much of their focus to the Vietnam War.

In 1968, student activists adopted a plan to convert an almost three-acre parcel of land in downtown Berkeley into a "Peoples' Park." The land, claimed by the university, had been partially developed, but the work had been stopped for more than a year due to insufficient funding. The students' plan called for a landscaped area that would provide a "free speech" zone for any interested parties. Over the course of several weeks, hundreds of volunteers cleared the area of debris, laid sod, planted apple trees and shrubbery, and built playground structures. The university at first took no action; then, in May, citing the construction of an outdoor athletic facility, it had the park fenced off. Reagan, who saw the Berkeley students as "communist sympathizers, protesters, and sex deviants," was determined to wrest control of the park from the students.

At a May rally on Sproul Plaza to debate US response to the tensions in the Middle East, one speaker drew the attention of the students in attendance to the contested, fenced-off property a few blocks away. The crowd, an estimated three thousand, immediately began marching down Telegraph Avenue, chanting "We want the park!" At the site, some protesters attempted to tear down the fence; others threw rocks and bottles at the police officers on guard, who responded by shooting tear gas. The state called in reinforcements, and the riot escalated. The officers, nearly eight hundred of them, chased the protesters, swinging nightsticks and firing shotguns. More than one hundred demonstrators were hospitalized. One young man from San Jose, James Rector, described by *Rolling Stone* as "the 25-year-old with the Zapata mustache," was killed when he tried to hide on a nearby rooftop and was hit by multiple shotgun blasts.

Governor Reagan declared a state of emergency and called in nearly three thousand National Guard troops, who patrolled the streets of Berkeley for the next two weeks. Some protesters began distributing a leaflet that paraphrased Bob Dylan's **"Maggie's Farm,"** which insinuated that the local merchants might not appreciate the fact that "the National Guard stands around his door."[13] Dylan's song, one of the three he'd performed with his electric band during his notoriously divisive appearance at the 1965 Newport Folk Festival, was widely interpreted as his statement of refusal to be the voice of protest folk music. But it also worked as a general statement of nonconformity:

> *Well, I try my best*
> *To be just like I am*
> *But everybody wants you*
> *To be just like them*

Several days after the riot, thousands of Berkeley students gathered on Sproul Plaza for a memorial service honoring Rector. After the service ended and much of the crowd had dispersed, a National Guard helicopter sprayed the remaining several hundred with a thick trail of tear gas. "Berkeley has always been the enemy to Reagan," wrote *Rolling Stone*'s correspondents. "He holds the opportunity to make it the first permanently occupied college town in the country, and may prove loath to let it slip away from him."[14]

At a press conference attended by several members of the Berkeley administration, the governor rebuked the regents for failing to crack down hard enough on the dissenters: "All of it began the first time some of you who know better, and are old enough to know better, let young people think that they had the right to choose the laws that they would obey as long as they were doing it in the name of social protest," he admonished. But the heavy hand of the state had unintended consequences, pushing many neutral observers onto the side of the protesters. Many members of the Berkeley faculty signed a pledge not to teach until peace in their community could be restored. One university regent noted that the students had only been planting flowers in the park: "In the long run of history, I would have to say that flowers beat fences. And that young men beat old men every time."

By the latter half of the 1960s, the knowledge business was a growth industry, reportedly expanding at twice the rate of the rest of the economy. It was a pace comparable to that of the tycoons' railroad boom of the nineteenth century and the rapid rise of the automotive industry in the early twentieth. The University of California system had become the biggest public university in the country, with close ties to the military, nuclear energy, and dominant corporations such as IBM. Malvina Reynolds wrote a song from the perspective of the student who refuses to submit to the university's expectations, or give up her right to think critically: "Everybody thinks my head's full of nothing," begin the lyrics to **"No Hole in My Head."** "Wants to put his special stuff in."

"The point is that it was the culture that was sick," recalled one Berkeley activist, "the whole American way of looking at things that was sick."[15]

University students from New York to Chicago, and many more in cities overseas, were galvanized into action by the passion of the Berkeley activists and selfless leaders such as Savio. "The names, the sit-ins, the arrests, the headlines, the fact that they won their demands for on-campus activism—all this became legend to students entering a university in the mid-1960s," wrote Mark Kurlansky, who attended Columbia University.[16] Though Savio never again sought the spotlight, he would feel compelled to return periodically to the Berkeley campus. He spoke out against President Reagan's support for the effort to overthrow Nicaragua's democratically elected government in 1984; the following year, he denounced his alma mater's financial ties to apartheid South Africa. Savio died of heart trouble in 1996 at age fifty-three. One year later, the university installed a small bronze plaque commemorating the "Mario Savio Steps" in Sproul Plaza.

On April 30, 1970, Richard Nixon announced the US military's latest operation, the Cambodian Campaign. US forces would work in tandem with the Army of the Republic of Vietnam to root out thousands of troops of the People's Army of Vietnam and the National Front for the Liberation of South Vietnam (commonly known as the Viet Cong) amassed along the eastern border of Cambodia. Antiwar protesters were angered by this expansion of the Vietnam War into another country without a congressional declaration of war. On college campuses across the country, dozens of ROTC buildings were reportedly set ablaze in the days after the news broke.

At a rally the day after Nixon's announcement on the campus of Kent State University in Kent, Ohio, students symbolically buried a copy of the Constitution. Later that day, a Friday, several hundred members of a group called Black United Students rallied to address their concerns about the Ohio National Guard's presence on campus. Participants spread the news that activists were planning another demonstration against the Cambodian invasion, set for the following Monday afternoon. That night, in a part of town known as the "Strip," groups of bar-hopping students engaged in a series of spontaneous protests against the war. Some of the students grew violent, tossing bottles at police cruisers and smashing windows of downtown institutions.[17] The mayor of the city declared a state of emergency, and local police employed tear gas and nightsticks to disperse the crowd.

On Saturday night, an estimated two thousand students marched on campus to the old ROTC barracks, where protesters, after a few failed attempts and skirmishes with local police and firemen, eventually succeeded in burning the building down. The Ohio National Guard chased students back to their dormitories with bayonets drawn. The following day, tensions escalated as the National Guard stepped up its presence on campus. Ohio governor James Rhodes, facing an imminent primary vote in his campaign for one of the state's senate offices, arrived in Kent to deliver a speech. Sensing an opportunity to get out the law-and-order vote, he accused the Kent State protesters of trying to destroy higher education in Ohio. They were "the worst type of people we harbor in America," Rhodes claimed, "worse than the brownshirts and the communist element," and he vowed that the state would use "whatever force necessary" to stop them.[18]

Monday morning brought a new gathering of about fifteen hundred students and other young demonstrators to the Commons on the Kent State campus. The National Guard troops formed a skirmish line and quickly dispersed the crowd, methodically pursuing them up Blanket Hill and lobbing tear gas canisters, some of which the students threw back. As the students scattered, the Guard troops retreated back up the hill. When they reached the crest, a dozen or so members of Ohio National Guard Troop G suddenly pivoted in unison and began firing at the students. As investigations would later conclude, those soldiers fired a total of sixty-seven shots in thirteen seconds. Nine students were wounded. Four more were killed.

Across the country, public outrage was acute. The war in Vietnam was straining relations between elders and youth, left and right, those who sided with law enforcement and those who saw a moral imperative in speaking out. But the cold-blooded killing of four students—Jeffrey Miller, Allison Krause, Sandra Scheuer, and William Schroeder—was, for most Americans, plainly unconscionable. Within days, the nation was riveted by the coverage in *Life* magazine; its cover story, TRAGEDY AT KENT, included an unforgettable photo of fourteen-year-old runaway Mary Ann Vecchio wailing in distress, kneeling over Miller's prostrate body.

In Pescadero, California, David Crosby handed a copy of the magazine to Neil Young, "who got out his guitar and wrote the song right there in front of me," as Crosby would recall.[19] The song was **"Ohio,"** a bitter, incriminating inquiry into how protesting students could be mowed down in a country that considered itself "free."

> *Tin soldiers and Nixon's comin'*
> *We're finally on our own*
> *This summer I hear the drumming*
> *Four dead in Ohio*

Coincidentally, one of the slain students, Miller, was said to have been a big fan of Young's. Young had recently joined the group Crosby, Stills & Nash as its fourth well-known member, having previously played in Buffalo Springfield with Stephen Stills. The band recorded Young's new song just eleven days after the Kent State killings, releasing a single backed with another song ripped from the depressing headlines, Stills's "Find the Cost of Freedom." Despite a ban on Young's song by some AM radio stations, which objected to its explicit denunciation of the president, "Ohio" quickly became one of the signature protest songs of the era. "It felt really good to hear it come back so fast—the whole idea of using music as a message and unifying generations and giving them a point of view," as Young told his biographer.[20] "That was about the first time I had to have a conscience about something like that."

One Kent State student who was not especially moved by Neil Young's song was Gerald Casale, who had known two of the fatally wounded students. "At the time we just thought rich hippies were making money off of something horrible and political that they didn't get," he would recall.[21]

The Kent State massacre would have another direct, if not quite so immediate, impact on popular music. "I was a white hippie boy and then I saw exit wounds from M1 rifles out of the backs of two people I knew," Casale once said. "We were all running our asses off from these motherfuckers. It was total, utter bullshit. Live ammunition and gasmasks—none of us knew, none of us could have imagined. . . . They shot into a crowd that was running away from them! I stopped being a hippie and I started to develop the idea of devolution. I got real, real pissed off."[22]

For Casale and his colleagues—his brother Bob, brothers Mark and Bob Mothersbaugh, and Alan Myers—the shootings brought a seriousness of purpose to an idea Casale and fellow artist Bob Lewis were already toying with: their notion that the human race had stopped making progress and was undergoing a process of "devolution." Like the Dadaists, whose deeply absurd performance art emerged in response to the horrific madness of World War I, these Kent State students found an outlet for their anguish in a nonsensical form of expression. If the culture was going to demand conformity and the suppression of dissent, then they would just have to embody that conformity to a farcical degree.

The band Devo debuted in 1973 at a Kent State performing arts festival, filming their performance for an experimental movie they called *The Truth about De-Evolution*. Willfully amateurish, the group dressed in matching factory jumpsuits and wore rigid, doll-like plastic masks, which made them look disturbingly mindless. Musically, Devo anticipated the coming wave of punk rock: they were confrontational, abrasive, and perfectly willing to alienate an audience, as they often did in their early years. One of their first original compositions took its name from a briefly trendy 1920s-era booklet called *Jocko Homo Heavenbound*, which argued against the theory of evolution. (To the author, B. H. Shadduck, a "jocko homo" was an apeman.)

The band's entire existence was one big work of conceptual art. Their first single featured "Jocko Homo" and "Mongoloid," a kind of punk descendant of Malvina Reynolds's "Little Boxes." The "mongoloid" of the second title was a mutant ("one chromosome too many") living undetected as a typical suburban father: "And he wore a hat, and he had a job/And he brought home the bacon, so that no one knew." Devo's themes were single-minded, from their "Mechanical Man" to a "Blockhead" who does precisely what's expected of him ("cube top, squared off, eight corners, ninety-degree angles," as Mark Mothersbaugh intones mechanically). The band's commercial breakthrough came with an overwrought cover of the Rolling Stones' "(I Can't Get No) Satisfaction," a song about the unattainable promises of consumer culture.

Though she came from a very different background, Reynolds was a kindred spirit. "Our best words—'sincere,' 'love,' 'hope,' 'happy'—have been so misused, that they are only good enough for a joke," she once wrote. "Or an emetic. They are used to sell hair spray, real estate, political platforms, wars; they are worn out, and can't be used to talk with anymore."[23]

"A band of the '80s has to understand that democracy is over; hippies are over," keyboardist Mark Mothersbaugh said around the time of Devo's debut album, in 1978. "We're in a corporate society, headed for recombinant DNA. . . . You have to face that and use it creatively."[24] One of the first indications that their weird futurism was striking a chord in the disillusioned 1970s came, oddly enough, when Neil Young recruited the band, as yet unsigned but enjoying their first wave of success, to participate in his off-kilter film *Human Highway*, a dark comedy about the impending doom of a nuclear holocaust.

By then, punk rock had replaced the topical folk music of the 1960s as the musical conveyance for dissatisfaction. Like Devo, the very existence of England's Sex Pistols was effectively a protest—a strident objection to stultifying economic conditions and the corporate takeover of everyday life. Punk rock also represented the unceremonious dismissal of 1960s-era idealism and the grave disenchantment that sometimes seemed to be its only vestige. "I belong to the blank generation," yowled a dead-eyed young man who called himself Richard Hell, leader of the band called the Voidoids. The Ramones, four street urchins in black leather jackets and ripped jeans, proudly declared celebrated "Teenage Lobotomy." In the San Francisco Bay Area, the birthplace of the "love-in," where Devo found a willing fan base among the emerging cynics—some of whom had only recently been the same "gentle people with flowers in their hair" that one pop song promised—a new band called Dead Kennedys instantly lived up to its deliberately off-putting name. The name was chosen, frontman Jello Biafra insisted, not out of disrespect, but as a two-word requiem for the American dream.

Dead Kennedys' first single, "**California uber Alles**," satirized their home state under the leadership of Governor Jerry Brown (son of the former Governor Pat Brown). According to Biafra, the younger Brown had instituted a kind of statewide "Zen fascism"—tolerant of all views, except those that differed from the Left. "You will jog for the master race/And always wear the happy face," Biafra quavered like he was narrating a horror show. The band's subsequent singles included "Kill the Poor," which envisioned a class cleansing by well-to-do liberals, and "Holiday in Cambodia," which fantasized about sending privileged college students to the "killing fields" of the Khmer Rouge.

Punk rock, defined by its stark, rudimentary, predominantly fast-tempo style, could also be categorized by its fixation on social issues. Punk is "gut rebellion and change," wrote Craig O'Hara in his treatise *The Philosophy of Punk: More Than Noise*.[25] The music was, and remains, "a formidable voice of opposition." O'Hara quoted one fanzine writer who disputed the mainstream assumption that all punk involves a hateful, nihilistic attitude. In fact, he suggested, the music can be deceptively idealistic: "Freedom is something we can create every day; it is up to all of us to make it happen."

But the members of Devo remained deeply cynical, even after their anti-conformist stance stumbled into commercial success. Obsessed with visual imagery, the band was poised to capitalize when the music industry turned its attention to MTV (Music Television) in the early 1980s. Because their look was stylized and their sound was more keyboard- than guitar-driven, Devo shed the "punk rock" tag they'd first earned in favor of the more commercially viable category known as New Wave. Though they called their third (and, as it would happen, most commercially successful) album *Freedom of Choice*, the message was distinctly ironic. On the cover, the band wore identical shiny black jackets and matching hats, red plastic "energy domes" that looked like inverted flowerpots. Their uniforms made the point clear: it would be ludicrous to believe in "**Freedom of Choice.**"

The title track, robotically danceable, mocks the idea that there is any such thing "in the land of the free." If choice exists at all, the band implies, it is only in the aisles of the supermarkets and department stores. There's an enigmatic verse about a dog that finds two bones and can't decide between them. Alluding to ancient fables and philosophical paradoxes, the lyric strongly suggests that modern men and women will gladly sacrifice their true free will in favor of the empty illusions provided by consumer goods. As the song winds down, the band hammers the point: "Freedom of choice is what you got/Freedom from choice is what you want."

Devo's high point of notoriety coincided with the election of President Ronald Reagan. To the band, ever attuned to facades and delusions, it was laughable and regrettable that the politician who had once vowed to put down the student uprising at UC Berkeley by force had adopted a kindly, grandfatherly image. "It's like *Invasion of the Bodysnatchers*," Casale told the British music paper *NME* of the mindless acceptance of the status quo in the aftermath of the 1960s. "They don't seem particularly uptight about it.... People's quest for happiness when they don't have any idea what it is, it's like some psychotic thing."[26]

Though Devo's underlying theme was mass conformity, no one actually looked like the band, in their energy domes and their matching hazmat suits. No one sounded quite like them, either—as if the sentient machines were on the permanent fritz. Yet the band unleashed a new strain of critical thinking in popular music. Alice Cooper, the hard-rock singer known for his theatrically ghoulish stage show, had the most successful single of his short-lived New Wave phase with **"Clones (We're All),"** a 1980 release. "I'm all alone, so are we all/We're all clones/All are one and one are all," he sang, appealing to all the students grappling with the enduring high school dilemma: how to fit in and stand out at the same time.

"Out of all the bands who came out of the underground and actually made it in the mainstream, Devo is the most subversive and challenging of all," said Kurt Cobain in 1992, when his band, Nirvana, was conquering the music world with its own complex critique of middle-class complacency on **"Smells like Teen Spirit"**: "Here we are now, entertain us."[27]

"One thing we learned from the hippies was that rebellion was obsolete," Mothersbaugh explained. "Hippies turned into safe little yuppies, and punks turned into safety-pin-wearing paraphernalia consumers. You can't fight the system head to head. It's like, 'I fought the law and the law won.' They will kick your butt each time." Recognizing that, Devo took the indirect route to its unique brand of protest: by lashing out with parody, by fighting foolish consistency with more of the same.

Gay rights demonstration at the Democratic National Convention, July 11, 1976.
Credit: Library of Congress, Prints & Photographs Division, photograph by Warren K. Leffler.
http://www.loc.gov/pictures/resource/ppmsca.09729/

7 GAY PRIDE

At first glance, the song titles listed on the jukebox at the Stonewall Inn in the summer of 1969 looked a lot like the same chart hits that might have been on the jukebox in any bar in America. There were upbeat songs by Stevie Wonder and Sly and the Family Stone, several classics by the girl groups of the early 1960s, and innocuous pop sentiments such as Jackie DeShannon's "Put a Little Love in Your Heart." Each night at closing time, they played the same crowd-pleaser, Connie Francis's pining 1960 ballad **"Where the Boys Are."**

For the clientele at the Stonewall, that song—"Where the boys are, someone waits for me"—meant something very different than it might have elsewhere. Most of the patrons at the Stonewall were gay men, at a time when gay men were *personae non gratae* in American culture. In Manhattan, the Stonewall was one of the few nightclubs where queer men were not-so-secretly welcome. Most of its visitors were well aware that the place was owned and operated by the American Mafia, who saw it as a money-making machine: the Mob watered down the beer and alcohol, which were typically hijacked from delivery trucks, and they knew the customers would not complain. The Mafia also owned the cigarette machines, and the jukebox.

"Where the Boys Are" was just one of dozens of songs that held double meaning for the LGBT community. Commissioned as the title theme of the 1961 coming-of-age comedy of the same name (which helped establish Fort Lauderdale as a spring break destination), the song was co-written by the Brill Building writer and pop star Neil Sedaka and Howie Greenfield, a prolific songwriter who was openly gay at a time when few dared to be so.

A year later, in late 1962, a singer from Nashville named Jackie Shane scored a modest regional hit with a version of the measured soul song **"Any Other Way."** Written and originally recorded by the R&B singer William Bell, the song depicts a lover hoping to send word to an old flame:

> *Tell her that I'm happy*
> *Tell her that I'm gay*
> *Tell her I wouldn't have it*
> *Any other way*

Jackie Shane flirted with stardom, drawing interest from the Atlantic and Motown record labels and from the *Ed Sullivan Show*. But Shane ultimately sidestepped the music industry for a quiet life as a transgender woman.

Though she presented as a man, wearing suits in her early years onstage, Shane has said she always knew she was born female. "Most people thought I was a lesbian," she told the *Guardian* when her music was rediscovered in 2017. "One taxi driver said, 'I don't know why, as pretty as she is, she wears suits.'"[1]

Gay men and women, whose relationship with the rest of America historically ranged from being ignored to vilified, had been particularly careful to conceal their sexuality since the turn of the 1950s, when the anti-communist hysteria fomented by Senator Joe McCarthy and the House Un-American Activities Committee gripped the entire nation in a hunt for "the enemy within." Three weeks after McCarthy made his speech claiming that there were hundreds of card-carrying Communist Party members working in the US State Department, Undersecretary of State John Peurifoy testified before a Senate committee about State Department employees who had been forced to resign as potential security risks since the end of World War II. "Ninety-one persons in the shady category," he said. "Most of these were homosexuals."[2]

Gay employees of the government could be susceptible to blackmail. Rumors spread that the Soviet Union under Stalin had come to possess a list of tens of thousands of gay people around the world who could be coerced into espionage or terrorism. In the press, homosexuality was freely reviled. Gay people were "deviants," "perverts," "pansies." "Mind you, I don't say every homosexual is a subversive, and I don't say every subversive is a homosexual," Nebraska senator Kenneth Wherry told the *New York Post*. "But a man of low morality is a menace in the government, whatever he is, and they are all tied together."[3]

Harry Hay, for one, recognized the need for solidarity. In 1950, the long-time Communist Party activist and a few of his music students in Los Angeles formed the Mattachine Society, the first real gay advocacy group of its kind in the United States. It was named, according to Hay, after a congregation of unmarried men in medieval France who wore masks during ritualized protests against oppression. Much like America's Communist Party members, those who joined the Mattachine Society declared loyalty to a secretive, pyramid-style organization; many members of the lower orders were not aware of the identities of the members in longer standing. When one of the society's founders was arrested in Los Angeles for soliciting an undercover police officer, the organization took the case as an opportunity to raise awareness about entrapment. The defendant fought the charge by denying his guilt while admitting his homosexuality in court; the jury deadlocked. This victory, however qualified, emboldened the society's leadership, and by mid-1953, there were an estimated two thousand members from southern California to San Francisco, where the headquarters was about to move.[4] Chapters would soon be established in Chicago, New York, and other major cities.

As the group's communist ties were loosened, a new steering committee sought to emphasize public education over "radical" attempts to affect lawmaking (for example, demanding a repeal of sodomy laws), which, the moderates felt, would provide "an abundant source of hysterical propaganda" against gay people.[5] This new approach, in which advocates sought the support and guidance of psychologists and other professional "experts" to show the world that homosexuality was a fact of life, came to be known as the "homophile" movement. Meanwhile, in San Francisco in 1955, Del Martin and Phyllis Lyon cofounded the Daughters of Bilitis, a lesbian social club named for the French poet Pierre Luoÿs's collection of erotic lesbian poems, *Les Chansons de Bilitis*.

Because participation in these groups was fraught with consequences, most members used aliases. When the Denver chapter of Mattachine held a convention, inviting legislators and a representative of the Colorado Civil Liberties Union, they invited the press and granted interviews using their real names. A few weeks later, police officers raided the homes of the convention's organizers, confiscating the group's mailing list and arresting one member for possession of pornography. The damage to the Denver chapter was extensive, and long-lasting.

There were, however, some signs that attitudes might be changing. In San Francisco, the gay population had grown in part due to large numbers of former military men and women who'd been dishonorably discharged there.

For many, the decision to stay in the city was easy; families were often unhappy with or unaware of their lifestyle, and California was the only state at the time that did not prohibit gay men and women from gathering in public places. According to some estimates, San Francisco could claim as many as thirty gay bars by the late 1950s. But a creeping perception that the city was becoming too permissive led to a backlash during the 1959 mayoral race, when a challenger accused incumbent George Christopher of allowing the city to become "the national headquarters of the organized homosexuals in the United States."[6] Christopher, sensitive to the charge, won re-election and quickly ordered a police crackdown.

Resistance came in the form of songs—subversive, campy songs. At the Black Cat, a long-running, bohemian North Beach hangout that had developed a large gay clientele, a flamboyant waiter named Jose Sarria began staging one-man operas while waiting tables in red heels, singing parodies of *Carmen*, discreetly changing the lyrics to warn patrons of impending police raids. Each night at closing time, Sarria got the Black Cat's customers to join him in singing "God Save Us Nelly Queens." Sarria's popularity grew to be such that in 1961 he declared his candidacy for San Francisco Board of Supervisors, making him the first openly gay person to run for elected office in the United States.

The official mobilization against gay life in San Francisco spurred the formation of several new advocacy groups, including the Society for Individual Rights (SIR) and, in an alliance with the liberal church, the Council on Religion and the Homosexual (CRH). In January 1965, those groups, together with Mattachine and the Daughters of Bilitis, threw a fundraising ball for six hundred guests. Though police had promised the CRH they would not interfere, officers instead descended on California Hall with photographers and paddy wagons. They spent the night marching in and out of the hall, conducting "inspections" and harassing the crowd. At one point, four lawyers—two gay, two heterosexual—were arrested for attempting to stop them from re-entering the building. The following day, the ministers held a press conference, accusing the officers of "bad faith." In court, the lawyers facing charges cited more than two dozen of the city's best known lawyers as counsel; before the defendants even made their case, the judge instructed the jury to declare them not guilty. The incident became known as "San Francisco's Stonewall."

As the 1960s unfolded, the gains of the civil rights movement helped establish a broader cultural climate in which other minority groups could similarly demand their own rights. A few gay Americans began organizing their own demonstrations, however modestly at first. In Washington, DC, a former civil servant named Franklin Kameny helped found a new chapter of Mattachine with a much more forceful agenda than its predecessors in other cities. Kameny had become politicized when he lost his job as an astronomer for the US Army Map Service after an old charge of lewd conduct was brought to light. "My dismissal amounted to a declaration of war against me by my government," he said.[7] Kameny was staunchly opposed to his peers' customary reliance on the testimony of medical and psychological professionals, many of whom, he felt, hindered the cause more than they helped, categorizing same-sex attraction as a "sickness." Instead, Kameny led the DC chapter in aggressive lobbying efforts, arguing the injustice, for example, of gays' exclusion from the military and the civil service. Under his leadership, the campaign for gay rights gradually began to coalesce into a movement.

In 1963, after police raided a gay bar in the nation's capital, Kameny convinced several men who'd been arrested to lodge a formal complaint against the police department for mistreatment. One year later, a group of ten conservatively dressed men and women picketed the White House, holding signs that declared sexual preference "irrelevant to federal employment" and accusing the Civil Service Commission of being "un-American." At the next demonstration, nearly fifty people participated.

By the latter part of the decade, the spirit of activism was rampant across the culture, and the commercial radio airwaves reflected it. "C'mon people now, smile on your brother," sang Jesse Colin Young of the band the Youngbloods in their version of a song first recorded by the Kingston Trio. The Youngbloods' **"Get Together,"** released to modest reception in 1967, gained its highest chart position when it was reissued two years later, based on its popularity as part of a public service announcement.

The assorted ideas of freedom and personal liberation were clearly in the air. During the chaotic summer of 1968, with news of international student uprisings giving way to the assassinations of Dr. Martin Luther King, Jr., and Robert F. Kennedy, the Rascals spent five weeks at the top of the charts with their song "People Got to Be Free." "All the world over, so easy to see/People everywhere just want to be free," they sang, pleading for basic civility. At the beginning of the following year, the Bay Area soul group Sly and the Family Stone landed their first number one single with "Everyday People." This song, too, called for simple understanding and forgiveness, and the senselessness of our failures to achieve them. "Different strokes for different folks," the group sang, infectiously. On **"It's Your Thing,"** another top hit of 1969, the Isley Brothers joyfully agreed they had no right to tell another person "who to sock it to." ("Sock it to me!" had become a popular, all-purpose slang phrase, dragged into the mainstream on the prime-time sketch comedy show *Laugh-In*.)

Each of those songs were preferred selections on the jukebox at the Stonewall Inn, where a group of patrons and their supporters were about to change the narrative about what it meant to be gay in America. The Stonewall first opened for business in 1930, during Prohibition, as a tearoom; renovated from two former horse stables on Christopher Street in Greenwich Village, the club was named Bonnie's Stone Wall, after a lesbian memoir called *The Stone Wall* published that year. Over time, the place was transformed into a full-fledged banquet hall, the Stonewall Inn Restaurant, a popular site for (straight) wedding receptions. After a fire, it lay dormant for a time in the 1960s, then reopened, in 1967, as the Stonewall Inn. The location was just steps from the intersection of Christopher Street and Greenwich Avenue, the most highly trafficked neighborhood in the city for gay men, known in the 1960s to cruising New Yorkers simply as "the Corner."

The man who refurbished the nightclub was Tony Lauria, son of a well-known Manhattan mafioso. Everyone knew him as Fat Tony. He painted the whole interior of the club black—a theme among gay bars of the time, but also a cost-saving measure, to cover any charred wood left over from the fire. From the beginning, the Stonewall stood out among the city's other gay bars because there was room enough for men to dance together, and little inclination on the part of the management to stop them. For the clientele, the opportunity to dance to a popular song like Martha Reeves and the Vandellas' Motown hit **"Third Finger, Left Hand"** was a rare pleasure. The song describes the sheer bliss of being asked to marry, even after "friends said it couldn't be done." At the Stonewall, the men were free to put themselves in the shoes of the singer. "A song like this would be like a big, celebratory thing, every word," as one patron put it.[8]

In 1969 there was not a single law, local or federal, to protect gay men and women from losing their jobs or being denied housing due to their sexual orientation. The Stonewall, like most other gay bars of the era, was run like a semi-secretive operation; clients typically had to be recognized at the door or vouched for by regulars to gain entry. Yet gay men and women were beginning to make their voices heard in New York life.

Earlier in the decade, a young activist named Randy Wicker, newly arrived from the University of Texas, took it upon himself to counter the media's stereotypical depictions of gay men. He convinced the local Mattachine chapter to advertise its lectures, drew crowds when he made soapbox speeches in Greenwich Village about the rights of gays to gather in public places, and distributed buttons that read "Equality for Homosexuals." He also convinced the progressive radio station WBAI to let him assemble a panel of gay men to speak on air about their experiences. The report drew some predictable outrage—one aggrieved newspaper columnist declared that the station should have been rebranded WSICK—but it also earned respectful notices from the *New York Times* and *Newsweek* magazine. It was invaluable positive press for the incipient gay rights movement.[9]

Meanwhile, the Oscar Wilde Memorial Bookshop, specializing in gay and lesbian literature, opened on Mercer Street in the Village in 1967. Owner Craig Rodwell modeled the store after a Christian Science reading room, explaining that his reading in the faith, which stressed "the dignity of all things human," helped him develop his commitment to gay liberation. The beginnings of today's LGBT community were emerging in other ways, too. The same year Rodwell opened his bookstore, students at Columbia University earned the institution's recognition for the Student Homophile League, the first of its kind at a major college. (The organization is now known as the Columbia Queer Alliance.) The following year, a front-page *Wall Street Journal* article about militancy in the gay movement generated so much reader response that the editorial board ran a full page of letters on the subject. And the biggest-selling album of 1969, the soundtrack to *Hair*, would feature several gay-positive lyrics co-written by creators James Rado and Jerry Ragni, who were at one time lovers. According to author David Carter, when 1969 got underway many gay men in New York City were sharing a simple thought: "Maybe this will be our year."[10]

Still, there was plenty of concern for the safety and well-being of the gay community, with reports of off-duty police officers and neighborhood vigilantes attacking young men in known cruising districts around the city. As the summer began, officers from Greenwich Village's "morals unit" raided several gay bars, closing a few of them—the Checkerboard, the Sewer—for good. The morals squad had been watching especially closely the criminal activity of the owners of the Stonewall, and in the early morning hours of June 28, eight policemen led by Deputy Inspector Seymour Pine entered the bar and arrested the employees for operating without a liquor license. The officers also detained several customers who were in violation of an obscure city law that forbade citizens from wearing insufficient articles of "gender-appropriate" clothing.

Outside the bar, other patrons who had been forced out of the building jeered as police began loading the detainees into a paddy wagon. Craig Rodwell, walking past the scene with a friend, immediately took up a post on the top step of a nearby stoop, where he blurted, "Gay power!" Instead of dispersing, the crowd grew, as gays, lesbians, and transgender people began to sense a culmination of the fear and frustration most of them had experienced for much of their lives. The Stonewall had just been raided days before. According to one eyewitness, the customers were fed up: "When did you ever see a fag fight back? . . . Now, times are a-changin'. Tuesday night was the last night for bullshit."[11]

Some bystanders cracked jokes while the police herded first the Mafia men, then several drag queens into the van. The collective attitude grew more hostile when one officer clubbed one of the less cooperative transvestites. Some protesters banged on the paddy wagon. They began throwing pennies ("dirty coppers!"), and then beer bottles. When a butch lesbian emerged from the bar and was clubbed by an arresting officer, "the scene became explosive," as the *Village Voice* would later report.[12] "Why don't you guys do something?" she reportedly yelled to the nearest bystanders. Chanting began: "Leave her alone! Let her go!" A male detainee tried to resist arrest by bracing against the back doorway of the paddy wagon. Someone dislodged a cobblestone from the street and threw it onto the trunk of one of the squad cars. At this point the police, stunned by the growing unrest, barricaded themselves inside the bar.

A few of the rioters, sensing they had gained the upper hand, attempted to set fire to the building, with the officers inside. Members of the city's Tactical Patrol Force soon arrived, clearing the streets to allow the officers to exit the bar. The officers, enraged by their humiliation, began chasing demonstrators around the narrow, helter-skelter streets of the West Village. Comically, like a slapstick scene from a silent film, they'd turn a corner to find a larger crowd advancing and pivot, suddenly being chased in the opposite direction. More violence erupted on both sides, but so did some very effective street theater: at one point a group of transvestites taunted the police by forming a kick line, singing a favorite queer parody of the familiar vaudeville song "Ta-ra-ra-Boom-de-ay": "We are the Stonewall girls, we wear our hair in curls/We don't wear underwear, we show our pubic hair!"

Ultimately, the Stonewall riot would fester for days. The business, though in shambles, reopened the next night, and the protesters returned. The bar's facade was quickly covered in graffiti: "Support Gay Power," read one. "Legalize gay bars and lick the problem."[13] Outside, Craig Rodwell led a leafleting campaign demanding the removal of the Mafia and the police from the gay bars. "Christopher Street belongs to the queens!" the crowd chanted. One Stonewall regular would recall the sight of so many demonstrators as "exhilarating . . . like the beginning of a lesbian and gay value system. From going to places where you had to knock on a door and speak to someone through a peephole in order to get in. We were just out. We were in the streets. I mean, can you imagine?"[14]

A few days after the rioting finally subsided, a group of leading activists, including Rodwell, Randy Wicker, and Frank Kameny, boarded a bus for Philadelphia, where they planned to participate in the Annual Reminder, a formal, orderly picket line that had been staged outside Independence Hall each Fourth of July since 1965. When Kameny physically separated a lesbian couple who'd broken the rules of the march—they were holding hands— Rodwell quickly asked several of his colleagues to break with tradition and hold hands themselves. The ten or so gay couples who did so drew more media attention than the Annual Reminder ever had before. "Did you hear about what's going on in New York and the riots last week?" a combative Rodwell asked a reporter who'd been speaking with Kameny, the event's designated spokesman. "We're tired of not being able to hold hands in public, and the leadership of our demonstration has to change."[15]

Within days, Mattachine members had begun calling the new movement the Gay Liberation Front. The group began renting halls and sponsoring dances; for the first time, the gay community in New York City could celebrate itself without resorting to Mafia-run establishments in which to do so. Revenues from the first dances were earmarked for a new underground newspaper covering LGBT issues called *Come Out!* In late 1969, a splinter group identifying itself as the Gay Activists Alliance (GAA) drafted a constitution, calling for "the right to our own feelings," "the right to love," "the right to our own bodies," and "the right to be persons." They chose as their logo the lambda, the eleventh letter of the Greek alphabet, symbolic of a change of energy. The logo would be established in 1974 as the international symbol for gay and lesbian rights by the first International Gay Rights Congress, which met that year in Edinburgh.

On June 28, 1970—the one-year anniversary of the Stonewall riots— several hundred demonstrators gathered around Sheridan Square to kick off the first Christopher Street Liberation Day march. The event had been conceived to replace the stodgy old Annual Reminder protest in Philadelphia. Instead, gay activists would commemorate the dawning of a new era of committed activism, triggered by the spontaneous Stonewall riots. Though the number of gay rights groups had ballooned since the riots (according to Kameny, there were fifty or sixty gay groups in the country at the time of Stonewall; now he estimated at least fifteen hundred), Rodwell and his colleagues were nervous about the turnout for their march, and the reception they could expect.

The participants planned to march from Greenwich Village all the way up Sixth Avenue to Central Park, where they hoped to stage a "Gay-In" in the park's Sheep Meadow. When the march began, the crowd moved so quickly, fearing potential violence from bystanders, that some would later refer to it jokingly as the "first run." Gradually, however, clusters of onlookers began stepping off the sidewalks to join the group. By the time they reached the park, at least two thousand marchers had joined together. Along the way, the demonstrators chanted the slogan the various factions had agreed upon ahead of time, "Say it clear, say it loud. Gay is good, gay is proud," a play on the title of James Brown's recent "message" song, "Say It Loud—I'm Black and I'm Proud." The first Christopher Street Liberation Day would mark the official origin of what we now know as the annual Gay Pride parades that take place across the globe.

For years, some have suggested that the death at age forty-seven of the singer-actress Judy Garland a week before the Stonewall riots helped inspire them. Garland, the star of *The Wizard of Oz*, was beloved by generations of gay men, who saw the innocence in her character Dorothy and heard the over-whelming heartache in her signature song, "Over the Rainbow." In the gay underground before the liberation movement, to be a "Friend of Dorothy" was a subtle way of admitting one's sexuality. The author of the book *Celluloid Closet*, Vito Russo, who attended Garland's funeral in New York on the day the riots began, effectively quashed that bit of lore. The timing of Garland's death was, however, undoubtedly symbolic, he agreed, marking "the end of the old gay world and the beginning of a new one."[16]

There were some members of the gay community who resented the emphasis on a seedy nightclub as the battleground for the gay rights movement. (In fact, the Stonewall Inn would be closed a mere three months after the riots.) But in a rebuttal published on the occasion of the five-year anniversary, the president of the Gay Activists Alliance pointed out that though the bar was without question "illegal, dingy, dirty, and exploitative," it had been, in 1969, "virtually all we had. . . . There is no getting away from the fact that the Stonewall Inn is a symbol of the past. It was a departure point for Gays like the Bastille was for the French people."[17]

On the evening of Valentine's Day, 1970, the invited guests began arriving at David Mancuso's loft apartment at 647 Broadway. Mancuso had been raised in a Catholic orphanage in upstate New York, where the nuns held record-playing parties for the children. The boy spent a lot of time by himself outside, listening to the sounds of the natural world: the birds, the crickets, the burbling brooks. "One day I realized: What perfect music," Mancuso once recalled.[18]

As a young man living in New York City, Mancuso became active in the civil rights, antiwar, and gay rights movements. He also began hosting private dance parties for his friends, playing music through state-of-the-art stereo equipment. "I was always into sound, and I was more into the psychedelic sounds in jazz, R&B, and all that stuff," he said.[19]

After a few years of hosting parties, Mancuso sent out an invitation for his first official dance. It was billed as Love Saves the Day. No alcohol was served, just fruit punch and snacks. The parties, which quickly became routine, moved from invitation-only to membership-based, which was free, with modest admission fees. "Life is a banquet," Mancuso liked to say, and from his DJ booth high above the dance floor—designed like an old Wurlitzer jukebox—he regaled his audiences with carefully curated playlists. In the early years of the Loft, the DJ's sets might include extended R&B tracks such as Little Sister's "You're the One" ("I'm the one my life has taught to fight/To turn around would never make it right"), produced by Sly Stone; the Pointer Sisters' "Yes We Can Can," written by the New Orleanian Allen Toussaint, which called for a universal kindness that would "make this land a better land than the world in which we live"; and "Girl You Need a Change of Mind" by Eddie Kendricks, formerly of Motown stars the Temptations, which addressed the women of the Equal Rights era: "All men don't discriminate/ This man emancipates."

Mancuso's social experiments in dance utopia were linked in spirit to similar movements that predated the disco era of the 1970s. In Nazi Germany before the start of World War II, an underground network of teenagers opposed to Adolf Hitler's compulsory "Hitler Youth" identified themselves as the Swing Jugend, or Swing Kids, acting out their rebellion by attending clandestine, late-night dance parties featuring African-American jazz, which the Gestapo tried to outlaw. In Paris, similar groups of young people were known as Les Zazous, who congregated at a small basement bar in the Quartier Latin known as La Discothèque and, after the war, at the Whisky à Go-Go in the 1st Arrondissement.

Some years later, the American dance craze the Twist paved the way for a succession of popular disco-style nightclubs in New York City, including Le Club, Ondine, and El Morocco. By the middle of the decade, the last of these had been transformed as Arthur, where celebrities and the fashionable young mingled with a fringe element from the Manhattan streets, creating the same kind of eclectic, combustible mix of clientele that would come to define the disco era. Other legendary venues followed, notably the Sanctuary, a former German Baptist church where gay men flush with the success of the movement infamously took their newfound liberation to new extremes. The groundbreaking DJ at Sanctuary, Francis Grasso, has been credited as an inventor of "beatmatching," the modern disc jockey's technique of mixing one track into the next for a seamless, free-flowing dance experience.

All this activity represented a collective instinct to express oneself in terms apart from the mainstream, in which, from a musical perspective, DJs were historically paid to play the hits of the day. To Mancuso, the freedom of his "members only" dance parties was its own kind of social statement. "For me," he said in an interview not long before his death in 2016 at age seventy-two, "the core is social progress. How much social progress can there be when you're in a situation that is repressive? You won't get much social progress in a nightclub."[20]

By the mid-1970s, the social phenomenon of disco had emerged from the gay underground into the mainstream. Radio stations were saturated with the propulsive, "four on the floor" beat of the discotheques, with songs by Barry White's Love Unlimited Orchestra, KC and the Sunshine Band, Donna Summer, and others enjoying major commercial success. But critical backlash was strong. The style was accused of being vacuous and narcissistic, and many saw the scene's hedonism as an inevitable tilt away from an earnest era that had been stripped of its idealism by the disappointments of the 1970s—the ugly, state-sanctioned violence of Kent State, the ongoing war in Vietnam, the economic hardships that led to severely stratified, desolate urban areas. But the very existence of disco, writes Peter Shapiro, was in itself a kind of political statement: "Disco didn't have to hit anyone over the head with slogans or bore you into submission with earnest missives; its 'message' was its pleasure principle. Disco was born of a desire that was outlawed and branded an affront to God and humanity, so its evocation of pleasure was by necessity its politics, and by extension its politics was pleasure."[21]

In San Francisco, one expression of that pleasure came in the form of an outrageous post-hippie theatrical group known as the Cockettes. Formed by a group of a dozen or so flamboyant performers of various sexual persuasions, the Cockettes made their official debut as part of a futuristic, multimedia New Year's Eve celebration in 1969. They dressed in vintage dresses and thrift-shop accessories, applying glitter and plentiful makeup. They created outlandish burlesques such as *Pearls over Shanghai*, based on a scandalous 1920s-era Broadway play called *The Shanghai Gesture*. The group's over-the-top glamour prefigured the campy, gender-bending pop culture that was shortly to come, including David Bowie's "Ziggy Stardust" era, Lou Reed and the New York Dolls, the midnight movie phenomenon *The Rocky Horror Picture Show*, and the forgotten would-be pop star known as Jobriath, the first openly gay performer to sign with a major record label.

One of the undeniable stars to emerge from the Cockettes' fast-burning constellation was a distinctive falsetto singer who answered to the stage name Sylvester. Sylvester was a showcase performer, often stealing the night with his dramatic interpretations of torch songs by Billie Holiday, Etta James, Ethel Waters, and other leading ladies of song. Sylvester James, Jr., grew up singing in a gospel choir in his family's Pentecostal church, and brazenly walking the streets of Los Angeles in full drag. After performing with the Cockettes and making a fitful attempt to establish a career in rock—his debut album with his Hot Band featured covers of Neil Young's "Southern Man" and a mostly instrumental, scarcely recognizable version of the patriotic anthem "My Country 'Tis of Thee"—Sylvester regrouped in San Francisco, where he was signed by Harvey Fuqua, a onetime member of the doo-wop group the Moonglows.

There had been a few other examples of frankly gay disco songs before Sylvester's breakthrough. Most notable among them was **"I Was Born This Way,"** a 1975 single release by the Motown artist Charles Harris, who called himself Valentino. Written by Chris Spierer and Bunny Jones with the gay pride movement in mind, the song was recorded independently, for a small label called Gaiee. Curiously, neither Jones, a Christian housewife and lyricist, nor Spierer identified as gay. Jones once owned a Harlem beauty parlor, where many of her employees were gay. "I began to feel that gays are suppressed more than Chicanos, blacks, or other minorities," she told *The Advocate* in 1975. "You hear of great designers or famous hairdressers, and that's about as far as society will let gays go."[22] She sold fifteen thousand copies of the record out of the back of her car before enticing Motown founder Berry Gordy to pick it up for distribution.

"No major company has ever had to deal with a gay protest record before," Jones claimed. "No one ever stood up and said, 'I'm gay.'" The song drew a modest underground following in the United States, but it was a dance-floor hit in London, landing the number one chart position for disco singles there. "I'm walking through life in nature's disguise/You laugh at me and you criticize/Just because I'm happy, I'm carefree, and I'm gay," Harris sang. Discovered in a Long Island revival of *Hair*, the singer told *The Advocate* that nightclub crowds would stop dancing when the song reached the declaration that he was gay. "It's really strange how one word can upset so many people," he said.

Two years later Jones approached another singer, hoping to gain some of the traction that had eluded her song in America. Carl Bean was an openly gay gospel singer with an expressive voice that Jones admired. "They came looking for me and they didn't even know I was gay," said Bean, who had appeared in the Broadway production *Your Arms Too Short to Box with God*. It was serendipity, he felt, "like providence. They came to me with a song I have been looking for my whole life." Bean's version of "I Was Born This Way," also issued by Motown, was covered in the music press as a potential "Gay National Anthem." "People have so many questions and misunderstandings," Bean told a reporter. At the time, the singer and former beauty contestant Anita Bryant was making news for her successful campaign against a Miami ordinance banning discrimination against gay people. Bryant followed that by pressuring the Florida state legislature to pass a measure barring gays from adopting children. For Bean, the message of "I Was Born This Way" was personal. "I feel this is my mission," he told *Soul* magazine. "I'm not trying to change anybody, just to help people understand."[23]

Sylvester, meanwhile, was about to become disco's first true gay star. After cultivating a devoted following at the Elephant Walk, a gay bar in San Francisco's Castro district, he released his second solo album, *Step II*, in late 1978. The record featured the number one dance hit **"You Make Me Feel (Mighty Real),"** which Sylvester sang in an exuberant falsetto. The song would quickly become "the cornerstone of gay disco," writes Shapiro. On the same day in 1979 that San Francisco mayor Dianne Feinstein presented the singer with the keys to the city, Sylvester recorded a live performance at the San Francisco War Memorial Opera House that featured his hits "You Make Me Feel (Mighty Real)" and "Dance (Disco Heat)" alongside covers of Billie Holiday's "Lover Man" and an uptempo version of the Beatles' "Blackbird," written by Paul McCartney as a subtle tribute to the civil rights movement.

In the 1980s, having earned the nickname "Queen of Disco," Sylvester became a vocal supporter of the fight against HIV/AIDS, promoting awareness about the immunodeficiency syndrome that was devastating his community. When he was honored at the 1988 Castro Street Fair, he was too unwell—dying of AIDS-related complications—to attend, but he could hear the crowds outside his apartment chanting his name. Throughout his performing career, Sylvester was unequivocal about his identity. Asked his opinions about gay rights, civil rights, his Christianity, or his transvestitism, his typical reply was simply, "I am Sylvester."[24]

In New York City, two French producers were busy concocting a conceptual pop group that would infiltrate the mainstream with a unique kind of subversion in the form of a fatuous, bubblegum brand of disco. Henri Belolo and Jacques Morali conceived of the Village People when they encountered a gay bar employee in the West Village dancing on tabletops in full Native American regalia. Their idea was to celebrate the "gorgeous mosaic" of the American male, and the performers they recruited would famously represent its stereotypes, including a cop, a cowboy, a soldier, a biker, and a construction worker. The group would smuggle a mild form of gay erotica onto the radio airwaves, from the sufficiently innocuous anthems "Macho Man" and "Y.M.C.A." (their biggest hits) to more explicit album tracks, such as **"I Am What I Am"** ("People have the right to be just who they are. . . . No one has the right to choose my love for me"). Though the group's very existence was a statement, its members claimed otherwise: "We are just a party band. We are not here to save trees or the planet."[25]

A celebration of identity, glamour, and self-indulgence, dance music was much more than just musically antithetical to the bombastic hard rock of the time. Disco's rise was symbolic of a rapidly changing national culture, in which the homogeneity of young people who grew up on *Leave It to Beaver* was being challenged by a rainbow coalition of gay men, women, African Americans, Latinos, and other minorities. As the new decade approached, even the most repressed Americans were proving defenseless to disco's flamboyant sense of fun. By 1979, the straight mainstream had helped make disco a $4 billion industry—"bigger than television, movies, or professional sports in America."[26]

One night during the 1977 baseball season, the Chicago White Sox hosted "Disco Night" at Comiskey Park. The White Sox, owned by the inveterate showman Bill Veeck, were known for their colorful attractions. They were the team that briefly wore shorts as part of their uniform, and once took the field on "Salute to Mexico" night wearing sombreros.

Disco Night was a success, but that didn't stop Veeck and his son, Mike, from organizing an anti-disco event two seasons later. In a backlash to disco's sudden domination of the culture, rock 'n' roll fans around the country began loudly proclaiming their disdain for the inescapable dance music. Among the biggest-selling records of the previous year: several Bee Gees songs from the *Saturday Night Fever* soundtrack, the disco-tinged pop music of *Grease*, and the dance single "Boogie Oogie Oogie." Even the Rolling Stones were flirting with a conversion, with an extended version of their dance hit "Miss You."

In Chicago, a local disc jockey named Steve Dahl had built a reputation as a leading voice of the swelling "Disco Sucks" movement. A few days before the ballpark event, he'd made a crass promotional stunt of smashing a copy of Van McCoy's hit single "The Hustle" to mark the performer's sudden death of a heart attack.[27] When he called for listeners to donate copies of disco singles so he could blow them up in a follow-up stunt, the idea caught the imagination of the Veecks. They advertised a "Disco Demolition" at the ballpark, to take place between games of a scheduled doubleheader. Fans who brought a disco record to destroy would get a discounted admission of ninety-eight cents.

On the outfield grass between games, Dahl, outfitted in army fatigues and a helmet, led a chant of "Disco Sucks!" As soon as his crew set off an assortment of explosives under the crate of records, thousands of fans surged onto the field. The White Sox, who had been warming up for the second game, fled to the safety of their clubhouse. The rioters made a bonfire of records; they ripped up chunks of sod, stole the bases, and destroyed the batting cage. Twenty minutes after the melee ensued, Chicago police arrived in full riot gear.

While that event was an unmitigated fiasco, the anti-disco attitude was catching on across the country. New York's WPIX—the first station in the country to devote a programming block to disco—switched to an all-rock format that year. On a Los Angeles beach, a KROQ disc jockey organized a "disco funeral," burying records in the sand. Advertisements began appearing in *Rolling Stone* for T-shirts that read "Death to Disco" and "Shoot the Bee Gees." The widely publicized incident in Chicago simply brought to the fore the growing white, male desire to find a scapegoat in disco.

As depictions of gay lifestyles became more commonplace—on television, the popular prime-time sitcom *Soap*, which ran from 1977 to 1981, featured a young actor named Billy Crystal playing one of the medium's first openly gay characters—so too did the reactionary forces of antigay advocates casting themselves as protectors of "family values." Such groups included James Dobson's Focus on the Family, the Reverend Lou Sheldon's Traditional Values Coalition, and the Reverend Jerry Falwell's Moral Majority, each of which denounced the relaxation of social mores. The discovery of and panic over the HIV virus in the early 1980s led to the swift condemnation of gay sexuality. In 1983, President Ronald Reagan's communications director, Pat Buchanan, declared the virus "nature's revenge on gay men." Three years later, the decade's antigay hysteria reached a peak when the US Supreme Court upheld a Georgia law that criminalized anal sex between consenting adults. (The Court would overrule its decision, declaring anti-sodomy laws to be unconstitutional, in 2003.)

None of this divisiveness and discrimination would be lost on Nile Rodgers and Bernard Edwards, cofounders of the Manhattan-based dance band Chic. Though themselves in conventional relationships, the two musicians were well aware that their band's emergence as a mainstream institution, on the strength of major crossover hits including "Le Freak," "I Want Your Love," and "Good Times," was indebted largely to the gay-friendly disco community. Their first hit, "Dance, Dance, Dance (Yowsah, Yowsah, Yowsah)," borrowed its parenthetical interjection from the Sydney Pollack film *They Shoot Horses, Don't They?* (1969), which found a grim metaphor for the futility of the American dream in the marathon, sometimes deadly dance contests of the Depression era. "It was spectacle entertainment, it was like being in the Colosseum in Rome," as Rodgers once explained.[28] One of Chic's club hits was a song called "My Forbidden Lover," the title of which seemed to allude to the furtive lifestyle that disco's gay habitués were ready to shed once and for all. Rodgers, an influential guitarist, and bassist Edwards were suddenly in high demand as studio session players and producers. They made pop celebrities of the family group Sister Sledge, and Rodgers would soon produce albums for David Bowie and Madonna. Before that, however, in 1980 he would partner with his first true superstar, Diana Ross.

For the members of Chic, the band represented a kind of urban sophistication that recalled the heyday of swing. "Everything about Chic is based on the black musicians from the Depression era, the black musicians who were allowed to entertain for whites but couldn't stay in the same hotel that they were performing in," said Rodgers, who'd been a teenage Black Panther. To insist upon their dignity, he continued, those earlier musicians assumed names like royalty: Duke Ellington, Count Basie. "A person doesn't want to think of themselves as beneath somebody," Rodgers said, "they want to think of themselves as an equivalent. . . . Like they say, 'How are you gonna keep 'em on the farm once they've seen Paris?'"

As the disco era began to show signs of waning, Rodgers recalled, Diana Ross was "the biggest star in the world." Or at least she was on the New York club scene, where the embodiment of Motown's "finishing school" approach to pop stardom had seamlessly incorporated disco production into her chart-topping, post-Supremes solo career. Ross's dizzying, heavily syncopated 1976 single "Love Hangover," nearly eight minutes long in its extended version, hit number one on the *Billboard* Hot 100, soul, and dance charts simultaneously. By then, she had transcended the music world to become a Hollywood star. She'd debuted as an actor playing Billie Holiday in *Lady Sings the Blues* (1972), scored a soundtrack hit on the troubled production for *Mahogany* (1975), and starred as Dorothy in the 1978 film adaptation of *The Wiz*, the widely hyped, African-American Broadway musical based on *The Wizard of Oz*.

One night in an underground New York nightclub called the Gilded Grape, Rodgers had an epiphany. At the time, he and Edwards were frequenting the predominantly gay and transvestite clubs, where the partying was rampant and the music was designed for the hardcore dance fetishists. "I was standing there in the bathroom, urinating," Rodgers recalled in a 2011 interview, "and I looked next to me, and there were five guys in drag, and they all looked like Diana Ross. Talk about an artistic light bulb. I said, what if Diana were gay, and she said to the world, I'm coming out?"

Edwards and Rodgers, who were co-producing Ross's next album, *Diana*, quickly introduced her to the concept for the song. When she balked, wondering whether her fans would think she was announcing she was gay, Rodgers had a diplomatic reply. Ross's dissatisfaction with Motown had been evident for some time; she'd clashed with label founder Berry Gordy, her onetime lover, on the set of *Mahogany*, and she'd begun to realize that she'd been grossly undercompensated by Motown, despite being its biggest star. By 1980, she was negotiating a deal to leave the label. *Diana* would prove to be her last release for Motown before signing a $20 million contract with RCA, making her the best-paid performer in the business at the time.

Though Rodgers understood the singer's concern that the lyric content of "I'm Coming Out" could cost her some of her mainstream audience—it was, he noted, the summer of "Disco Sucks"—he insisted the idea behind the song had nothing to do with sexuality. "You're leaving Motown, changing your life," he told her. "You're an independent woman. You're coming out of your shell."

In fact, however, "I'm Coming Out" soon became one of the key anthems of gay pride. Drag performer Morgan Royel, a longtime Ross impersonator, once said that the song has been a lifelong inspiration. "Anything that was hiding inside of us, we had a moment to be proud about it and come out," she said. Though Ross was skeptical at first, it didn't take her long to embrace her status among the gay community. For years she has opened her concerts with

"I'm Coming Out." In 1996, she filmed a video for her own version of Gloria Gaynor's anthemic "I Will Survive" on Santa Monica Boulevard in West Hollywood, where she shared a parade float with the drag queen RuPaul.

By then, fifteen years after the outbreak of the AIDS epidemic, protesters had managed to dispel many of the misinformed notions about the disease and the gay community that had been devastated by it. In the mid-1980s, 150,000 people were becoming infected annually, and gay and lesbian civil rights were under attack, blamed as the cause of a rapidly spreading virus that was infecting intravenous drug users as well as sexual partners. Alarmed at the medical industry's perceived indifference to the problem, a group of activists formed the radical direct-action group ACT UP: AIDS Coalition to Unleash Power. In a series of high-profile demonstrations that began with blockades on Wall Street to denounce the high price of medications to manage the infection, members of ACT UP took to the streets, demanding faster clinical trials for experimental drugs. "From the start, ACT UP acted with aggressiveness, audacity, and a panache that had been mostly missing from radical activism for decades," writes L. A. Kauffman in *Direct Action: Protest and the Reinvention of Radical Activism* (2017).[29] The group protested the government's inaction by shutting down the Golden Gate Bridge and tossing the ashes of dead loved ones on the White House lawn. Their memorable slogan, accompanied by a symbolic pink triangle, was "Silence=Death."

In 1990, supporters of ACT UP formed another protest group, Queer Nation, to counter the rise of homophobia that accompanied the AIDS epidemic. The coalition made masterful use of guerrilla public relations tactics, coining the slogan, "We're here, we're queer, get used to it!" By most measures the American public has done just that, due in part to the visibility of ACT UP, Queer Nation, and many other advocacy groups, and the role of popular culture in making gay lives more visible. According to Gallup polling, 38 percent of the country in 1992 believed that homosexuality should be considered an acceptable alternative lifestyle; ten years later, that number had risen to 51 percent.[30] In 1996, 27 percent of the population felt that same-sex marriage should be recognized by law. Twenty years later, that figure had more than doubled, to 61 percent.[31]

The Red Hot Organization, a not-for-profit company established in 1989, increased public awareness of the AIDS crisis through its ongoing series of compilation albums, videos, and messaging campaigns. Red Hot's first benefit release, *Red Hot + Blue* (1990), was a tribute to the music of the urbane Broadway composer Cole Porter, which featured various stars singing "I've Got You under My Skin," "Love for Sale," "Don't Fence Me In," and other songs from Porter's extensive catalogue. In 1993 Bruce Springsteen accepted the filmmaker Jonathan Demme's challenge to write and record a song for his film *Philadelphia*, which starred Tom Hanks as a lawyer dying of AIDS. Demme, as Springsteen told *The Advocate* in a 1996 cover story, wanted to make a movie "for the malls": "I think he wanted to take a subject that people didn't feel safe with and were frightened by and put it together with people that they did feel safe with like Tom Hanks or me," he said. On **"Streets of Philadelphia,"** a kind of AIDS-era update of the classic Depression lament "Brother, Can You Spare a Dime?," the singer who'd built his superstardom on "a very straight image" (by his own admission) put himself in the shoes of a scared and lonely AIDS victim.

> *I was bruised and battered, I couldn't tell what I felt*
> *I was unrecognizable to myself*
> *Saw my reflection in a window and didn't know my own face*
> *Oh brother are you gonna leave me wastin' away*
> *On the streets of Philadelphia*

"That's all anybody's asking for—basically some sort of acceptance and to not be left alone," Springsteen told *The Advocate*. "There was a certain spiritual stillness that I wanted to try to capture. Then I just tried to send in a human voice, as human a voice as I possibly could."

All those human voices joining the chorus of support for same-sex couples would eventually lead to vindication in the court of law. In June 2015, the US Supreme Court handed down a landmark ruling in favor of marriage equality. A few years earlier, Barack Obama became the first president to declare his support for same-sex-marriage while still in office. The occasion led one LGBT writer to address the continuing relevance of Diana Ross's unwitting anthem, "I'm Coming Out." "Each of us, in our own way, by being out, contributes to changing the future," he wrote. "Our authentic selves, on full display for the world to see, have great power to influence hearts and minds. And thanks to a chance encounter in a gay bar more than thirty years ago, Nile Rodgers gave us an anthem to break down the oppressive closet doors."[32]

Solidarity Day march, September 19, 1981.

Credit: Library of Congress, Prints & Photographs Division, photograph by Frank Espada.

http://www.loc.gov/pictures/resource/ds.02975/

8 IMMIGRATION AND THE "OTHER"

Deportee – America – Immigration Man – American Tune – The Ballad of Ira Hayes – The Immigrant – Black, Brown, and White – American Skin (41 Shots) – Without a Face – Migra

On the first day of November each year—El Dia de los Muertos, the Mexican Day of the Dead—an anonymous visitor left flowers on the mass gravesite. The marker was embedded in the grass in a corner of the Holy Cross Catholic Cemetery in Fresno, California. The interred bodies belonged to twenty-eight Mexican citizens who'd died decades before, in 1948, in a plane crash in the mountains outside Coalinga, a modest oil and farming community about fifty miles southwest of Fresno.

Most of the deceased had been working as braceros, guest workers with US government permission to enter the country for hire during the seasonal harvest. The braceros were being flown back to Mexico after their work was complete. A few others were undocumented immigrants who'd been rounded up and were being deported. Most news reports at the time of the crash gave the names of the pilot, the first officer, the flight attendant, and the immigration officer assigned to accompany the flight. But the rest of the occupants of the chartered DC-3 were commonly identified only as "Mexican nationals."

So Woody Guthrie gave them names. "Goodbye to my Juan, goodbye, Rosalita," he wrote. "Adios, mis amigos, Jesus y Maria." His lyric tribute to the dead, **"Deportee,"** would turn out to be one of Guthrie's last major contributions to American music. Suffering from an as-yet undiagnosed case of Huntington's disease, he would not record, and rarely performed, after 1948.

Almost ten years later, Pete Seeger held a concert in Fort Collins, Colorado. Afterward, a student at the university then known as Colorado A&M hosted a small gathering at his home in honor of the visiting folk singer. Martin Hoffman, a member of a local songwriters' club, told his hero he'd set Guthrie's verses about the plane crash to music. Seeger, who had been trying not to fall asleep on a couch, perked up at the news of Hoffman's work. As Hoffman strummed his guitar, Seeger pulled out a small notepad to mark the chord changes.

A few months later, Hoffman received a letter from the promoter Harold Leventhal, informing him that Seeger had begun performing "Plane Wreck at Los Gatos (Deportee)" and wished to credit the composer. (The song, eventually recorded by a wide range of artists including Joan Baez, Dolly Parton, Bruce Springsteen, and Guthrie's son Arlo, has been credited with various titles).[1]

> *The skyplane caught fire*
> *Over Los Gatos Canyon*
> *A fireball of lightning*
> *Shook all our hills*
> *Who are all these friends*
> *Who are scattered like dry leaves*
> *The radio said*
> *They were just "deportees"*

Though Guthrie, who was living in New York City at the time, was unaware, a few local newspapers had in fact been diligent in reporting the names of the victims at the time of the accident. Outside of the area, however, the victims remained anonymous, as they did for decades to the visitors at Holy Cross Cemetery. It was not until 2013 that the names of the twenty-eight "deportees" were finally memorialized on a large gravestone commissioned to replace the old marker. One local history teacher told her students the story, and they raised $14,000 toward defraying the cost of the headstone and memorial service by holding a bake sale.

"They connected right away because many of their parents are farm workers from Mexico," Berenice Guzman said at the dedication. "This is an agricultural community. For many of us here, the people in that crash could have been family."[2]

In America, we are *A Nation of Immigrants*, as John F. Kennedy wrote in his book by that title, published in 1958. As Alexis de Tocqueville had observed in his renowned report on the new democratic experiment across the Atlantic Ocean from his native France, America from the beginning was a society of immigrants, all recreating themselves, and all doing so on equal footing. "This was the secret of America," wrote Kennedy, the future president: "a nation of people with the fresh memory of old traditions who dared to explore new frontiers, people eager to build lives for themselves in a spacious society that did not restrict their freedom of choice and action."[3]

But from its origins, the United States has harbored another not so well-kept secret: historically, many Americans have resented the "equal footing" afforded those who arrived on these shores after they did. One version of the country's story can be told through its successive waves of immigrants. By the seventeenth century, British newcomers had colonized New England and Virginia, and Dutch settlers had established New Amsterdam at the southern tip of the island of Manhattan. Meanwhile, Spanish settlers had occupied Florida for more than two centuries by the time Spain ceded the territory to the United States in 1819. One year later, the US Census for the first time classified black Americans as a separate race, accounting for more than 1.5 million, against a total population of 9,638,000. (Black Americans were initially identified on the census as "slaves"; later censuses added distinctions between slaves and free men and women, as well as further distinctions between mulatto, quadroon, and octoroon).[4]

By the mid-1850s, Irish immigrants, many of them fleeing the Great Famine, led the latest wave of American newcomers. They were followed by thousands of Chinese arrivals who came through the port of San Francisco during the Gold Rush in search of decent wages; it was Chinese workers who built much of the First Transcontinental Railroad. But economic hardships—there were multiple recessions after the Civil War, followed by the Panic of 1873, a depression that lasted nearly six years—led to fierce calls for immigration reform. With the Chinese accused of taking jobs that might have gone to "real" Americans, Congress passed the Chinese Exclusion Act in 1882. It was the first time, but not the last, that the government would target a particular ethnic group. Intended to expire in ten years, the act was instead renewed, and would not be repealed until the Magnuson Act of 1943.

Another crackdown on immigration occurred in the 1920s, in response to the steady flow of millions of European immigrants passing through the busy Ellis Island immigration station. During World War II, more than one hundred thousand Japanese resident aliens and American-born citizens with Japanese ancestry were notoriously incarcerated in camps along the west coast.[5]

Yet another considerable source of new ethnic Americans was Puerto Rico, which became an unincorporated territory of the United States following the Spanish-American War of 1898. Beginning in the 1950s, Puerto Rican immigration to the US mainland—specifically, to the New York City neighborhoods that earned the nicknames Spanish Harlem and Loisaida—increased dramatically, with seventy-five thousand islanders relocating to the city in 1953 alone. A decade later, people of Puerto Rican descent accounted for nearly 10 percent of New York City's total population.[6] But better job prospects didn't mean immunity to discrimination. The influx of Puerto Rican families meant that other ethnicities in New York City, among them Germans, Irish, and Italians, had a new social group to look down upon.

The story of feuding tribes, of course, is timeless. More than three centuries after Shakespeare deployed it in *Romeo and Juliet*, the choreographer Jerome Robbins recast that tale with the ethnic divisions of World War II fresh in mind. Robbins conceived of a play that would reimagine Shakespeare's work as an ill-fated love between a New York City boy from an Irish-Catholic family and a girl who survived the Holocaust. Playwright Arthur Laurents called his script *East Side Story*.

Though the initial project was shelved, it was revived several years later, with some major changes: Maria, the Jewish girl, was now a new arrival from Puerto Rico. The production, renamed *West Side Story*, opened on Broadway in September 1957, with music by the composer and conductor Leonard Bernstein, who would be well-known in American households for his series of instructional Young People's Concerts for CBS television. The lyrics were by a newcomer named Stephen Sondheim. The show ran on Broadway for 732 performances. When it was released in a film adaptation in 1961, it was enthusiastically embraced across the country. Of its eleven Academy Award nominations, the movie won ten, including Best Picture. The soundtrack album still holds the record for the longest run atop the *Billboard* album chart: fifty-four weeks.

One of the show's most memorable numbers is **"America,"** written as a dialogue between Bernardo, the leader of the Sharks, the Puerto Rican gang, and his girlfriend, Anita. She's glad to be done with island living, but he is quick to note the shortfalls of their families' adopted home. When she sings of the good fortune of "lots of new housing with more space," he replies, "Lots of doors slamming in our face!" When she says, "I'll get a terrace apartment," he shoots back, "Better get rid of your accent." Then their friends trade lines:

> *Life is all right in America*
> *(If you're all white in America)*
> *Here you are free and you have pride*
> *(Long as you stay on your own side)*
> *Free to be anything you choose*
> *(Free to wait tables and shine shoes)*

The song as it appears in the film adaptation of *West Side Story* was a distinct reworking of the version in the theatrical play. On stage, the number focused on the Sharks girls—Anita extolling the conveniences of America as her friend Rosalia expresses her longing for the old country. The film version was much more incisive, with the cast indexing the downsides of being a minority in this country.

An exuberant moment in a popular musical, "America" nevertheless amounted to a full-throated protest on behalf of all the newcomers who've ever been made to feel unwelcome. "The lyrics were unusual in their willingness to puncture a near-sacrosanct illusion that the United States is a land of plenty and abundant opportunity for every new arrival," writes Misha Berson in her book on *West Side Story* in the American imagination. "Such a poke at the American dream was most uncommon in Broadway musicals of the time—almost as rare as the inclusion of Puerto Rican characters in a show."[7]

On a bright October day in 1965, President Lyndon Johnson stood at the foot of the Statue of Liberty. He'd ferried to Liberty Island to sign a piece of legislation that would dramatically alter the future of the country.

The bill would "repair a very deep and painful flaw in the fabric of American justice," Johnson promised. "It corrects a cruel and enduring wrong in the conduct of the American nation." The Immigration and Nationality Act of 1965—also known as the Hart-Celler Act, after the two Congressmen who co-sponsored the bill—abolished the national origins quota system, which had been in place since the 1920s. Under the old law, the United States heavily favored immigrants from northern and western Europe, with far less opportunity for people applying to come to America from southern and western Europe. For Asians and Africans, coming to America was even tougher. Acknowledging the discrepancy, President Truman commissioned a report in his last year in office on immigration and naturalization, titled *Whom We Shall Welcome*. The report, which would help pave the way for the Hart-Celler Act, opened with a relevant quote from George Washington: "The bosom of America is open to receive the not only Opulent and respectable stranger, but the oppressed and persecuted of all Nations and Religions."[8]

The new law, Johnson explained, would assess hopeful immigrants on the basis of the skills they offered and "their close relationship to those already here. . . . The fairness of this standard is so self-evident that we may well wonder that it has not always been applied," he said.[9] Though Johnson maintained that passage of the bill would not drastically alter the makeup of the American populace, it did just that, and quickly: as the president pointed out, nearly 70 percent of all legal immigrants in the 1950s were from the British Isles and Canada. By 1970, five years after the passage of the Immigration and Nationality Act, Asian immigration to the United States had more than quadrupled. Overall immigration, which accounted for 11 percent of the total population growth in the 1960s, ballooned to 33 percent of that figure in the next decade.[10]

With a boost from Hart-Celler, America was rapidly on its way to becoming the minority-majority nation that has proved an inevitability in the twenty-first century. (It's just about here: according to the Census Bureau, of the twenty million children under the age of five in the United States in 2014, more than half of them were nonwhite).[11]

Some protest songs have collective justice in mind; others are sparked from more personal resentments. The British musician Graham Nash was moved to write **"Immigration Man,"** a frustrated rant about border control, when he found himself on the receiving end of a minor incident of what he found to be unfair treatment. After performing in Vancouver in early 1970 with Crosby, Stills, Nash & Young, Nash was briefly detained while passing through customs to return to California. The singer, who would become a US citizen some years later, felt he was singled out by a border patrol officer because of his British accent. "It infuriated me," as he would remember in his autobiography. "I don't like being left out, and I especially don't like bullies."[12] As soon as he returned home, he sat down at the piano and began jotting down lyrics about the experience. For paper, he used the margins of the book he was reading—Ray Bradbury's *The Silver Locusts*, the British version of the science fiction writer's *Martian Chronicles*, a series of vignettes that describe the conflict between a sentient species on Mars and the refugees from Earth who have settled their planet. "I was trying to express my disgust with people who always want your papers," Nash recalled.

> *Let me in, immigration man*
> *Can I cross the line and pray*
> *I can stay another day?*
> *Let me in, immigration man*
> *I won't toe your line today*
> *I can't see it anyway*

Nash released the song on *Graham Nash David Crosby*, the first album by the duo following the breakout success of their supergroup with Stephen Stills and Neil Young, in 1972. In part, Nash was inspired by the same photograph of Earth from space that appeared on the cover of Stewart Brand's

Whole Earth Catalog. "When you look at a photograph of the earth you don't see any borders," Nash said. "That realization is where our hope as a planet lies."

The 1970s were a time of despair, as the idealism and apparent progress of the previous decade banged up against the solid wall of a stagnant economy, widespread urban distress, and the national identity crisis of the Vietnam War and the Watergate era. Paul Simon was working on his second solo album following the breakup of Simon and Garfunkel when he wrote **"American Tune,"** a somber meditation based on a seventeenth-century Lutheran hymn. Simon's lyric imagines a bone-weary narrator who dreams he flies over the Statue of Liberty, which is "sailing away to sea."

> *And I don't know a soul who's not been battered*
> *I don't have a friend who feels at ease*
> *I don't know a dream that's not been shattered*
> *or driven to its knees*
> *But it's all right, it's all right*
> *We've lived so well so long*
> *Still, when I think of the road*
> *we're traveling on*
> *I wonder what went wrong*
> *I can't help it, I wonder what went wrong*

The song's title was instructive: this tune could have spoken for any American. "For the child of an immigrant family," writes one Simon biographer, "one of the hundreds of millions of citizens whose forebears were delivered to this land on a vessel of some sort, the contrast between hope and reality is almost too stark to contemplate."[13] Years after the song's release, Simon would acknowledge it as a rarity in his catalog: "I don't write overtly political songs, although 'American Tune' comes pretty close, as it was written just after Nixon was elected."[14]

In the history of the country, there has been just one minority group that was not the product of immigration. During the civil rights era, the US government began referring to the descendants of American Indian tribes as "Native Americans." Ironically, the term had been used by an altogether different group a century prior—by the Anglo-Saxon Protestants whose opposition to Irish and German Catholic immigration was the founding principle behind the "Know-Nothings," the nativist political party that briefly framed the debate over the future of the American melting pot.

By the 1960s, generations of Americans who grew up on the cowboys and Indians of Western movies and television shows, from *Stagecoach* to *The Lone Ranger*, recognized that the indigenous peoples of North America had been the first victims in a long history of American injustice toward the "other." The songwriter Peter La Farge, who grew up in New Mexico and competed in rodeos as a teenager, felt a particular kinship: his father was a noted scholar of Native American history, and La Farge claimed to have Narragansett ancestry on his mother's side of the family, who came from New England.

La Farge served time in the US Navy during the Korean War before moving to New York, where he devoted himself to music, playing on the Greenwich Village folk circuit. Bob Dylan sang La Farge's song "As Long as the Grass Shall Grow," which recounted a land dispute between the Seneca Nation of New York and the US government, at Pete Seeger's 1962 Carnegie Hall Hootenanny. La Farge, Dylan would later recall, was the real protest singer on the folk scene.[15]

La Farge's short recording career launched with an album titled after his best-known song, **"The Ballad of Ira Hayes."** The song told the sad tale of the real-life Pima Indian who was one of the Marines who raised the American flag during the Battle of Iwo Jima in World War II, the moment captured in an iconic photograph by Joe Rosenthal for the Associated Press. Hayes, whose celebrity from his war heroics could not shield him from discrimination upon his return to civilian life, became an alcoholic and died of exposure in 1955, after a night of heavy drinking.

> *Call him drunken Ira Hayes*
> *He won't answer anymore*
> *Not the whiskey drinking Indian*
> *Or the marine that went to war*

"The way Ira Hayes was treated was the way Peter felt he had been treated," the folk singer Oscar Brand has said. "I thought when he performed he carried the weight of the whole Indian nation with him."[16]

La Farge's last album, *Peter La Farge on the Warpath*, was dominated by songs about Native Americans, including "Johnny Half-Breed" and "I'm an Indian, I'm an Alien." La Farge died in late 1965, reportedly of an accidental overdose of Thorazine. The previous year, he'd had his biggest success as a songwriter when Johnny Cash recorded five of La Farge's songs on his concept album *Bitter Tears: Ballads of the American Indian*. Cash, who believed at the time that his family had some Cherokee ancestry, fought back against what he felt was the record industry's reluctance to promote the album, taking out a full-page ad in *Billboard* in which he called radio programmers "gutless" for neglecting to play his version of "Ira Hayes." The campaign made an impact: the song eventually rose as high as the third spot on *Billboard's* country singles chart, and the album reached number two. "To me, Cash's album is one of the earliest and most significant statements on behalf of native people and our issues," said Dennis Banks, a cofounder of the American Indian Movement (AIM).[17]

Buffy Sainte-Marie was another outspoken advocate for the rights of indigenous peoples. Best known for her antiwar song "Universal Soldier," the Cree folk singer from Saskatchewan, Canada, was often inspired, in songs such as "Now That the Buffalo's Gone" and "My Country 'Tis of Thy People You're Dying," to write about their plight. By the early 1970s the culture was inundated with Native American imagery, from the prolonged occupation of the abandoned prison facility on Alcatraz Island (1969–1971) to the seventy-one-day standoff at Wounded Knee in 1973. Both actions were undertaken to raise awareness of the rampant poverty on Indian reservations and the US government's disregard of treaties it had entered with various tribes. In 1971, an advocacy group called Keep America Beautiful debuted a public service announcement that would become one of the most memorable television commercials of all time—the so-called "Crying Indian" ad, in which an actor portraying a Native chieftain (in actuality, an Italian-American actor who went by the alias Iron Eyes Cody) shed a tear over a bag of fast-food wrappers dumped on a highway. Two years later, the pop star Cher had a number one hit with "Half-Breed," a song written expressly for the singer. Cherilyn Sarkisian was born to a father of Armenian heritage and a mother who claimed her family had English, Irish, German, and Cherokee roots. (Years later Cher was taken to task on social media for the Vegas-style headdress and white bikini she wore in promotional materials at the time.) Set to a danceable pop orchestra with more than a dollop of tribal thunder, the lyrics described the child of a Cherokee man and a white woman, whose marriage displeased both of their families and drew the scorn of locals: "We never settled, went from town to town/When you're not welcome, you don't hang around."

Packing up and moving all over again: it's a scenario familiar to countless people who have been made to feel they don't "belong." For decades, Mexican immigrants have found themselves at the center of the endless debate about American citizenship, and which newcomers are welcome in this country. The debate has grown hotter as the rate of immigration climbs. According to the US Census Bureau, the number of Mexican immigrants in the United States has zoomed from a little over two million in 1980 to nine million in 2000 and more than 11.5 million—about half of them illegally—just six years later. (Mexican immigration has actually leveled off since; by 2013, both China and India had overtaken our neighbor to the south as the countries sending the most newcomers to the United States each year.)[18]

Long before Mexican "illegals" found themselves a flashpoint in the culture wars, migrant workers like the ill-fated ones who inspired Woody Guthrie's "Deportee" were on Merle Haggard's mind. The country stalwart was sometimes assumed to be a conservative figure in terms of personal politics, but the reality was far more complicated than that. Haggard's best-known song, "Okie from Muskogee," has been endlessly debated: was it an anti-hippie rant, or a tongue-in-cheek sendup of traditional small-town values? In 1978 Haggard released a song simply titled "**The Immigrant.**" This time there was little mistaking his intention, despite the lyric's broad, sometimes cartoonish strokes. The song, co-written with Dave Kirby, addressed the hypocrisy of the well-to-do American ranchers who rely on Mexican migrants for their hard labor, only to "haul 'em back over the border" when the work is done. "They sneak 'em through customs 'til time comes to bust 'em," Haggard croons.

> *Viva la Mexico, go where they let you go*
> *Do what you can for the land*
> *Take home dinero and buy new sombrero*
> *And come back again when you can*

Racial profiling has been another controversial, much-discussed subject of in the twenty-first century, from the anti-Muslim rhetoric that roared in the aftermath of the September 11 attacks on the World Trade Center to the incidents of police brutality that sparked the Black Lives Matter movement. The history of the practice is long, and often systemic.

Victor Hugo Green was a mailman for the US postal service. Green, who lived and worked in Harlem, knew from firsthand experience that driving long distances to tour the countryside attracted plenty of unwanted attention for people of color in the era of Jim Crow. He began compiling information about restaurants, hotels, and storefronts that were amenable to African-American travelers, which he published, beginning in 1936, in an annual guidebook. Though he sold about fifteen thousand copies each year, eventually enabling his retirement from the postal service, Green looked forward to the obsolescence of his own lifework.

"There will be a day sometime in the near future when this guide will not have to be published," he wrote of *The Negro Motorist Green Book: An International Travel Guide*. "That is when we as a race will have equal opportunities and privileges in the United States. It will be a great day for us to suspend this publication for then we can go wherever we please, and without embarrassment."

The Green Book, as it became widely known, identified businesses that were friendly to African Americans, but it also identified municipalities that were considered "sundown" towns, where people of color were not welcome on the street after dark. In more recent years, the specter of African-American drivers facing intimidation by local authorities has earned a bitter descriptive term: "Driving While Black."

The country blues singer Big Bill Broonzy addressed the discrimination he lived with when he began performing his song **"Black, Brown, and White,"** probably sometime in the 1930s. If you're white, it's all right, he sang. If you're brown, stick around. But if you're black, "get back, get back, get back." This obsession with varying skin tones would become known as "colorism."

Despite his successful recording career, Broonzy could not find an American label that would issue a studio version of "Black, Brown, and White." They all claimed it wouldn't sell, but Broonzy knew otherwise. Pete Seeger once explained that he first met Broonzy at a New York City hootenanny in the 1940s. Afterward, Broonzy mailed a demo recording of the song to Seeger, imploring him to cut his own version. "I can't sing this in the kind of places I work at," Broonzy wrote, "but maybe you can."

"Officers in Bronx Fire 41 Shots, and an Unarmed Man Is Killed," read a *New York Times* headline in February 1999, when a West African immigrant named Amadou Diallo was killed in the doorway of his apartment building. Officers later claimed they'd mistaken the wallet he took out of his pocket for a gun. "We have a very undemocratic society back home, and then we come here," said one of Diallo's friends. "We don't expect to be killed by law enforcement officers."[19]

Diallo's death inspired Bruce Springsteen to write **"American Skin (41 Shots)."** He debuted the song at a concert in Atlanta, a few months after the officers were acquitted.

Is it a gun?
Is it a knife?
Is it a wallet?
This is your life

Springsteen included the song in his set list for a subsequent ten-date run at Madison Square Garden. Though he stressed that the song wasn't "anti-police"—"I worked hard for a balanced voice," he would later write; "I knew a diatribe would do no good."[20]—members of the New York Police Department expressed their displeasure at the song by refusing to provide security at the shows. "I personally don't particularly care for Bruce Springsteen's music or his songs," said Police Commissioner Howard Safir, who supported the boycott. Springsteen has revisited the controversial song often in the ensuing years, dedicating it to the memory of Trayvon Martin after the Florida teenager was shot and killed in 2012.

In 2000 the politically energized hard rock band Rage against the Machine recorded a version of Springsteen's "The Ghost of Tom Joad" for an album of socially conscious cover songs. Springsteen and Rage guitarist Tom Morello were mutual admirers; some years later, Morello began a long stint as a frequent guest member of Springsteen's E Street Band.

Formed in the early 1990s in the San Fernando Valley just north of Los Angeles, Rage against the Machine, as the name implied, embodied a comprehensive, fully committed kind of dissent rarely seen since the 1960s. Inspired by the anti-corporate politics of hardcore punk bands such as Washington, DC's Fugazi and the brash, combustible hip-hop of Public Enemy, Rage came out for the opening bell with fists flying. Led by Tom Morello, a Harlem-born, Harvard-educated leftist with innovative guitar techniques that often simulated the percussive scratching of hip-hop DJs, and vocalist Zack de la Rocha, son of the Mexican-American artist and activist Robert "Beto" de la Rocha, the band's debut album sold more than three million copies. Their immediate success hinged on the popularity of the track "Killing in the Name," a ferocious song that charged racism in police work. The song and album were released six months after the Los Angeles riots that followed the acquittal of the LAPD officers in the infamous Rodney King trial.

"Killing in the Name" set a blueprint for the unique vocal style for which de la Rocha would become known, in which he repeats an incendiary line again and again, often rising from a hush to a caterwaul. "Fuck you, I won't do what you tell me!" he howls repeatedly on "Killing in the Name," after accusing "chosen whites" of hiding behind the badge. The single and the band's debut album both featured a cover image of a Pulitzer Prize–winning photograph, the horrifying self-immolation of a Buddhist monk in a 1963 protest against the Vietnamese government's suppression of his faith. The band would go on to release a brief catalog (four albums) of diatribes about the status quo in America and across the globe, with songs such as the military-industrial condemnation "Bulls on Parade" and the media rant "Testify," which borrows from Orwell's *1984*: "Who controls the past now controls the future/Who controls the present now controls the past."

On their second album, *Evil Empire*, which took the number one spot on the *Billboard* album chart in mid-1996, Rage against the Machine addressed the rising furor over Mexican immigration and calls for increased border security. This was two decades before Donald Trump's presidential campaign pledge to "build a wall" across the entirety of America's southern border. "Got no card, so I got no soul," de la Rocha spews on the tension-and-release thrasher **"Without a Face,"** narrating from the perspective of a border-crossing migrant who knows his life is probably endangered: "To survive, one motive no hope/It's hard to breathe with Wilson's hand around my throat." ("Wilson" was Pete Wilson, at the time the governor of California. The governor was a vocal proponent of the 1994 ballot initiative known as Proposition 187, which aimed to deny social services to undocumented immigrants.)

At a show in the Netherlands around the time of the album's release, de la Rocha explained the catalyst for the song. "It seems as soon as the wall in Germany fell, the US government was busy building another one on the border between the U.S. and Mexico," he said. "Since 1986, as a result of a lot of the hate talk and hysteria that the government of the United States has been speaking, fifteen hundred bodies have been found on the border. We wrote this song in response to it."

By 2000, de la Rocha had grown disillusioned with the band's decision-making process, and he announced his departure, effectively ending the group. A year later, during the collective trauma in the wake of the 9/11 attacks, the band earned a dubious distinction: when the Clear Channel radio network distributed a memorandum with a long list of "lyrically questionable" songs for programmers to avoid, Rage against the Machine were the only band whose entire catalog was banned from the company's airwaves.

De la Rocha's Mexican heritage had relatively few predecessors in the world of rock music. In 1999, however, the most influential Mexican American in American popular music staged a blockbuster comeback. Thirty years after launching the band that bore his surname to worldwide fame from the stage at Woodstock, Carlos Santana earned eight Grammy Awards for his album *Supernatural*. It was a historic haul, including awards for Album of the Year, Song of the Year, and Record of the Year for the hit single "Smooth." Sneaked in among the album's high-profile collaborations was one song that expressed the bandleader's grave concern for the undocumented immigrants from his own homeland. The song was no dour lament, but a joyous (if urgent) reminder of our shared humanity. Sung in Spanish, **"Migra"** took its title from Spanish slang for the US Immigration and Naturalization Service (now US Citizenship and Immigration Services, a division of the Department of Homeland Security):

> *Malicia veo en tus ojos*
> *Desprecio en tu corazón*
> *Es hora de reconocer*
> *Que todos somas una voz*
> *Abraza el concepto*
> *Venimos de la misma voz*
> *I see malice in your eyes, contempt in your heart*
> *It's time to admit that we are all one voice*
> *Embrace the idea that we are all the same*

"I'm not Latino, or Spanish," Santana said in an interview on the publication of his memoir in 2014. "What I am is a child of light."

Demonstration outside US Nuclear Regulatory Commission headquarters, Rockville, Maryland, 1990.

Credit: US Nuclear Regulatory Commission.

https://commons.wikimedia.org/wiki/File:Anti-Seabrook_demonstration_outside_NRC_HQ_(1990)_(13609031664).jpg

9 NO NUKES

Take It Away – Old Man Atom – We Will All Go Together When We Go – The Great Atomic Power – Morning Dew – A Hard Rain's a-Gonna Fall – Eve of Destruction – We Almost Lost Detroit – Before the Deluge – 1999

"I Write This As a Warning to the World." Readers of London's *Daily Express* were greeted with this grim headline on the morning of September 5, 1945. The Australian correspondent Wilfred Burchett had accompanied the first US Marines onto the Japanese mainland days after the bombs were dropped in Hiroshima and Nagasaki, in early August. Burchett's dispatch was the first to detail the massive devastation and loss of human life wreaked by the first and only time nuclear weapons have been used in war.

Hiroshima, Burchett wrote, looked as if "a monster steamroller had passed over it and squashed it out of existence." Citizens who were apparently uninjured in the bombing were dying nevertheless, "mysteriously and horribly," he wrote, "from an unknown something which I can only describe as atomic plague."[1]

Though the US military did its best to suppress the full extent of the destruction—a three-hour documentary on the effects of the bombings, filmed and edited by members of the US Strategic Bombing Survey, was considered classified information for more than twenty years after the war—the American public and their fellow world citizens were alarmed by the potency that had been unleashed by the work of the physicists of the Manhattan Project. Four years after the conclusion of World War II, the Soviet Union tested its first nuclear weapon, and the impending end of the human race became an all-consuming source of public anxiety. Beginning in 1950, American schoolchildren were required to watch the educational film *Duck and Cover*, and a generation grew up dreading the prospect of an enemy nation dropping "the big one."

Eight years after Hiroshima, President Dwight D. Eisenhower spoke to the United Nations General Assembly as part of the US government's coordinated effort to change public perception about nuclear power. Uranium, the president suggested, could be harnessed for use in nuclear reactors that would empower the world. "My country wants to be constructive, not destructive," Eisenhower said. "It wants agreement, not wars, among nations." The United States, he claimed, would pledge itself "to help solve the fearful atomic dilemma—to devote its entire heart and mind to find the way by which the miraculous inventiveness of man shall not be dedicated to his death, but consecrated to his life." The title of the president's speech, and the subsequent awareness campaign, was Atoms for Peace. Construction on the nation's first nuclear power plant began a year after Eisenhower's speech, in western Pennsylvania.

On the West Coast, an experimental reactor went online in Ventura County in the spring of 1957, followed by a commercial project near the San Francisco Bay Area suburb of Pleasanton, a joint venture between General Electric and Pacific Gas & Electric, the primary utility serving northern California. PG&E set its sights next on Bodega Bay, a rugged coastal community about forty miles north of the Golden Gate. The population of the utility's service area was growing rapidly, and the company needed new ways to supply its customers with power. With expansion in mind, the company acquired a parcel of land on the pristine, privately owned area known as Bodega Head, which had been earmarked for a future state park and discussed as a possible site for a University of California marine laboratory. When the power company approached Rose Gaffney, who had inherited property that gave her the claim to nearly half of Bodega Head's 947 acres, she refused to sell. The public had been told that PG&E was planning a steam-electric generating plant, but a company representative confided in Gaffney, as she later revealed, that the plant would in fact produce nuclear power. Having acquired the rest of the land at a premium, the company assumed that Gaffney would eventually relent.

But she had concerns about the environmental damage of any kind of development on the site, which was rife with birds and marine life. More ominously, locals voiced their unease about the intelligence of building a power plant on land situated directly along the San Andreas fault. David Pesonen, a staff member with the Sierra Club, was dispatched to assess PG&E's plans while all parties awaited the approval of the federal Atomic Energy Commission. "I had a feeling of the enormousness of what we were fighting," Pesonen would recall. "It was anti-life."[2] PG&E's resolve to see the project through, he said, "didn't involve people's well-being." Pesonen soon left the Sierra Club to establish an advocacy group opposing the power plant.

Another interested observer was Lucius "Lu" Watters, a geologist with a particular interest in earthquake studies. Watters was also a jazz trumpeter, a traditional Dixieland bandleader who had been a Bay Area celebrity since the 1930s. Though he'd retired from the music business, he assembled an ad-hoc group to record a topical album called *Blues over Bodega*, which included an instrumental called "San Andreas Fault" and a couple of guest vocals by the folk and jazz singer Barbara Dane.

Dane's friend Malvina Reynolds, the composer of "Little Boxes," wrote a song based on the Bodega Bay dispute called **"Take It Away,"** which was published in the folk newsletter *Broadside* in January 1963. In it she called out PG&E by name, accusing its leadership of being a "killer gang": "We need that electric power to make our country run/But what's the use of electric juice if the people are all gone?"

All around Eureka town
Dosimeters are set
To see, when the plant gets running,
What kind of a dose we'll get

Two of those meters, Reynolds noted, were mounted on an electric pole at a primary school.

Another Bay Area music act recorded a novelty jug-band song similarly inspired by the clash, called "Don't Blame PG&E, Pal." The song, by a group called the Goodtime Washboard Three, satirized the company as "a most benevolent utility/Always acting for the welfare of consumers/And that means all of us, you must agree." The company had pledged "millions to beautify our California shore," the group sang, with a heavy portion of sarcasm.

On Memorial Day in 1963, Pesonen's activists released fifteen hundred helium balloons from Bodega Head. Each balloon included a note explaining that its path could just as likely be the path of radioactive molecules that would be released in the event of an accident at the reactor. The balloons fell to earth across several counties, from Sonoma and Solano all the way to the Central Valley, nearly one hundred miles to the east. But the real blow was dealt when organizers summoned Pierre Saint-Amand, the geologist whose report on the 1960 Valdivia earthquake in Chile—still the most powerful ever recorded—was considered definitive. While PG&E publicly maintained that the company's design for the reactor accounted for any potential earthquake damage, Saint-Amand's report told a very different story. "A worse foundation condition would be difficult to envision," he concluded. A major earthquake reported in Alaska in March 1964 further set the public on edge; later that year, the Atomic Energy Commission agreed that the fears of the antinuclear activists were justified, and within a matter of days PG&E canceled plans for the project.

For her role in opposing the utility, Rose Gaffney has been called the "mother of ecology," and the successful opposition to PG&E's plans has been identified as "the birth of the antinuclear movement." When PG&E backed out, the company left behind a deep hole that had been dug for the proposed reactor. The pit, still jokingly referred to as the "Hole in the Head," has been reclaimed by the natural world: it is now a pond.

The threat of nuclear annihilation brought not just fear but a dark sense of humor to American popular culture. One of the first songs to consider the implications of nuclear fission was a "talking blues" written by Vern Partlow, a journalist who interviewed nuclear scientists for a Los Angeles newspaper after the bombs were dropped in Japan. "The people of the world must pick a thesis/Peace in the world, or the world in pieces," Partlow wrote.

At first he thought about writing a "Mother Goose–type" song, which he would call "Jack and Jill Went Up." Then he considered another wry title: "One of Our Hemispheres Is Missing."[3] Eventually known as **"Old Man Atom"** (and sometimes recorded as "Talking Atom" or "Atomic Talking Blues"), Partlow's lyrics were published in the quarterly bulletin of People's Songs, the progressive musicians' organization formed by Pete Seeger, his fellow Weavers member Lee Hays, archivist Alan Lomax, and others. A rash of recordings of the song soon followed, including versions by Seeger, Fred Hellerman (another member of the Weavers), and the Western singing group Sons of the Pioneers.

The most successful version, however, was cut by Sam Hinton, a marine biologist who was also a folk singer. It was placed in regular rotation by the influential New York disc jockey Martin Block, whose twice-daily program "Make Believe Ballroom" could single-handedly create hit records. But just as the song was reaching critical mass—Columbia Records picked up Hinton's small-label release for distribution, and Bing Crosby was reportedly preparing his own major-label version—grassroots organizers began demanding its removal from the airwaves, claiming its antiwar message had to be the work of communist sympathizers. The *New York Times* was one of several prominent publications to lament the effort to get radio programmers to ban the song, calling it "a new high in absurdity" and arguing that if the song was any kind of propaganda, "it is by rights American, not Russian, propaganda."[4] Despite the support, Partlow, the songwriter, was called before the House Un-American

Activities Committee. He lost his job at the *Los Angeles Daily News* and was blacklisted from journalism.

Though he paid a personal price for it, Partlow's song expressed the country's growing concern for the "thing that Einstein says he's scared of, and when Einstein's scared—brother, I'm scared," as Hinton recited. Albert Einstein, who had worked with the Manhattan Project, said after the bombs were dropped on Japan, "To the village square we must carry the facts of atomic energy. From there must come America's voice." Hinton's recording of the song featured a segment sung in a haunting falsetto, a simple, melodic citation of the place names associated with the bomb: "Hiroshima, Nagasaki, Alamogordo, Bikini." (The latter two, in New Mexico and the Marshall Islands, respectively, were the sites of early nuclear testing.) Hinton's version ended abruptly, with the sound of a detonation.

No less ominous, if a little more absurd, was Tom Lehrer's show tune-without-a-show, **"We Will All Go Together When We Go."** The mathematician and part-time songwriter, who'd gone to summer camp as a boy with Stephen Sondheim and began his studies at Harvard at age fourteen, released his second album of witty topical songs, *An Evening Wasted with Tom Lehrer*, in 1959, after completing his postgraduate studies and a stint in the Army. In concert, he typically introduced the song as a "modern, positive, dynamic, uplifting song in the tradition of the great old revival hymns. This one might be more actually termed a 'survival hymn.'" The timeless human anguish over the end of life—the mourning of the loved ones left behind—would be eradicated, the song promised, by the thorough obliteration of the coming nuclear holocaust: "Universal bereavement—an inspiring achievement!/Yes, we will all go together when we go." Lehrer, who was beloved for his inventive rhymes, brought the sardonic tune toward its closing flourish with the inspired couplet "When the air becomes uraneous/We will all go simultaneous."

There was just one way to assure salvation in the event of nuclear calamity, according to the Louvin Brothers. The gospel-country duo recorded one of their most enduring songs in 1952, **"The Great Atomic Power."** "Are you ready?" the brothers asked of their listeners. Are you ready for the "terrible explosion" that will mete out "horrible destruction?" There was only one way: be prepared to meet your Lord and savior.

He will surely stay beside you
And you'll never taste of death
For your soul will fly to safety
And eternal peace and rest

As Charlie Louvin recalled, the concept for the song originated with a song-writing partner named Buddy Bain. "The song was his idea, something he came up with after they dropped the big one," he said. When Bain struggled to set his thoughts to a lyric, Ira Louvin finished the job. Like Partlow's "Old Man Atom," a flurry of similarly themed country tunes emerged in the years following World War II, about two dozen in all, including "Jesus Hits like an Atom Bomb" and "There Is a Power Greater Than Atomic." For country-raised believers like the Louvins, the development of atomic power was "absolute proof that the deity exists and his power is infinite," as the historian Charles K. Wolfe once told the *New York Times*. "Here you have people who have put themselves through all sorts of hardship and struggle during the war, and all of a sudden it's ended, wham, just like that—what kind of power can do that?"[5]

There were reminders everywhere you looked. At the movies, radiation produced such metaphoric monsters as the enormous mutant ants, spawned by the nuclear test at Alamogordo, in *Them!*, and the Tokyo-crushing "gorilla-whale" Godzilla. A decade later Stanley Kubrick directed the classic black comedy *Dr. Strangelove or: How I Learned to Stop Worrying and Love the Bomb*, which ended with a montage of mushroom clouds accompanied by the British singer Vera Lynn's bittersweet World War II–era ballad "We'll Meet Again."

In England, meanwhile, the designer Gerald Holtom unveiled his logo concept for the Campaign for Nuclear Disarmament, which would soon be adopted as the most widely recognized international symbol for peace.

In 1961 the mounting opposition to nuclear energy converged in the co-ordinated efforts of the activist group known as Women Strike for Peace. Cofounded by Dagmar Wilson and the future congresswoman Bella Abzug, on the first day of November the group assembled an estimated fifty thousand women at marches and gatherings across dozens of cities, including a rally at the base of the Washington Monument that President Kennedy witnessed from a White House window. The demonstrators appealed to the public by emphasizing their maternal instincts: they pointed out that Strontium-90, the radioactive product of nuclear fission, was turning up in mother's milk and store-bought cow's milk. By raising such awareness, the women's movement deftly shifted the debate about the opposition to nuclear power from a referendum on communism—an argument that had clouded every peace initiative for decades—to a call for common sense about the health of the nation's newborns. The group's slogan crystallized their mission: "End the Arms Race, Not the Human Race."

Five years before the publication of Rachel Carson's *Silent Spring*, another book, a work of fiction, had gripped the public with the fear of a nuclear holocaust. Nevil Shute's *On the Beach* imagined a small group of survivors in Melbourne, Australia, anxiously awaiting the arrival of radioactive fallout after a nuclear war has annihilated the Western world. In 1959 the novel was adapted into a feature film starring Gregory Peck and Ava Gardner. The film alarmed a young Canadian folk singer named Bonnie Dobson, as it did so many of her generation.

In 1962, the same year Carson's book was published, Dobson released a live album that featured her song **"Morning Dew."** Inspired by the film, the somber folk song pictured a couple unable to step outside for fear of nuclear contamination: "You can't go walking in the morning dew today." The song was recorded in 1964 by the folk duo Martin & Neil (Vince Martin and Fred Neil, the latter of whom would later leave the music world to cofound the Dolphin Project, a Florida-based marine research group). Tim Rose, who'd performed in a trio with "Mama" Cass Elliott before she joined the Mamas and the Papas, also recorded the song, and in 1967 "Morning Dew" was recast as an acid rock ballad on the debut album by the San Francisco rock band the Grateful Dead. They played the song as their opening number at the Human Be-In, the January 1967 gathering in San Francisco's Golden Gate Park that foreshadowed that year's "Summer of Love."

Organized as a response to a newly passed California law that banned the recreational use of LSD, the Human Be-In opened with the poet Gary Snyder blowing on a conch shell. With much of the crowd—an estimated twenty or thirty thousand—under the influence of the drug, an afternoon succession of speakers included Ginsberg, who led a Buddhist chant; the psychedelic proselytizer Timothy Leary, who'd recently coined his phrase "Turn on, tune in, drop out"; and writer Lenore Kandel, who read from *The Love Book*, a collection of poems which had lately been seized on obscenity charges from City Lights Booksellers and the Haight-Ashbury's Psychedelic Shop.[6] The Be-In would prove to be one of the early clarion calls to the young people of the emerging counterculture, many of whom would descend on the Haight-Ashbury in the summer months to come, instigating a massive political shift with lifestyle choices that underscored the rapidly growing generation gap.

Dobson's "Morning Dew" was part of a barrage of songs that expressed the anxiety of the "baby boom" generation (born 1946–1964) over nuclear proliferation. Bob Dylan's early, politically motivated recordings included **"A Hard Rain's a-Gonna Fall,"** which was written, he claimed to the writer Nat Hentoff, in response to the Cuban Missile Crisis. (In fact, he'd written the song before the standoff, and not specifically about atomic bombs, as he would later explain to the interviewer Studs Terkel: "In the last verse, when I say, 'the pellets of poison are flooding the waters,' that means all the lies that people get told on their radios and in their newspapers.") Another song Dylan wrote around the same time, "Let Me Die in My Footsteps," was inspired, as he told Hentoff, by the sight of a construction crew building an enormous underground bunker.

> *I will not go down under the ground*
> *'Cause somebody tells me that death's comin' round...*
> *And some people thinkin' that the end is close by*
> *'Stead of learnin' to live they are learnin' to die*

Under the alternate title "I Will Not Go Down under the Ground," the song was released as a duet with Happy Traum (with Dylan credited as "Blind Boy Grunt") on the topical 1963 compilation album *The Broadside Ballads, Vol. 1*. It was Dylan's "blunt answer to the yawping of Madison Avenue Pitchmen trying to sell fallout shelters," according to that album's liner notes. Dylan's own version of the song, which had been cut from his second album in favor of "Hard Rain," would not be released for nearly three decades, finally appearing in 1991 on the first release in the singer's official *Bootleg* series. Years later, in Dylan's *Chronicles, Volume 1*, he suggested that the bomb shelters of his youth were actually considered something of a folly: "Not that people weren't concerned about the mushroom cloud—they were. But salesmen hawking the bomb shelters were met with expressionless faces."[7]

Dylan and his characteristic word surges were unmistakably on the mind of the songwriter P. F. Sloan when, at the green age of nineteen, he wrote **"Eve of Destruction."** By 1964, the New York native was writing for southern California acts including Jan & Dean and the Turtles, but it was his late-night fever dream about the state of the world in the early years of the Vietnam War, following the assassination of President John F. Kennedy, that would remain his lasting legacy. The song addresses "violence flarin', bullets loadin'," the nuclear launch "button," and segregation and the disintegration of "human respect," among other concerns: "And you tell me over and over and over again, my friend/You don't believe we're on the eve of destruction."

Sloan sometimes claimed he'd imagined the song as a dialogue with God. It was first recorded by the Turtles, the folk-rock incarnation of a former high school surf group, but its success came after the song was introduced to Barry McGuire, a folk singer who'd recently left the New Christy Minstrels. That group of choral folkies adapted their name from the Christy Minstrels, a nineteenth-century blackface act that helped popularize the songs of Stephen Foster. The "new" Minstrels' 1962 debut album, which won a Grammy Award, featured a perky popular version of Woody Guthrie's "This Land Is Your Land" that stripped the song of its some of its tart commentary.

McGuire wasn't smitten with Sloan's topical song when he first heard it; still, he agreed to record it as the B-side of another Sloan composition called "What's Exactly the Matter with Me." Disc jockeys quickly picked up on the provocative lyrics of the flip side, however, and their listeners confirmed its appeal. By September 1965, the song had supplanted the Beatles' "Help!" at the top of the *Billboard* Hot 100 chart.

For all its commercial success, though, "Eve of Destruction" incited an overwhelming backlash. Radio stations across the country forbade their programmers to play it, citing its "anti-American" attitude. Within weeks the music industry was flooded with "answer" songs. A US Marine officer named Barry Sadler co-wrote and recorded "The Ballad of the Green Berets" as a tribute to the first native Hawaiian to be killed in action in Vietnam; it went to number one. Meanwhile, a vocal trio from Philadelphia called the Spokesmen had a hit of their own with "Dawn of Correction," a near-parody of Sloan's wordy dissent. One key line from "Eve of Destruction" noted the disparity of the legal age in America—"You're old enough to kill but not for votin'." In "Dawn of Correction"—written and performed by John Madara and David White, the songwriting team behind "You Don't Own Me," along with a local radio personality named Ray Gilmore—the narrator argues that it's the duty of the citizens of the Western world to oppose "Red domination": "And maybe you can't vote, boy, but man your battle stations." Though the song was received as patriotic cheerleading, it was really conceived as an antidote to Sloan's pessimism:

> *You tell me that marches won't bring integration*
> *But look what it's done for the voter registration*
> *Be thankful our country allows demonstrations*
> *Instead of condemnin', make some recommendations*

Madara, who'd grown up in the Philadelphia projects, had participated in civil rights actions. He says he was at the March on Washington for Jobs and Freedom the day Dr. King delivered his "Dream" speech. He also traveled to Selma and Philadelphia, Mississippi, site of the June 1964 murders of activists James Chaney, Andrew Goodman, and Michael Schwerner. When the Spokesmen made the rounds of the rock 'n' roll TV shows based in California—*Shindig!*, *Where the Action Is*—to promote "Dawn of Correction," he was dismayed by his fellow musicians' reactions to the song's glass-half-full attitude at a time of mounting anxiety. On one bill that featured the Byrds, David Crosby approached Madara backstage and said, "Man, do you really believe that shit you're singing?"

Though McGuire's version of Sloan's song was a phenomenon, the writer was knocked off balance by the attention it attracted. "The media frenzy over the song tore me up and seemed to tear the country apart," he once wrote. "I was an enemy of the people to some and a hero to others, but I was still only 20 years old." The media, he felt, "headlined the song as everything that is wrong with the youth culture. . . . I told the press it was a love song. A love song to and for humanity, that's all. It ruined Barry's career as an artist and in a year I would be driven out of the music business too."[8]

Despite the efforts of activists such as Rose Gaffney, by 1974 there were fifty-five nuclear power plants representing $15 billion in investments operating in the United States. More than $100 billion had been pledged toward future construction. The nation's power companies hoped to have one thousand nuclear plants online by the year 2000, and Presidents Nixon and Ford both appealed to Congress to speed up the regulatory process in response to the growing energy crisis of the 1970s.

In Montague, Massachusetts, a small town of eight thousand or so residents situated along the Connecticut River, plans were announced in late 1973 for the development of what would be the country's largest nuclear reactor to date—twin cooling towers rising six hundred feet in the air, processing more than twenty million gallons of water from the river each day. A ragtag group of local protesters quickly organized against the developer, Northeast Utilities, under the name Nuclear Objectors for a Pure Environment: NOPE.

According to group leader Sam Lovejoy, the environmentalists who were then converging across the country in opposition to nuclear energy were "starting to realize there's a capitalist dialectic forcing nukes to be built in this country." Lovejoy was spurred to action after hearing a talk by a longtime opponent of the Vermont Yankee nuclear power plant in Vernon, Vermont, about twenty miles to the north of his hometown. The Vermont speaker believed the only thing that would stop the development of nuclear plants in the United States would be a major calamity. To Lovejoy, it was a startling admission. He felt duty-bound to stop the project in Montague: "They will have to build that plant over my body," he said.[9]

In the early morning on February 22, 1974—symbolically, it was Washington's birthday—Lovejoy, a young organic farmer with his hair pulled back in a ponytail, crept up to a 500-foot weather tower the utility had erected on the property it planned to use. The tower had been erected to study the regional wind patterns, to predict the path of "normal" radioactive emissions from the future plant. When the young man, working in the dark, loosened the turnbuckles that anchored the cables holding the slender tower in place, the tower came crashing to the ground. Having completed his act of sabotage, Lovejoy hitched a ride to the police station and turned himself in, presenting a four-page letter of explanation. One press account that reported Lovejoy's act of vandalism was headlined "Jack and the Nuclear Beanstalk."

A grand jury indicted Lovejoy on one count of willful and malicious destruction of personal property. At his trial later that year, he represented himself in court. Lovejoy claimed he was inspired in part by *Poisoned Power: The Case against Nuclear Power Plants*, a 1971 book co-written by Arthur R. Tamplin and John Gofman. Dr. Gofman, an early researcher for the Manhattan Project who had come to share Einstein's view about the terrifying prospects for nuclear power, testified on Lovejoy's behalf (as did the historian Howard Zinn). Outside the courthouse, Gofman scoffed at the utility spokesmen who touted the company's emergency preparedness. With one hundred tons of material burning at five thousand degrees Fahrenheit, melting through concrete into the soil, he speculated, when an engineer claims the damage would be minimal, "I look at them as a chemist, and I say, 'I have heard various forms of insanity, but hardly this form.'" Even if an accident never occurred on the site, the plant would generate an "astronomical" amount of radioactive "garbage," Gofman argued, with no effective long-term method of disposal.

Lovejoy was acquitted on a technicality, and he and his supporters quickly went to work launching the first truly integrated network of "no nukes" activists. Northeast Utilities pushed its plans back a year, then another four years. In 1980 the company officially canceled its plans for the project in Montague. It sold parts of the unfinished plant to an alternative energy company, which recycled the materials to build windmills.[10]

The movement against nuclear power made steady gains through the 1970s, with widely publicized blockades organized against the construction of plants in Seabrook, New Hampshire, along the Pacific Coast in San Luis Obispo County, California, and elsewhere. In defense of their actions, protesters frequently cited the narrowly averted disaster that occurred at a Michigan nuclear power plant in 1966. The Enrico Fermi Nuclear Generating

Station, named for the nuclear physicist who won the Nobel Prize for his work in the field in 1938, suffered a partial fuel meltdown when a malfunction in the sodium cooling system led to damage in two of the facility's one hundred-odd fuel assemblies. Fermi 1, as the plant was known, had been designed as a "breeder" plant, an innovative concept which could produce more nuclear fuel than it used. The belief was that such a plant, when fully operational, could produce plutonium that might be sold to the government for use in nuclear weapons or at other reactors. Given the volatility of liquid sodium, however, the risk factor at plants of such design was higher than at the more common water-cooled reactors. Citing that risk, the United Auto Workers unsuccessfully filed suit to stop its construction before Fermi 1 was activated in 1963.

Though no one was injured in the meltdown and the containment vessel did its job—no contamination was recorded outside the unit—the plant was shut down for repairs. It would be four years before Fermi 1 would go back online. In the meantime, hearsay about the accident stoked public concerns about the inevitability of human error in the nuclear industry. Some unsubstantiated reports suggested that the meltdown had been caused by a carelessly discarded beer can. (The cause turned out to be a dislodged metal plate, which had been installed inside the reactor as a safety measure.)[11]

In 1975 *Reader's Digest* published a book about the crisis at Fermi 1 by John G. Fuller, a longtime columnist for the *Saturday Review*. Called *We Almost Lost Detroit*, the title was based on a quote the author attributed to an anonymous engineer. Fuller's account was swiftly denounced by the power companies. Detroit Edison soon published an alternative account of the incident, *We Did Not Almost Lose Detroit*. Despite Edison's best efforts, Fuller's phrase took on a life of its own. The spoken-word artist and self-identified "bluesologist" Gil Scott-Heron, best known for his Black Power anthem "The Revolution Will Not Be Televised," recorded a song called **"We Almost Lost Detroit,"** a melancholy, piano-based ballad in which he charged that "when it comes to people's safety, money wins out every time." In his lyrics Scott-Heron referenced Karen Silkwood, the plutonium production worker who testified before the Atomic Energy Commission about safety standards in 1974. Her death under mysterious circumstances a few months later inspired the 1983 film *Silkwood*, in which Meryl Streep played the activist.

Two years after recording his song, Scott-Heron was one of dozens of artists invited to perform at the No Nukes concerts, a series of all-star shows at Madison Square Garden organized by Musicians United for Safe Energy, or MUSE. The group, led by the recording artists Jackson Browne, Bonnie Raitt,

Graham Nash, and John Hall of the band Orleans (a future two-term US congressman from New York), came together in response to another nuclear accident, the March 1979 partial meltdown at the Three Mile Island Nuclear Generating Station in Pennsylvania. That incident would be characterized, as Fermi 1 had been, as a narrowly averted catastrophe. For the nuclear industry, however, coverage of the Three Mile Island accident was a public relations disaster. Cleanup efforts would take more than a decade and cost well over a billion dollars, and in the five years after the meltdown, plans for more than fifty new reactors across the United States would be canceled.

In June 1979, MUSE staged a concert called "Survival Sunday" at the Hollywood Bowl to raise money for antinuclear protest groups. The cofounders of MUSE drew Bruce Springsteen, John Sebastian, and others as fellow performers. Three months later, the No Nukes organizers addressed a gathering of more than 200,000 in New York City's Battery Park, joining speakers including consumer advocate Ralph Nader, the actress Jane Fonda, and Tom Hayden, the onetime president of Students for a Democratic Society (and, at the time, Fonda's husband). Pete Seeger and Tom Paxton sang "If I Had a Hammer," the Seeger–Lee Hays ballad about empowerment that had been a Top 10 pop hit for Peter, Paul & Mary in 1962. "We believe all of us against nuclear energy have to think of ourselves as Paul Reveres and Pauline Reveres," said Fonda, "going through our country town by town, city by city warning the people about the dangers."[12]

The rally in Battery Park wrapped up five nights of high-profile concerts at Madison Square Garden, portions of which were released before the end of the year in a triple album that featured a handful of songs addressing the nuclear issue or sociopolitical concerns in general. (Sam Lovejoy, saboteur of the Montague power plant, was the executive producer of the *No Nukes* concert documentary.) Jackson Browne, who hosted Native American tribe members whose livelihood was affected by uranium strip-mining, sang **"Before the Deluge,"** a lament for the fate of the planet that MUSE adopted as its theme song. Some from Browne's generation, he sang, "were angry at the way the earth was abused/By the men who learned how to forge her beauty into power." John Hall showcased two songs written expressly for the nuclear opposition, "Power" and "Plutonium Is Forever." Hall, James Taylor, Carly Simon, and Graham Nash collaborated on a straightforward version of Dylan's most famous protest song, "The Times They Are a-Changin.'"

Other performances sought to rekindle the activist spark of the previous decade. Jesse Colin Young sang "Get Together," and the Doobie Brothers capped their sets with "Takin' It to the Streets." If the music was mostly inarticulate on the subject, the concerts and live album succeeded by raising awareness for the issue, in the way that Bonnie Raitt described at a No Nukes press conference. Responding to a reporter's suggestion that perhaps the rock world was in danger of becoming "too powerful or too pushy," she argued that it was the artists' responsibility to attract the media to the issue: "If just the movement people had been here today, you probably wouldn't have even covered this." Much of the drawing power was attributed to the participation of Springsteen, the biggest name on the bill, who hadn't toured in a year and had not yet released any live recordings in his fast-rising career. He also hadn't yet grown comfortable with his own activist streak, as he would in later years; at the time, his mere presence was more than enough. The No Nukes concerts were "the greatest conglomeration of fee-waiving heavyweights since George Harrison's benefit for Bangladesh in 1971," wrote *People* magazine's breathless correspondents, who added that, "[s]hort of the much-rumored Beatles reunion, it was the most potent spectacle the '70s pop culture could bring forth."[13] Hyperbole aside, the No Nukes shows did give the rock community "a sense of how powerful our voices could be," as Graham Nash would recall.[14]

For Nash's bandmate, David Crosby, rock 'n' roll and politics usually did not mesh. "I don't think musicians should go out seeking causes," he said. This one, however, was different: "I'm here because I'm scared. These reactors depend on people, and people always screw up." In a *Rolling Stone* cover story that followed the concerts, Browne did his best to explain MUSE's position on the nuclear issue to a readership that included the same fans who'd nearly drowned out Scott-Heron, Chaka Khan, and others at the MUSE concerts by begging for "Bruuuuce!" The utilities' emphasis on nuclear power over legitimate alternatives was in their own interest, not the public's, Browne argued. "Their thing is selling something to somebody that they don't need. That's Madison Avenue. That's Jiffy Pop. That's hair dryers. New and more expensive ways of using up power for the aggrandizement of oneself."[15]

One of the chief organizers of the No Nukes movement (he reportedly helped coin the name) was Harvey Wasserman, a journalist, spokesperson, and advocate. "This is a movement of national proportion," he told *Rolling Stone* in 1977, shortly after he and several colleagues began engineering a series of demonstrations against the proposed Seabrook Station Nuclear Power Plant in coastal New Hampshire. Inspired by the success of antinuclear protesters in Germany and Denmark, more than 1,400 nonviolent protesters were arrested in Seabrook in May 1977 for criminal trespassing as they tried to block construction of the power plant. The Clamshell Alliance, as the group was known, held signs reading SPLIT WOOD, NOT ATOMS and behaved "like Gandhians," the *Rolling Stone* reporter wrote, "saying 'yes sir' and 'thank you' to the police."[16] When the demonstrators refused to post bail, they were detained for nearly two weeks in nearby National Guard armories.

One of the group's leaders, Nina Simon, explained that hot-water discharge from power plants along both coasts had created miles of ocean that were "virtually dead." She also claimed that "giant sponges" were growing off the coast of San Francisco, caused, she said, by improperly disposed radioactive waste. (When Graham Nash repeated the claim during the No Nukes concerts, the *New York Times* gently chided him for sounding "more enthusiastic than knowledgeable.") Lovejoy, who'd come to Seabrook as a young hero of the antinuclear movement, was amused to be considered a "radical" activist: "This is no radical issue, unless you call protecting life radical," he said, "and if that's radical I'm radical as a motherfucker."

In fact, the Clams, as the members called themselves, subscribed to strict principles in their demonstrations. Drugs and alcohol were forbidden, and protesters were not to run, move after dark, carry weapons, or cause destruction or violence. "It was important to us that human dignity be kept at the forefront of the demonstration," said Elizabeth Boardman, an organizer and Quaker who helped the group conduct training sessions on how to respond to provocation. Their ultimate goal was public ownership of the power utilities, and their methods of achieving that goal were cut from the playbook of nonviolence. "It's good to go to Washington and rant a bit—that's important for a movement—but you also have to go home and revolutionize on your parents and on your neighbors, and that's what's happening here," Lovejoy told *Rolling Stone*.

Years later, upon the death of one of the original Clamshell leaders, Guy Chichester, a coalition of environmental groups dedicated in his name their successful lobbying effort to remove a $50 billion set-aside for new reactors from the federal budget. "He knew the power of a good laugh, a big hug, and a warm smile," said Wasserman. "One of the great things about the Clamshell Alliance was that we all loved doing this. It's fun to save the world."

But decades of anguish about the fate of humankind in the age of nuclear science would reach critical mass by the early years of the Reagan administration. The fortieth president assumed office in 1981 promising to increase defense spending, including a significant expansion to the nuclear arsenal.

In late 1981 the rising pop superstar Prince released his fourth album, *Controversy*. Born in 1958, Prince was a child of the Cold War. He expressed his fears about the bomb in explicit terms on "Ronnie Talk to Russia," an abrasive, punky song that took inspiration for its clattering, rapid-fire sound effects from Jimi Hendrix's Vietnam-era "Machine Gun." "Don't you blow up my world!" he railed.

"Mommy, why does everybody have a bomb?" Prince would ask, his voice disguised as that of a child, on the title track to his next album, the block-buster "1999." As biographer Ben Greenman has noted, Prince, who would join the Jehovah's Witnesses later in life, envisioned a Judgment Day on one of his biggest songs that corresponded to the Book of Revelation. If the end is near, he famously declared, then there was only one logical response: to party like it's 1999.

> I was dreamin' when I wrote this, forgive me if it goes astray
> But when I woke up this morning could have sworn it was Judgment Day
> The sky was all purple, there were people running everywhere
> Tryin' to run from the destruction, you know I didn't even care

In early 1982, a few months before Prince released the album named after "1999," President Reagan escalated the West's war of words with the Soviet Union in a speech he delivered to the British House of Commons. Reagan warned of the threat of global war, which, he noted, he and his fellow world leaders were obliged to contemplate every day. "And I don't have to tell you that in today's world the existence of nuclear weapons could mean, if not the extinction of mankind, then surely the end of civilization as we know it," he said. "We see around us today the marks of our terrible dilemma—predictions of doomsday, antinuclear demonstrations, an arms race in which the West must, for its own protection, be an unwilling par-ticipant." The choices were stark, he suggested: "Must civilization perish in a hail of fiery atoms? Must freedom wither in a quiet, deadening accommo-dation with totalitarian evil?"[17]

Around the time of Reagan's doomsday speech, arthouse movie audiences were lining up to see *The Atomic Cafe*, a montage-style docu-mentary that compiled old government training films and public safety announcements to accentuate the terrible absurdity of life under the con-stant spectre of annihilation. The film's soundtrack featured a vintage rock 'n' roll song called "Uranium," the Golden Gate Quartet's "Atom and Evil," and "Red's Dream," a classic Chicago blues in which Louisiana Red imagined confronting Castro, Khrushchev, and Kennedy about their dangerous missile games. One civil defense film urged families preparing to take cover in a bomb shelter to keep a stock of tranquilizers on hand "to ease the strain and monotony." In the most memorable line of the documentary, an Army instruction film assured viewers that, as long as observers were "not close enough to be killed, the atomic bomb is one of the most beautiful sights in the world."

Demonstration encouraging a boycott of Black Friday consumerism in solidarity with Ferguson, Missouri protesters, New York City, November 28, 2014.

Credit: Black Lives Matter Black Friday.

https://commons.wikimedia.org/wiki/File:Black_Lives_Matter_Black_Friday_(15741865229).jpg

10 INTO THE TWENTY-FIRST CENTURY

The Day after Tomorrow – We Can't Make It Here – Alright – Girl on Fire –
I Need to Wake Up – American Idiot – Born This Way – Trump Talkin' Nukes –
Immigrants (We Get the Job Done)

The day after his inauguration, the American woman trumped our forty-fifth president. In the largest multi-sited, coordinated protest in the country's history, women from all walks of life came together in cities large and small, calling not only for women's rights, but also for the rights of immigrants, an end to police brutality, acknowledgment of the effects of climate change, full acceptance for those who identify as LGBT, and more. On a chilly day in Washington, DC, an estimated half-million demonstrators gathered joyfully in and around the National Mall, wearing the pink hand-knit "pussy hats" that symbolized their collective power, and dwarfing the crowd at Donald Trump's swearing-in ceremony the day before. The *Los Angeles Daily News* reported that 750,000 attended the march in that city; by some counts, more than five million people participated in total across the United States.

The protests were widely noted as a reminder of the activist Vietnam War era. But the twenty-first century had already seen some extraordinary acts of advocacy, from protests against the Iraq War and the Occupy Wall Street vigils highlighting wealth inequality to the impassioned demonstrations against systemic racial profiling in America's police departments, which coalesced as the Black Lives Matter movement. For all the human progress of the twentieth century, as the next millennium begins, we're still searching for solutions to the eternal problems of war, poverty, intolerance, and the ecology. And we're trying to find these answers from within the mind-numbing cacophony of modern America.

As the year 2000 approached, the atmosphere was fraught. Americans shared fears about the Y2K bug ostensibly poised to cripple the world's computers, and Prince's apocalyptic "1999," first released in 1982, enjoyed a second life as a desperate party anthem. When the world's financial leaders convened in Seattle in late November for the World Trade Organization Ministerial Conference, at least forty thousand radical protesters gathered on the streets of the city. A unique alliance that included nongovernmental organizations, labor unions, and unaffiliated, self-proclaimed anarchists, the participants were determined to disrupt the event and voice their grave concerns for the global economy.

In the confrontation that came to be known as the "Battle of Seattle," some created human blockades by chaining themselves together and refusing to move. Others resorted to vandalism to attract attention to their pro-labor, anti-corporate message. ("A riot," Martin Luther King, Jr., once said, "is the language of the unheard.") Washington State governor Gary Locke called in the National Guard, and police arrested more than five hundred activists and bystanders before the conclusion of the two-day convention. It was a foreboding sign of the many confrontational, us-vs.-them disputes to come in the new century.

On September 11, 2001, television audiences across the country watched in horror as two airplanes piloted by hijackers crashed into the Twin Towers of the World Trade Center. In less than two hours, both of the burning towers collapsed, burying lower Manhattan in soot, rubble, and tattered personal effects. Nearly three thousand were dead.

A few days later, the media company Clear Channel Communications sent a list to its affiliated radio stations of more than 150 songs they were banning temporarily from their airwaves. Assuming the shell-shocked American public was too emotionally fragile after the attacks to hear songs with certain themes, the company instructed its affiliates to avoid the Gap Band's "You Dropped a Bomb on Me," Michael Jackson's "Earth Song," Tom Petty's "Free Fallin'," R.E.M.'s "It's the End of the World as We Know It (And I Feel Fine)," and even Louis Armstrong's "What a Wonderful World."

Within weeks, the United States and its British allies launched a bombing campaign against suspected terrorist cells in Afghanistan. Focus on the special operations there shifted westward in early 2003, when the United States led a coalition of forces in an invasion of Iraq, the second in thirteen years for US troops. The presidential administration of George W. Bush cited evidence of "weapons of mass destruction" in its justification for declaring war against Iraq. But as those claims proved misleading, and the conflict escalated from its initial bombing raids to a protracted ground war involving thousands of American troops, public support dwindled.

A new era of dissent was soon underway. Many musicians were eager to voice their growing dissatisfaction with what they saw as an ill-conceived crusade, and several specifically called out the leader of the free world. The rapper Eminem suggested that protesters strap the president "with an AK-47, let him go fight his own war" ("Mosh"). The Armenian-American thrash-metal band System of a Down won a Grammy Award for its 2005 song "B.Y.O.B." ("bring your own bombs"), which asked an age-old question about militarism: "Why do they always send the poor?" Songwriter Steve Earle dared to imagine the mind of John Walker Lindh, a young man from suburban America who converted to Islam and fought with the Taliban in Afghanistan. Earle's "John Walker's Blues" earned the veteran outlaw country star a hailstorm of condemnation.

But the best antiwar song to come out of the Iraq War era may have been one that expressed not outrage or defiance but heartbreak. The exceptional songwriter Tom Waits is known as a gruff-voiced balladeer, an avant-garde carnival barker, a well-studied bohemian in a weathered fedora. Written with Waits's wife and songwriting partner, Kathleen Brennan, and released in 2004, "The Day after Tomorrow" was conceived as a letter home from the frontline by an enlistee just turning twenty-one. The soldier is due to be discharged and fly home, but the song carries an ominous hint that he may not make it that far.

> *And tell me how does God choose*
> *Whose prayers does he refuse*
> *Who turns the wheel*
> *Who throws the dice*
> *On the day after tomorrow*

Around the same time, Waits made available for Internet download a seven-minute song about the futility of the long Arab-Israeli conflict, "Road to Peace." Asked in a magazine interview about a line in "The Day after Tomorrow" in which the soldier confesses, "I'm not fighting for justice, I am not fighting for freedom, I am fighting for my life," Waits replied, "All the guys who come home on leave say that. That's why when you ask them why they just don't stay home now that they're safe, they say, 'Because I've got buddies over there, and they need me. I'm not going over there for the government' . . . Do you think that a senator sleeping in a nice warm bed looks at a soldier as anything more than a spent shell casing? Nothing more. That's why we need more ammo, and the ammo is these children."[1]

Waits once professed a lack of faith in the power of protest music. "I hate to sound cynical," he said, "but it seems to me that protest songs are like throwing peanuts at a gorilla." In the next breath, however, he allowed that Pete Seeger's "The Big Muddy" was one instance in which a singer's message managed to become "more than a song."[2]

Some musicians are more optimistic. "Every successful progressive social movement has a great soundtrack," said Tom Morello, the Rage against the Machine guitarist, while touring Occupy Wall Street demonstrations around the country in late 2011.[3]

The Occupy Wall Street movement was a protest against the financial institutions that caused the economic fiasco of the previous years, which began in late 2007. "Occupy," as the protest became known, launched with a call to action published in *Adbusters* magazine and an encampment in Zuccotti Park (previously Liberty Park Plaza) in New York City's Financial District. The movement spread virally, with similar sites propagating in hundreds of communities around the country and the world. Occupy Wall Street popularized the notion that the wealthiest 1 percent of the population holds an imbalance of power over our democracy—the 1 percent were "writing the rules of an unfair global economy that is foreclosing on our future," as the movement's anonymous leadership claimed—and that the remaining 99 percent must be prepared to act in solidarity in response.[4]

True to the organic roots of these demonstrations, dozens of participants contributed original songs to the cause, with self-explanatory titles such as "Occupy the U.S.A.," "Stand Together," and "We the 99%."[5] Many established artists, meanwhile, showed up in support of the activists. Morello performed as his acoustic alter-ego, the Nightwatchman, at several rallies; Seeger, then ninety-two, marched thirty blocks from a concert venue to Zuccotti Park; rapper Talib Kweli performed there a cappella. David Crosby and Graham Nash represented the old-guard counterculture of the 1960s when they led the crowd in the park in a singalong of "Teach Your Children." They also sang a new, anti-materialist song called "They Want It All" and an evergreen ballad Crosby had written more than three decades prior, "What Are Their Names": "I wonder who they are/The men who really run this land."

The Occupy movement was designed as a model of diffuse leadership. Widely noted at the time, the only amplification permitted at the demonstrations was the "human microphone," with participants collectively repeating the words of each speaker for all to hear. In that spirit, no single song emerged as the movement's foremost anthem. But if there was one song that personified the frustrations of the protesters, it was a somber Americana ballad by the Texas songwriter James McMurtry. **"We Can't Make It Here"** featured vivid verses that described destitute military veterans, vacant textile mills and barren storefronts, dead-end jobs, and widespread resentment toward new immigrants who vie for the same minimum wage.

> *Now I'm stocking shirts in the Walmart store*
> *Just like the ones we made before*
> *Except this one came from Singapore*
> *I guess we can't make it here anymore*

Having released the song in 2005, McMurtry stopped playing it live after the election of Barack Obama, hoping that its bitterness had outrun its usefulness. But when "We Can't Make It Here" was adopted by some involved in the Occupy movement, he made the song available as a free download and encouraged listeners to create their own accompanying videos. "I'd be glad to let them use that song," he said at the time. "Whatever helps."[6]

As a writer, McMurtry has claimed he's more interested in storytelling than manifestos. "My goal is to write the best song, and usually the way to do that is stay in character," he once told *Rolling Stone*. "Once in a while you get away with getting your own point across."[7]

Protesters needed no poetic license to dramatize the next major social movement, which was triggered by a series of distressing real-life stories of young black men and their grim encounters with law enforcement. The Black Lives Matter marches and demonstrations that took place in Ferguson, Missouri, and other communities had a distinct hip-hop flavor, and some of the music's biggest names felt compelled to address the movement directly, with original songs. But hip-hop already had a long history of appeals for justice.

Frank songs about race relations and the burdens of being black in America reached a new prevalence with the rise of hip-hop in the 1980s, and particularly the black consciousness movement of the late decade. Hip-hop emerged in the 1970s as a party culture, from the block parties and underground dances of the Bronx, where a small core of pioneering DJs developed the art of mixing, scratching, and sampling vinyl records. Despite the early emphasis on good times, however, the genre's mainstream breakthrough came in the form of a protest song. Grandmaster Flash and the Furious Five's "The Message" was like a seven-minute documentary tour of impoverished New York. It came just a few years after the city's request for a federal bailout inspired the classic *Daily News* headline "FORD TO CITY: DROP DEAD." Rats, roaches, junkies, broken glass: the city of "The Message" is depicted as one big, demoralizing obstacle course. "Don't push me 'cause I'm close to the edge," the rapper Melle Mel warns on the chorus, deliberating on each word. "I'm trying not to lose my head." The epic song, which was added to the Library of Congress's National Recording Registry in 2002, ends with a skit that echoes Stevie Wonder's "Living for the City," with innocents being busted on the street and herded into a police car. ("Officer, what's the problem?" "You're the problem!")

In the early 1980s, two students at Long Island's Adelphi University started a rap group called Spectrum City. They changed the band name after recording a tape they titled *Public Enemy #1*. Carlton Ridenhour and William Drayton, better known as Chuck D and Flavor Flav, were the strident voices of a creative group that included the sound producers known as the Bomb Squad (brothers Hank and Keith Shocklee and Eric "Vietnam" Sadler) and the DJ Terminator X. Public Enemy made dense, chaotic music that stood as a metaphor for the systemic chaos the group took as its recurring theme. Almost all of the group's material was politically motivated, but their unrelenting black pride and ministerial thunder peaked on "Fight the Power," the kinetic protest rap that featured prominently in Spike Lee's film breakthrough, *Do the Right Thing*. "Nothing but rednecks for four hundred years if you check," as Chuck D snaps on one line. The song, which took its title from the Isley Brothers song of the same name, sampled elements of theirs, several cuts by James Brown, Syl Johnson's "Different Strokes," and many more classic soul records to produce its delirious, belligerent rhythmic soundscape. "Mine and Hank's goal, originally, was to destroy music," as Chuck D told the writer Brian Coleman.[8] The group's intensity, Coleman writes, made listeners "reconsider the power of music and lyrics in a way that arguably hadn't been done since Bob Dylan brought real issues to real music, two decades earlier."

One guest on Public Enemy's third album was the rapper Ice Cube. Aptly, given both his Los Angeles upbringing and his future movie stardom, his contribution came on the track "Burn Hollywood Burn." In his featured verse, Cube (born O'Shea Jackson) visualizes a routine encounter with police: "Roaming through Hollywood late at night/Red and blue lights, what a common sight." When he's pulled over and "played like a sucka," he suggests an aggressive course of action: "Don't fight the power"—we hear the *blam!* of a gunshot—"the motherfucker."

Though the violent images of "gangsta" rap drew loud calls of condemnation, revenge fantasies have always been a source of inspiration in popular song. American culture has produced countless examples of the "murder ballad." In the folklore of Stagger Lee, which has produced hundreds of re-corded variations since first being published in 1911, the bad man guns down an associate who has taken his hat. In Johnny Cash's "Folsom Prison Blues," the inmate admits that he "shot a man in Reno, just to watch him die."

But when young black men of the hip-hop generation began musing about retaliation against police officers, those lyrics were swiftly sensationalized. "Rap Group N.W.A Says 'Kill Police,'" read the headline in a publication of the prominent Christian group Focus on the Family. More precisely, what the group said was "Fuck tha Police."

There's a story in which the members of N.W.A (Niggaz Wit Attitudes)—Ice Cube, Dr. Dre, Eazy-E, MC Ren, and DJ Yella—were standing outside a recording studio in Torrance, California, when several police officers pulled up to the sidewalk. Unprovoked, the officers demanded the artists get on their knees and produce IDs. It's depicted in the film *Straight Outta Compton* as the catalyst that drove Ice Cube to write the group's most incendiary line, "Fuck tha police"—a phrase that would ignite a long debate about racial pro-filing, police brutality, and inner-city lawlessness, and one that continues to smolder today.

Though they became known as icons of gangsta rap, N.W.A preferred to call their music "reality rap." They were "telling the real story of what it's like living in places like Compton," said Eazy-E. "We're like reporters. We give them the truth."[9] But if N.W.A was reporting the realities of ghetto life in America, much of the country was alarmed to hear it as a form of enter-tainment. At a time when the Parents Music Resource Center had recently succeeded in getting the recording industry to affix warning stickers to albums with content they judged to be improper for children, many major retailers refused to stock the group's hit record at all.

After Focus on the Family published its article on the group, law enforce-ment officials around the country demanded that promoters cancel shows on N.W.A's national tour. In some cases, concerts took place without any po-lice protection. On the other end of the scale, at an all-star show in Detroit featuring LL Cool J, De La Soul, and Big Daddy Kane, the police presence was ominous, with more than two hundred officers on hand. At other venues on the tour, N.W.A had agreed not to perform "Fuck tha Police." But the members of the group had a perverse reaction to the cops' show of strength in Detroit. Throughout the set, the sold-out crowd of twenty thousand at Joe Louis Arena howled for the song, until Ice Cube and Dr. Dre locked eyes and decided to give the audience what they wanted. As soon as Cube bellowed the title phrase, undercover police rushed the stage from the back of the house, intent on shutting down the show. As the incident was portrayed in the film *Straight Outta Compton*, the group is arrested as they try to escape. In truth, police officers confronted them at their hotel after the show, but no arrests were made. As a peace offering, Ice Cube has claimed he offered to produce a song for the police called "Fuck N.W.A."[10]

The police beating of Rodney King in 1991 was the first major incident of police brutality in the videotaping era. It was the "most infamous beating in history," as one journalist would declare.[11] King, an off-duty cab driver, was driving while intoxicated when a California Highway Patrol cruiser attempted to pull him over after midnight on March 3, 1991. Fearing a violation of his parole on a previous robbery conviction, he tried to outrace the officers. Over the course of an eight-mile pursuit, several LAPD cruisers joined the chase, with a police helicopter following overhead. When King finally came to a stop, he and his two passengers were hauled out of the car. In his drunken state, King's behavior alarmed the responding officers, who later testified that his resistance led them to believe he was under the influence of PCP. A local resident who lived in an apartment building near the scene caught the arrest and assault on videotape, which clearly showed the officers subduing King with dozens of blows from their police batons.

One year later, three of the four officers were acquitted in a trial by jury. Within hours of the heavily anticipated verdict, South Central Los Angeles was a war zone, with thousands of rioters venting pent-up resentment about white privilege and race in America. Over six brutal days of rebellion, with the National Guard and members of the US Army and Marines called in to respond, more than fifty people lost their lives. Damage from widespread looting and arson was estimated at more than $1 billion. At the corner of Florence and Normandie avenues, young people who were smashing the windows of passing cars with baseball bats taunted responding officers, asking whether they were going to beat the perpetrators "like Rodney King." When two African-American officers cornered a sixteen-year-old boy who they claimed had been throwing rocks, they pinned him to the ground. "I can't breathe," he gasped. Police officers soon received orders to leave the scene, leading to full-blown anarchy in the street. At one point, King appeared on television to plead with the protesters to stop: "Can we all get along?"

More than two decades later, King's poignant question still hung in the air. The slaying of Trayvon Martin, a seventeen-year-old boy who was walking through a gated Florida community while visiting relatives, was the first entry in an infamous inventory—the unjust, and unpunished, deaths of black men. Eric Garner of Staten Island succumbed to a chokehold after a routine stop by police for selling loose cigarettes on the street ("I can't breathe," he said, echoing the boy held down by police during the L.A. riots). Tamir Rice, a twelve-year-old from Cleveland, was shot by police responding to a report of an armed man in a neighborhood park; the boy was holding a toy pellet gun. Walter Scott of Charleston, South Carolina, was shot in the back as he ran from the scene of a traffic stop, fearful of being arrested for his failure to make child support payments. Freddie Gray died of a spinal injury while riding unsecured in the back of a police transport vehicle in Baltimore. Alton Sterling of Baton Rouge, Louisiana, who was selling compact discs on the street when he was stopped by police, was shot twice after they found a gun in his pocket. Philando Castile of St. Paul, Minnesota, was shot by police during a traffic stop, after calmly informing the officer he had a licensed gun in the car.

Amid all these news reports, it was the death of Michael Brown in Ferguson, Missouri, an economically stagnant suburb of St. Louis, that helped bring international recognition to the social movement that took the name Black Lives Matter. Formed in 2013 after the acquittal of George Zimmerman, the neighborhood watch coordinator who shot and killed Trayvon Martin, Black Lives Matter first emerged as an awareness campaign on social media. Brown's death at the hands of police drew the loosely organized group's first coordinated protest action, with approximately five hundred associates arriving in Missouri to help stage ongoing demonstrations in Ferguson through the summer of 2014.

Within weeks of Brown's death, the rapper J. Cole appeared on *The Late Show with David Letterman* to perform his heartbroken ballad "Be Free": "All we wanna do is break the chains off/All we wanna do is be free." The song featured spoken interludes drawn from the eyewitness account of Dorian Johnson, a friend who was with Brown when he died. Cole released the song with a statement explaining his urge to speak out. "I'm tired of being desensitized to the murder of black men," he said. "I don't give a fuck if it's by police or peers. This shit is not normal."[12]

The following summer the singer and actor Janelle Monae led a coalition of artists on a fierce, gospel-influenced protest track called "Hell You Talmbout." The song urged justice warriors to "say their names": not only the names of Trayvon Martin, Walter Scott, Eric Garner, and Freddie Gray, but also Sandra Bland, a twenty-eight-year-old woman who was found hanged in an east Texas jail cell after a traffic arrest; Amadou Diallo, the Guinean immigrant whose 1999 murder inspired Bruce Springsteen's "American Skin (41 Shots)"; and Emmett Till, the teenage boy who was infamously lynched in Mississippi in 1955.

Later in the summer of 2015, another new song became the unofficial anthem of Black Lives Matter. Kendrick Lamar's rapturously received third major-label album, *To Pimp a Butterfly*, featured lyrics addressing African-American stereotypes, inequality, and self-esteem. On the track **"Alright,"** set to a skittering beat and fractured jazz vocals, Lamar acknowledges the long-standing antagonism between police and black America: "We hate po-po/ Wanna kill us dead in the street for sure." Collaborator Pharrell Williams raps the hook, reassuring in the face of adversity: "We gon' be alright/Do you hear me, do you feel me? We gon' be alright."

Demonstrators in Ferguson and elsewhere adapted the simple chorus as a mantra, and some media designated the song a new black national anthem. Writing for *Rolling Stone*, the veteran critic Greg Tate noted that others were calling "Alright" a new generation's "We Shall Overcome." *To Pimp a Butterfly* and D'Angelo's album *Black Messiah*, Tate wrote, were "the first tuneful meditations of this era to come within spitting distance of canonical conscious-groove masterworks like Curtis Mayfield's *Superfly* and Marvin Gaye's *What's Going On*."[13]

There were others in the hip-hop world who found themselves invigorated by outrage. The Grammy-nominated Chicago rapper Vic Mensa recorded "16 Shots" in response to the 2014 police shooting of seventeen-year-old Laquan McDonald. In the video that accompanied the song, Mensa recreated dashboard camera footage of the shooting, with himself wearing a jacket marked with the word RESIST. For Mensa, McDonald represented Emmett Till, the teenager whose lynching—and his mother's subsequent decision to keep an open casket at his wake, revealing the gruesome extent of his facial injuries— helped ignite an earlier plea for the dignity of black lives. "Since then a lot of things have changed," said Mensa, "but one main thing [that] hasn't changed is that our lives are not respected."[14]

Growing up on the South Side of Chicago, Mensa had plenty of his own encounters with police. He recalled officers screaming at him to get his hands out of the pockets of his hoodie "before I punch you in the fucking face." His music, he said, was an act of "self-defense."

As the first year of Trump's presidency lurched to its conclusion, the *Washington Post* estimated that nearly nine thousand protests had been staged across America.[15] The year 2017 saw demonstrations in support of the Affordable Care Act (the embattled health care initiative known as Obamacare), and in opposition to white supremacist rallies and the GOP's proposed tax overhaul. When the administration announced its plan to ban travelers from a selective list of largely Muslim countries, tens of thousands of protesters, many of them immigration lawyers, congregated at the nation's airports.

But no coordinated event had quite the symbolic impact as the Women's March of January 21, on the day after Trump's inauguration. In Washington, DC, a huge throng of women wrapped in multiple layers of cold-weather gear heard speeches from role models ranging from Gloria Steinem, Janelle Monae, and the Illinois senator and retired US Army Lt. Col. Tammy Duckworth to six-year-old Sophie Cruz, the child of undocumented Mexican immigrants. One of the day's most inspirational appearances came from the singer Alicia Keys, who quoted from Maya Angelou's poem "Still I Rise":

> *Out of the huts of history's shame*
> *I rise*
> *Up from a past that's rooted in pain*
> *I rise*
> *I'm a black ocean, leaping and wide,*
> *Welling and swelling I bear in the tide*

Then she thanked the crowd for coming, for their strength and courage, and for their "womanliness. . . . Let us continue to honor all that is beautiful about being feminine," she continued. "We are mothers, we are caregivers, we are artists, we are activists, we are entrepreneurs, doctors, leaders of industry and technology. Our potential is unlimited. We rise."[16]

After calling for women to refuse to allow their bodies to be "owned and controlled" by men, and for an end to hate and bigotry and bombing, Keys concluded by leading a chant of modified lyrics from her song **"Girl on Fire"**: "We're on fire, living in a world that's on fire/Feet on the ground, not backing down."

Several times throughout the DC Women's March, a street choir of women performed a rousing ballad called "Quiet." It was written by a West Coast songwriter named Connie Lim, who identified herself online as MILCK. The singers, who converged on the march from various corners of the country, practiced beforehand by video chat. Operating like a "guerrilla flash mob," as Lim explained, the choir gathered at several points throughout the day to engage the crowds. Lim's somber, hymnlike call to arms about confronting personal trauma—"I can't keep quiet/A one-woman riot"—became another theme song of the event. (It also prefigured the "Me Too" social media movement that surfaced later in the year, a viral show of solidarity among the vast numbers of women who have been victims of sexual abuse and harassment.)

"In this time of fear, propaganda, and discrimination," Lim wrote about her song project, "it is critical for our individual and collective voices to be heard.... I want to encourage others to give a voice to whatever they may have silenced, political or personal."[17]

Across the country, at the huge sister march in Los Angeles, seventy-five-year-old Helen Reddy made an unexpected appearance on the speakers' stage. The massive crowd sang along to her impromptu, unaccompanied version of "I Am Woman."

The new women's movement inspired many musicians to speak out about their own experiences through their art. After widely reported allegations of abuse directed at a former music producer, the singer Kesha performed her gospel ballad "Praying" at the 60th Grammy Awards ceremony in early 2018. The song expressed her wish that an unnamed abuser might find peace, "falling on your knees": "'Cause you brought the flames and you put me through hell/I had to learn how to fight for myself." The song joined a surge of "Me Too" lyrics, from Lady Gaga's "Til It Happens to You" to the country music veteran Vince Gill, who felt compelled to introduce his own long-dormant song about suffering sexual abuse, "Forever Changed."

No pop star has been a more ferocious advocate for womanhood in recent years than Beyoncé, whose regal commitment to female empowerment has earned her the nickname "Queen Bey." From "If I Were a Boy" and "Independent Women, Pt. 1" to "Run the World (Girls)," Beyoncé Knowles-Carter has made a career of leveling male dominance through a long string of vital pop-R&B hits. But her 2016 album, *Lemonade*, was a true cultural event, a powerful artistic response to the alleged infidelity of her husband, the rapper Jay-Z. "Middle fingers up, put them hands high," she urges on behalf of all aggrieved women on the album's second Top 40 single (of an eventual five), "Sorry."

Despite the title, she was not. "I ain't sorry," Beyonce drawls again and again, as if she's speaking on behalf of all those who have felt defiance.

After serving two terms as vice president under Bill Clinton and losing the disputed presidential election in 2000 to George Bush, Al Gore re-emerged as an improbable voice of the counterculture. His 2006 documentary, *An Inconvenient Truth,* was a feature-length, big-screen version of the presentation he'd been giving about the dire implications of the rising temperature of Earth's atmosphere. The film was a surprise box-office success, becoming one of the ten highest-grossing documentaries to date. Its marketing plan featured a series of sensational taglines, including "By far the most terrifying film you will ever see," and "We're all on thin ice."

In 2007 Gore was honored as a co-recipient of the Nobel Peace Prize, sharing the award with the Intergovernmental Panel of Climate Change, an advisory group established by United Nations resolution in 1988. "I don't really consider this a political issue," Gore said on camera. "I consider it to be a moral issue." His film was a rousing success in terms of getting the public to think proactively about our care for the planet and the individual choices we make regarding energy use and carbon footprints. The film's end-credit theme song, written and recorded by the rock singer Melissa Etheridge, took a personal approach, with the narrator admonishing herself (as did many viewers) for her past inattention to the problem. The song, **"I Need to Wake Up,"** won an Academy Award for Best Original Song—the first time the award went to a documentary. "Now I am throwing off the carelessness of youth," Etheridge sang, "to listen to an inconvenient truth."

In July 2007, Etheridge performed "I Need to Wake Up" at the all-star Live Earth concert at Giants Stadium in New Jersey. The event, part of a coordinated series of benefit events across the globe, was developed in the spirit of earlier "cause" performances such as the 1979 No Nukes concerts. The accompanying video for Etheridge's song featured alarming news footage from global devastation caused by extreme weather events, including floods, wildfires, melting polar caps, and the human toll of Hurricane Katrina, which had just recently crippled the city of New Orleans.

"In 2000, it rained in Antarctica," read one title card in the video. "2005 was the hottest year on record," read another. At the time, the global warming trend was undoubtedly disturbing. But the situation grew darker each year: by 2017, the average temperature for the year 2005 had slipped all the way to seventh place on the list.

In spite of the scientific evidence, in 2017, the first year of the Trump administration, the very concept of climate change came under assault. Under the leadership of Trump appointee Scott Pruitt, staff members at the Environmental Protection Agency were instructed to scrub the term and related materials from a website previously identified as "Climate and Energy Resources" for state and local governments. Pruitt, the former attorney general of Oklahoma, came to the job as an avowed climate change "denier," a policymaker who disagreed that human beings and their carbon dioxide emissions have been a primary cause of global warming.

"Climate change" was not the only language declared off-limits in the Trump era. In December 2017, reports surfaced claiming the administration had urged the Centers for Disease Control and Prevention to refrain from using a list of specific words in official documents. Tone-deaf to irony, the administration presented a list that was seven words long—the same number as the "Seven Words You Can Never Say on Television," the iconic comedy routine of the late George Carlin, which mocked the idea of banning any part of the English language. A few days after the announcement of the CDC "ban" (the agency insisted it had not been forbidden to use the words), the civil rights organization known as the Human Rights Campaign mounted a protest in the form of a public art installation. Working in conjunction with the visual artist Robin Bell, the group projected each of the suddenly contentious words and terms—"transgender," "diversity," "science-based," "fetus," "vulnerable," "evidence-based," and "entitlement"—onto the facade of the Trump International Hotel in Washington, DC, along with the declaration WE WILL NOT BE ERASED. (The hotel, standing a little more than a mile from the White House, had already been targeted as an emblem of the new administration's rampant conflicts of interest; one evening earlier in the year, Bell had projected the words "Pay Trump Bribes Here" on the building, with an arrow pointing to the front door.)

In tumultuous times, words are often the first casualties. They're obfuscated, or euphemized, or infused with contrary meaning. In the aftermath of 9/11, with the country engaging in combat in Afghanistan and Iraq, the American public was deeply divided between those who opposed the Bush administration and those who labeled any form of dissension "unpatriotic." Of particular debate was the so-called Patriot Act, the legislative measure passed weeks after the September 11 attack, which suspended various individual rights to privacy in the name of increased security against terrorism.

By the time the band Green Day released their "punk rock opera" *American Idiot* in 2004, public support for the war in Iraq was flagging. After Iraqi president Saddam Hussein was captured in late 2003 and tried for crimes against humanity, a growing majority of Americans wanted the United States to remove its troops from Iraq. A decade beyond their emergence as the mischievous, proudly juvenile pacesetters of the pop-punk revival, Green Day tapped an unexpected reserve of earnestness on their concept album. Lead singer Billie Joe Armstrong was determined to write a cycle of songs that would express his disgust with his government and the mainstream mindset that had initially supported it. A few years earlier, the brash young rocker had sung of his consuming desire to side with the underdog: "I want to be the minority." Now he'd written a whole concept album about disaffection. On the song

"Holiday," a clarion call against complacency, Armstrong urged listeners not to stand by in apathy—"on holiday"—as cynical politicians decided the fate of his generation. On the album's disarmingly perky title track, **"American Idiot,"** he made clear that he'd never join the horde: "Can you hear the sound of hysteria?/The subliminal mind-fuck America."

The main verse of that song "appeared in his head like a banner," wrote the late Green Day biographer Marc Spitz. "Armstrong thought of Bush, campaigning on a war ticket across the country. He thought of the man's message, which he considered to be a lie. The raising of the terror alert every time the administration was scrutinized. The using of the media to play him and his family and friends like puppets."

"We've had enough and we're ready to say 'I feel confused and disenfranchised,' " bassist Mike Dirnt told Spitz. "As individuals we feel like we're losing our individuality."[18] The record struck a chord, and not just with the band's confirmed fans: it became Green Day's best-selling album since their debut ten years earlier, and it would soon be adapted—in a development that surely would have surprised the punk rockers in their do-it-yourself warehouse days—as a hit Broadway musical.

As they approached middle age, the members of Green Day used their commercial clout to voice their support for various issues in the culture wars that continued to roil the nation. In 2010, the band threw itself into a controversy when officials in a Mississippi school district canceled a high school prom because a lesbian student had planned to bring her girlfriend. The band was one of several sponsors of the "Second Chance Prom," an event in Tupelo that was open to all LGBT students in the state and their allies. A Mississippi federal court ruled that the school district violated the student's First Amendment rights when it canceled the prom.

The band was attending rehearsals for the *American Idiot* musical when the news broke about the school district canceling the prom. While discussing ways the band could help, Mike Dirnt suggested that Green Day simply throw a prom for the students themselves. "My high school was a little more open-minded," he said. "There were a lot of girls dressed in tuxedos showing up for the prom. I didn't live in Mississippi, though. Sometimes you've got to force change."[19]

The children of the so-called Generation Z, born after the mid-1990s, have consistently demonstrated themselves to be far more tolerant about gender and sexuality than their elders. In a survey conducted by a trend forecasting agency in 2016, just 48 percent of Gen Z respondents identified as "exclusively" heterosexual. More than half said they were acquainted with someone who used gender-neutral pronouns such as "they" and "them," and a strong majority—70 percent—supported gender-neutral bathrooms.[20]

Curiously, in recent years the country music world—so often assumed to be culturally conservative, and rigidly so—has attracted considerable notice for more than one song supporting same-sex relationships. In 2006, Willie Nelson released a version of the satirical song "Cowboys Are Frequently, Secretly Fond of Each Other." The song had been written twenty-five years earlier by the musicologist and composer Ned Sublette, who said he had Nelson's voice in mind when he wrote it. After a member of the *Saturday Night Live* house band introduced the song to Nelson, he recorded a private demo version; for years, he'd play it for friends on his tour bus. Upon the success of the 2005 film *Brokeback Mountain*, a Best Picture nominee about two male ranchers who fall in love, Nelson decided it was time to bring his version of Sublette's song "out of the closet."

Eight years after Nelson's recording debuted, country singer Kacey Musgraves earned Song of the Year honors at the Country Music Association (CMA) awards for "Follow Your Arrow," her celebration of self-respect. While the song included lyrics about going to church (or not), taking a drink (or not), and other personal choices, its most memorable lines addressed sexuality:

> *Make lots of noise*
> *Kiss lots of boys*
> *Or kiss lots of girls*
> *If that's something you're into*

For her gay-positive message, Musgraves was invited to perform at the GLAAD (Gay & Lesbian Alliance against Defamation) Media Awards, but she also drew some pointed criticism. If she'd sung the song a hundred years earlier, one Colorado pastor contended, "somebody would've called for a rope."[21]

If such vicious homophobia was waning, casual discrimination was still ingrained in the culture. On his hit single "Same Love," the rapper Macklemore noted that his peers were still cavalier about using "gay" as a term of disapproval: "Have you read the YouTube comments lately?/'Man, that's gay' gets dropped on the daily." When the song was released as a single, the cover art featured a photograph of the rapper's uncle and his husband. "Same Love" was adopted as an anthem during the campaign for a referendum in Washington,

Macklemore's home state, which confirmed public support for legislation that legalized same-sex marriage.

But the song that perhaps best exemplified the continuing efforts to achieve full acceptance for LGBT was a direct descendant of the disco-era cult favorite "I Was Born This Way." Since becoming an arena-scale pop star, the New York City native who calls herself Lady Gaga has been one of the country's most outspoken supporters on behalf of gay rights. Her 2011 single **"Born This Way"** was a number one hit in the United States and several other countries. "Don't be a drag, just be a queen," Gaga urged, repeating a certain bit of advice her mother told her never to forget: "I'm beautiful in my own way/'Cause God makes no mistakes." Gaga followed the success of her song with proactive engagement on the issue of LGBT acceptance. She announced the establishment of her Born This Way nonprofit foundation for youth empowerment at Harvard University, and she brought a bus on tour with counselors on board prepared to speak with young people struggling with bullying or discrimination. After forty-nine people were murdered at a gay nightclub in Orlando, Florida, in 2016—the largest mass shooting attack in US history to that point—Gaga spoke emotionally at a vigil for the victims at Los Angeles City Hall, reading the names of each. "Tonight I will not allow my anger and outrage over this attack to overshadow our need to honor those who are grieving truly for their lost ones, lost members of the LGBT community," she said.

For myriad reasons, the Trump presidency brought demonstrators to the nation's streets in numbers not seen since the depths of the Vietnam War. They gathered and marched for science and for women's rights, on behalf of immigrants and gun control. Those issues were debated long before the 2016 election, of course. One issue that most Americans had not fretted over in years involved the worst fears of the Cold War, which ended with the fall of the Soviet Union in 1991, or so the world believed. But the president's war of words with North Korean leader Kim Jong-un renewed the long-dormant prospect that our government's posturing against a sworn enemy might lead to a nuclear calamity.

At the outset of the new administration, a coalition calling itself Our First 100 Days announced a song project to raise money for the causes "that will come under threat," including immigration, reproductive rights, measures to combat climate change, and LGBT issues. To this collection of one hundred original recordings, the comedian and musician Tim Heidecker contributed a new song called **"Trump Talkin' Nukes."** Though it seemed intended as a satire similar to Tom Lehrer's "We Will All Go Together When We Go,"

Heidecker was the first to admit his song was no laughing matter. Set to an elegiac piano riff, the song explained how the singer, born in 1976, grew up worrying about intercontinental ballistic missiles and the early-1980s movie *Red Dawn*, which posited a US invasion by the Soviet Union after a nuclear strike against Washington, DC.

"But my dad had it worse than me," Heidecker sings in a melancholy lilt. "He'd have to hide under a desk/As if that would stop the blast from destroying everything." After the arms control treaties of the 1980s, he points out, suicide bombers and other terrorist attacks diverted our concerns about nuclear arms. Such incidents were "terrible tragic," he goes on, but they weren't "a mushroom cloud."

Before a live Internet performance of the song, violinist Andrew Bird asked Heidecker whether the lyric was meant to imply a sort of perverse longing: "You're talking about nostalgia for a time when we were terrified of being obliterated," Bird said. If Trump wanted to "Make America Great Again," as his campaign slogan claimed, did he in fact want to revive the Cold War? It was Trump's promise to dramatically increase the country's nuclear arsenal "by tenfold," as Heidecker replied, that inspired the song, which ends with a dark, repeated thought: "Crazy how it only takes a maniac."

Ten days after Trump's election in 2016, his vice president–elect, former Indiana governor Mike Pence, requested tickets for a Broadway show. An avowed Christian, Pence had come to prominence in part due to his staunch opposition to abortion and LGBT rights. Upon hearing of his request, the cast of *Hamilton* prepared for the incoming vice president's visit.

Hamilton: An American Musical is the hip-hop flavored show written by Lin-Manuel Miranda based on Alexander Hamilton, the Revolution-era statesman who served as a delegate to the Constitutional Convention, published the Federalist Papers, and was appointed the first US Secretary of the Treasury. The show, a sensation that set box-office records, highlighted Hamilton's achievements as an American immigrant—he was born on the island of Nevis, in the Caribbean—by casting a multicultural range of actors to play the Founding Fathers. Pence was booed when he arrived to take his seat. Three hours later, as he hustled out of the theater during the curtain call, the actor Brandon Victor Dixon, playing Hamilton rival Aaron Burr, spoke on behalf of the cast as he thanked the politician for attending. Then he explained why the show's cast and many of its fans were concerned about the incoming administration.

"We are the diverse America who are alarmed and anxious that your new administration will not protect us, our planet, our children, our parents, or defend us and uphold our inalienable rights, sir," Dixon said. "But we truly hope this show has inspired you to uphold our American values and work on behalf of *all* of us."

Several of the show's musical numbers took on additional layers of meaning in the presence of the vice president–elect. Playing King George, the actor and gay rights activist Rory O'Malley gestured toward Pence's seat as he delivered the concluding line in a song about the difficulty of leadership, "What Comes Next?": "When your people say they hate you, don't come crawling back to me." And the audience leaped to their feet to applaud one of the show's most memorable lines: "Immigrants—we get the job done."[22]

After Miranda, the show creator, organized a "mixtape" of songs from *Hamilton* performed by various artists, he released a powerful six-minute video to accompany the song **"Immigrants (We Get the Job Done)."** The video was used to promote fundraising efforts on behalf of a new coalition of nonprofit organizations, named after the song, which would provide legal representation and social services to incoming refugees and asylum-seekers. The footage opened like a short film, with an enactment of anxious immigrants huddled in a boxcar, listening to a radio commentator. "It's really astonishing that in a country founded by immigrants," the voice on the radio says, " 'immigrant' has somehow become a bad word."

A diverse crew of rappers, with roots in Somalia, Mexico, Pakistan, and Puerto Rico, perform the lyrics, while a cast of actors wordlessly depict the latest wave of American newcomers and their symbolic productivity: delivering babies, sewing the Stars and Stripes. "Look how far I come," the performers chant. In an interview, director Tomas Whitmore pointed to the increasing incidence of xenophobia in American discourse as "a really unique opportunity to give a voice to the immigrant narrative, and to shine a spotlight on, as the song says, 'America's ghost writers'—a lot of people that make this country great and that we don't often get to see in mainstream media."[23]

But when the song asks whether Americans have in fact achieved freedom, the voice of George Washington responds with two simple words.

"Not yet."

ACKNOWLEDGMENTS

I distinctly recall hearing or reading somewhere, when I was growing up amid the malaise and narcissism of the 1970s and the '80s, that we'd entered a time with "no more heroes." I also remember thinking how that could not possibly be true, because I myself had so many.

I had lots of heroes who were supremely talented in some way. They were better than most of their peers as athletes, as writers, as comedians and musicians. But if there's one thing I've learned in twenty-five or so years as a journalist, it's that most heroes are admirable not so much for their talent (though they often have plenty of it), but for their sheer determination to stand up in the name of doing the right thing.

What follows is a short, woefully incomplete list of heroes—some of whom I've interviewed, others I would have been honored to meet, a few of whom I'm proud to call a friend. They're brave and righteous people all.

To W. Kamau Bell, the late Sam Berns, Billy Bragg, Kelly Carlin, Jeff Chang, Alex Charalambides, Barbara Dane, Bobbi Gibb, Otis Gibbs, Greg Gibson, Dave Hoffman, Daniel Johnson, Alan Kaufman, Diane Legg, James Meredith, Jerry Moore, James Parker, Will Power, Sonny Ochs, the late David Rakoff, Patti Smith, Erika Spanger-Siegfried, Amanda Torres, Josh Wilker, and Karen Wulf, to name just a few: thank you for the lives you've led.

Thank you to my agent, Paul Bresnick, who has stuck by me for five books now. (Not sure I believe it, either.) To Suzanne Ryan at Oxford University Press, who saw the value in this idea and helped hammer it into shape. To all of my editors at the *Boston Globe*, my former colleagues at the *San Francisco Chronicle*, and the various assignment editors at the long list of newspapers, magazines, and websites who have helped keep an improbably long freelance career afloat. To all of the librarians. A toast of locally brewed beer to Bill

McKibben, whose unexpected enthusiasm for this project helped keep it on track.

And all my love to Monica, who stands up every day for her beliefs and her many, many friends, and to Sam, Will, and Owen, our three boys: You'll always be my heroes.

NOTES

INTRODUCTION

1. Robert Hilburn, *Johnny Cash: The Life* (New York: Little, Brown & Company, 2013), 384–87.
2. Alfred F. Young, *The Shoemaker and the Tea Party: Memory and the American Revolution* (Boston: Beacon Press, 1999).
3. Irwin Silber, *Songs of Independence* (Harrisburg, PA: Stackpole Books, 1973), 35–37.
4. Ibid., 45.
5. Ibid., 45–46.
6. Alfred Owen Aldridge, *Man of Reason: The Life of Thomas Paine* (Philadelphia: Lippincott, 1959), 84–86.
7. L. A. Kauffman, *Direct Action: Protest and the Reinvention of American Radicalism* (New York: Verso, 2017), ix–x.

CHAPTER 1

1. Nicholas Smith, *Stories of Great National Songs* (Milwaukee: Young Churchman Co., 1899), 155.
2. Ronald D. Cohen and Will Kaufman, *Singing for Peace: Antiwar Songs in American History* (New York: Routledge, 2015), 103–4.
3. Hannah Gurman, *Hearts and Minds: A People's History of Counterinsurgency* (New York: The New Press, 2013), 60.
4. David Hadju, *Positively Fourth Street: The Lives and Times of Joan Baez, Bob Dylan, Mimi Baez Farina, and Richard Farina* (New York: Farrar, Straus and Giroux, 2001), 144.
5. https://www.washingtonpost.com/posteverything/wp/2017/01/24/why-phil-ochs-is-the-obscure-60s-folk-singer-america-needs-in-2017/?utm_term=.cde19eb68e69.
6. *New York Times,* April 30, 1968, 40.

7. Scott Miller, *Strike Up the Band: A New History of Musical Theatre* (Portsmouth, NH: Heinemann Drama, 2006), 105.

8. Ibid., 107.

9. Ibid., 108.

10. Allen Ginsberg, *Planet News* (San Francisco: City Lights Books, 1968).

11. Cohen and Kaufman, *Singing for Peace*, 78.

12. Ibid 32.

13. David King Dunaway, *How Can I Keep from Singing?: The Ballad of Pete Seeger* (New York: McGraw-Hill, 1981), 252.

14. Alec Wilkinson, *The Protest Singer: An Intimate Portrait of Pete Seeger* (New York: Knopf, 2009), 98.

15. Dunaway, *How Can I Keep from Singing?*, 264.

16. Deanna R. Adams, *Rock 'n' Roll and the Cleveland Connection* (Kent, OH: Kent State University Press, 2002), 166–69.

17. Ralph Young, *Dissent: The History of an Idea* (New York: New York University Press, 2015), 332.

18. Groucho Marx, *The Groucho Letters* (New York: Simon & Schuster, 1967).

19. John Shaw, *This Land That I Love: Irving Berlin, Woody Guthrie, and the Story of Two American Anthems* (New York: Public Affairs, 2013), 134.

20. Ibid., 151.

21. Sheryl Kaskowitz, *God Bless America: The Surprising History of an Iconic Song* (New York: Oxford University Press, 2013).

CHAPTER 2

1. Robert McAfee Brown, *Unexpected News: Reading the Bible with Third World Eyes* (Louisville, KY: Westminster John Knox Press, 1984), 19.

2. Daniel Weinstein, *Boston Globe*, December 27, 2016, A9.

3. Earl Robinson, with Eric A. Gordon, *Ballad of an American: The Autobiography of Earl Robinson* (Lanham, MD: Scarecrow Press, 1997).

4. William M. Adler, *The Man Who Never Died: The Life, Times, and Legacy of Joe Hill, American Labor Icon* (New York: Bloomsbury, 2011), 206.

5. Ibid., 325.

6. Ibid., 17.

7. Philip Dray, *There Is Power in a Union: The Epic Story of Labor in America* (New York: Doubleday, 2011), 12.

8. Ibid., 26–27.

9. Ibid., 29.

10. Rosalyn Fraad Baxandall and Linda Gordon, eds., *America's Working Women: A Documentary History, 1600 to the Present*, Sarah F. Yoseloff Memorial Publications (New York: W. W. Norton, 1995), 68–69.

11. Dray, *There Is Power in a Union*, 33.

12. http://www.hymntime.com/tch/htm/h/o/l/holdfort.htm.

13. Clark D. Halker, *For Democracy, Workers, and God: Labor Song-Poems and Labor Protest, 1865–95* (Urbana: University of Illinois Press, 1991).

14. Philip S. Foner, *American Labor Songs of the Nineteenth Century* (Urbana: University of Illinois Press, 1975).

15. http://www.kansasmemory.org/item/209680/page/12.

16. Sarah Eisenstein, *Give Us Bread but Give Us Roses: Working Women's Consciousness in the United States, 1890 to the First World War* (New York: Routledge, 1983), 32.

17. http://www.breadandroses.org/about/history/mimi-farina/tribute.

18. Foner, *American Labor Songs*, 188.

19. Ibid., 189.

20. Ibid., 194–95.

21. Alessandro Portelli, *They Say in Harlan County: An Oral History* (New York: Oxford University Press, 2012), 177.

22. Ibid., 181.

23. Ibid., 187.

24. Ibid., 187.

25. Ibid., 236.

26. http://www.folkstreams.net/context,284.

27. Jim Garland, *Welcome the Traveler Home: Jim Garland's Story of the Kentucky Mountains* (Lexington: University Press of Kentucky, 1983), 33.

28. Shelly Romalis, *Pistol Packin' Mama: Aunt Molly Jackson and the Politics of Folksong* (Urbana: University of Illinois Press, 1998), 86–87.

29. http://xroads.virginia.edu/~ma05/luckey/amj/kentucky.htm.

30. http://www.folkstreams.net/context,284.

31. http://www.folkstreams.net/film,164.

32. https://singout.org/2015/01/12/conversations-death-4-black-lung.

33. https://www.youtube.com/watch?v=voQyNgCcdpE.

CHAPTER 3

1. Joan Baez, *And a Voice to Sing With: A Memoir* (New York: Simon & Schuster, 2009), 103.

2. Drew D. Hansen, *The Dream: Martin Luther King, Jr., and the Speech That Inspired a Nation* (New York: Ecco, 2003), 57.

3. Baez, *And a Voice to Sing With*, 103.

4. William Eleazar Barton, *Old Plantation Hymns: A Collection of Hitherto Unpublished Melodies of the Slave and the Freedman, with Historical and Descriptive Notes* (Boston: Lamson, Wolffe & Co., 1899), 25.

5. David Margolick, *Strange Fruit: Billie Holiday, Cafe Society, and an Early Cry for Civil Rights* (Philadelphia: Running Press, 2000), 17.

6. http://forward.com/articles/153734/strange-evolution-of-legendary-song.

7. Paul Robeson, *Paul Robeson Speaks: Writings, Speeches, Interviews, 1918–1974*, ed. Philip Foner (New York: Brunner/Mazel, 1978), 119.

8. Judith E. Smith, *Becoming Belafonte: Black Artist, Public Radical* (Austin: University of Texas Press, 2014), 27.

9. Ibid., 121.

10. Ibid., 128.

11. Ibid., 203.

12. Ibid., 206.

13. Ibid., 140.

14. http://www.nytimes.com/2008/12/03/arts/music/03odetta.html?_r=1&hp.

15. Jon Else, *True South: Henry Hampton and "Eyes on the Prize," the Landmark Television Series That Reframed the Civil Rights Movement* (New York: Viking, 2017), 286.

16. Ibid., 287.

17. Todd Gitlin, *The Sixties: Years of Hope, Days of Rage* (New York: Bantam, 1987), 75.

18. Robert Cantwell, *When We Were Good: The Folk Revival* (Cambridge, MA: Harvard University Press, 1996), 289.

19. Dunaway, *How Can I Keep From Singing*, 222.

20. Ibid., 5.

21. Ibid., 223.

22. Brian Ward, *Just My Soul Responding: Rhythm and Blues, Black Consciousness, and Race Relations* (Berkeley: University of California Press, 1998), 185.

23. Todd Mayfield, with Travis Atria, *Traveling Soul: The Life of Curtis Mayfield* (Chicago: Chicago Review Press, 2016), 101.

24. Ibid., 102.

25. Ibid., 111.

26. Ibid., 131.

27. Ibid., 143.

28. Ward, *Just My Soul Responding*, 191.

29. Peter Guralnick, *Dream Boogie: The Triumph of Sam Cooke* (New York: Little, Brown and Company, 2005), 526–27.

CHAPTER 4

1. http://www.esquire.com/entertainment/music/a29785/tami-show-facts.

2. http://www.spectropop.com/JohnMadara.

3. Dave Marsh, *The Heart of Rock & Soul: The 1001 Greatest Singles Ever Made* (New York: Plume, 1989), 590.

4. Robert Palmer, *Rock & Roll: An Unruly History* (New York: Harmony, 1995), 35.

5. Trevor Tolliver, *You Don't Own Me: The Life and Times of Lesley Gore* (Milwaukee, WI: Backbeat Books, 2015).

6. http://msmagazine.com/blog/2015/02/18/lesley-gore-and-her-feminist-anthems.

7. http://www.startribune.com/it-s-lesley-gore-s-party/80951892/?c=y&page=all&prepage=1.

8. http://www.afterellen.com/people/43863-interview-with-lesley-gore.

9. Robert James Branham and Stephen J. Hartnett, *Sweet Freedom's Song: "My Country 'Tis of Thee" and Democracy in America* (New York: Oxford University Press, 2002), 84.

10. Richard Crawford, *America's Musical Life, A History* (New York: W. W. Norton & Co., 2001), 815.

11. Angela Davis, *Blues Legacies and Black Feminism: Gertrude "Ma" Rainey, Bessie Smith, and Billie Holiday* (New York: Pantheon, 1998), 30–31.

12. https://www.arts.gov/honors/heritage/fellows/lydia-mendoza.

13. https://www.npr.org/sections/therecord/2015/09/25/443209089/rhiannon-giddens-patty-griffin-and-shakey-graves-a-musical-conversation.

14. Davis, *Blues Legacis and Black Feminism*, 92.

15. Susan Faludi, *Backlash: The Undeclared War against Women* (New York: Crown, 1991), 49.

16. Ibid., 50.

17. Ibid., 51.

18. Ibid., 54.

19. Betty Friedan, *The Feminine Mystique (50th Anniversary Edition)* (New York: W. W. Norton, 2013), 82.

20. Ibid., 101.

21. Jerry Lieber and Mike Stoller, with David Ritz, *Hound Dog: The Leiber & Stoller Autobiography* (New York: Simon & Schuster, 2009), 236.

22. Ibid., 235.

23. Tammy Wynette, with Joan Dew, *Stand by Your Man: An Autobiography* (New York: Simon & Schuster, 1979), 190.

24. David Cantwell and Bill Friskics-Warren, *Heartaches by the Number: Country Music's 500 Greatest Singles* (Nashville: Vanderbilt University Press, 2003), 9–11.

25. Ibid., 10.

26. Gail Collins, *When Everything Changed: The Amazing Journey of American Women from 1960 to the Present* (New York: Little, Brown and Company, 2009), 59.

27. http://now.org/about/history.

28. Howard Zinn, *A People's History of the United States, 1492–Present* (New York: Harper & Row, 1980), 497.

29. David Ritz, *Respect: The Life of Aretha Franklin* (New York: Little, Brown and Company, 2014), 152.

30. Ibid., 158.

31. Ibid., 161–62.

32. Ibid., 161.

33. http://nymag.com/news/politics/har.

34. Cantwell and Friskics-Warren, *Heartaches by the Number*, 89.

35. http://www.ourbodiesourselves.org.

36. Marjorie J. Spruill, *Divided We Stand: The Battle over Women's Rights and Family Values That Polarized American Politics* (New York: Bloomsbury USA, 2017), 2.

37. Ibid., 3.
38. Gillian G. Gaar, *She's a Rebel: The History of Women in Rock and Roll* (New York: Seal Press, 2002), 120.
39. Spruill, *Divided We Stand*, 6.
40. Ibid., 8.

CHAPTER 5

1. http://www.aljazeera.com/indepth/interactive/2011/05/2011512141926468292.html.
2. http://www.geog.ucsb.edu/~kclarke/Papers/SBOilSpill1969.pdf.
3. https://archive.epa.gov/epa/aboutepa/guardian-origins-epa.html.
4. Liner notes, *The Best of Tom Paxton: I Can't Help but Wonder Where I'm Bound*.
5. http://www.nelsonearthday.net/earth-day/beginnings.php#1.
6. Linda Lear, introduction to Rachel Carson, *Silent Spring: Fortieth Anniversary Edition* (New York: Mariner Books, 2002), xiii.
7. Ibid., xvii.
8. http://www.npr.org/2015/08/06/a/it-took-a-musicians-ear-to-decode-the-complex-song-in-whale-calls.
9. http://www.nationalgeographic.com/radiox/humpback/hw_archive.html.
10. http://articles.latimes.com/1996-12-08/entertainment/ca-6804_1_early-songs#mod-a-body-after-second-para.
11. *Sounds* magazine, October 1976.
12. https://www.epa.gov/clean-air-act-overview/evolution-clean-air-act.
13. Howard Fineman, *The Thirteen American Arguments: Enduring Debates That Define and Inspire Our Country* (New York: Random House, 2008), 217.
14. http://www.pophistorydig.com/topics/cuyahoga-river-fires.
15. *Rolling Stone*, April 7, 1988.
16. *Rolling Stone*, April 21, 1988.
17. Steve Knopper, *MJ: The Genius of Michael Jackson* (New York: Scribner, 2015), 233.
18. Ibid., 321.

CHAPTER 6

1. http://www.nytimes.com/2003/01/29/us/praising-san-francisco-s-champion-of-conformity.html.
2. http://www.ocweekly.com/music/the-life-and-times-of-malvina-reynolds-long-beachs-most-legendary-and-hated-folk-singer-7474438.
3. David Halberstam, *The Fifties* (New York: Villard, 1993), 136.
4. Ibid., 142.
5. Ibid., 140.
6. https://www.census.gov/prod/2012pubs/p20-566.pdf.

7. http://www.ditext.com/searle/campus/1.html.

8. http://tapewrecks.blogspot.com/2012/12/oh-come-all-ye-mindless-conceptless-and.html.

9. http://www.americanrhetoric.com/speeches/mariosaviosproulhallsitin.htm.

10. Baez, *And a Voice to Sing With*, 119.

11. Seth Rosenfeld, *Subversives: The FBI's War on Student Radicals and Reagan's Rise to Power* (New York: Farrar, Straus and Giroux, 2012), 219.

12. http://www.berkeley.edu/news/media/releases/2004/06/08_reagan.shtml.

13. Rosenfeld, *Subversives*, 462.

14. https://web.archive.org/web/20070830211157/http://www.beauty-reality.com/travel/travel/sanFran/peoplespark3.html.

15. Jentri Anders, quoted in *Berkeley in the Sixties* (film).

16. Mark Kurlansky, *1968: The Year That Rocked the World* (New York: Ballantine, 2003), 93.

17. https://www.m4tf.org/chronology.html.

18. https://www.m4tf.org/chronology-day3.html.

19. Jimmy McDonough, *Shakey: Neil Young's Biography* (New York: Random House, 2002), 345.

20. Ibid., 346.

21. Ibid., 346.

22. http://boingboing.net/2010/05/04/devos-jerry-casale-o.html.

23. http://people.wku.edu/charles.smith/MALVINA/inmrmp.htm.

24. Liner notes, *Greatest Misses*.

25. Craig O'Hara, *The Philosophy of Punk: More Than Noise!* (Edinburgh and San Francisco: AK Press, 2001), 41.

26. Evie Nagy, *Devo's Freedom of Choice* (New York and London: Bloomsbury Academic, 2015), 71.

27. McDonough, *Shakey*, 524.

CHAPTER 7

1. https://www.theguardian.com/music/2017/oct/23/trans-pioneer-jackie-shane-i-dont-bow-down-i-do-not-get-down-on-my-knees.

2. Neil Miller, *Out of the Past: Gay and Lesbian History from 1869 the Present* (Boston: Alyson Books, 2006), 259.

3. Ibid., 261.

4. Ibid., 335.

5. Ibid., 337.

6. Ibid., 346.

7. Ibid., 343.

8. David Carter, *Stonewall: The Riots That Sparked the Gay Revolution* (New York: St. Martin's Press, 2004), 85.

9. Ibid., 23–25.

10. Ibid., 115.

11. Ibid., 143.

12. Ibid., 151.

13. Ibid., 183.

14. Ibid., 185.

15. Ibid., 217.

16. Ibid., 261.

17. Ibid., 266.

18. Peter Shapiro, *Turn the Beat Around: The Secret History of Disco* (London: Faber & Faber, 2005), 31.

19. Ibid., 31.

20. http://pitchfork.com/thepitch/1365-10-classic-songs-from-the-loft-david-mancusos-influential-dance-party.

21. Shapiro, *Turn the Beat Around*, 65.

22. http://queermusicheritage.com/jun2002v.html.

23. Ibid.

24. http://www.popmatters.com/column/167895-queen-of-disco-the-legend-of-sylvester.

25. http://www.getintothis.co.uk/2016/10/disco-didnt-suck-dancing-social-politics.

26. Andrew Kopkind, "The Dialectic of Disco: Gay Music Goes Straight," *Village Voice*, February 12, 1979.

27. Shapiro, *Turn the Beat Around*, 232.

28. Ibid., 163.

29. L. A. Kauffman, *Direct Action*, 109.

30. http://www.gallup.com/poll/6961/what-percentage-population-gay.aspx.

31. http://www.gallup.com/poll/1651/gay-lesbian-rights.aspx.

32. http://www.dallasvoice.com/im-coming-out-resonates-10118312.html.

CHAPTER 8

1. Tim Z. Hernandez, *All They Will Call You* (Tucson: University of Arizona Press, 2017), 194–95.

2. http://www.nytimes.com/2013/09/04/us/california-memorial-names-crashs-forgotten-victims.html.

3. John F. Kennedy, *A Nation of Immigrants*, rev. ed. (New York: HarperPerennial, 2008), 2.

4. https://blogs.voanews.com/all-about-america/2015/06/22/how-us-has-defined-black-americans-since-1820.

5. https://www.libertyellisfoundation.org/immigration-timeline.

6. http://palante.org/History.htm.

7. Misha Berson, *Something's Coming, Something Good: "West Side Story" and the American Imagination* (Milwaukee: Applause Theatre & Cinema Books, 2001), 98–99.

8. https://archive.org/details/whomweshallwelco00unit.

9. http://www.lbjlibrary.org/lyndon-baines-johnson/timeline/lbj-on-immigration.

10. https://www.libertyellisfoundation.org/immigration-timeline#1930.

11. https://www.usnews.com/news/articles/2015/07/06/its-official-the-us-is-becoming-a-minority-majority-nation.

12. Graham Nash, *Wild Tales: A Rock & Roll Life* (New York: Viking, 2013), 204.

13. Peter Ames Carlin, *Homeward Bound: The Life of Paul Simon* (New York: Henry Holt & Co., 2016), 213–14.

14. http://www.paulsimon.com/news/paul-simon-discusses-political-references-songs.

15. Antonino D'Ambrosio, *A Heartbeat and a Guitar: Johnny Cash and the Making of Bitter Tears* (New York: Nation Books, 2009), 97–99.

16. Ibid., 98.

17. Ibid., 171.

18. http://www.pewresearch.org/fact-tank/2017/03/02/what-we-know-about-illegal-immigration-from-mexico, https://www.migrationpolicy.org/article/mexican-immigrants-united-states.

19. http://www.nytimes.com/1999/02/05/nyregion/officers-in-bronx-fire-41-shots-and-an-unarmed-man-is-killed.html.

20. Bruce Springsteen, *Born to Run* (New York: Simon & Schuster, 2016), 435.

CHAPTER 9

1. https://www.fairobserver.com/region/north_america/wilfred-burchett-atomic-plague-99732.

2. http://www.sonomamag.com/nuclear-fault-line.

3. http://www.folkarchive.de/atom.html.

4. *New York Times*, September 9, 1950.

5. http://www.nytimes.com/2005/03/15/science/listening-to-the-beat-of-the-bomb.html.

6. Joel Selvin, *Summer of Love: The Inside Story of LSD, Rock & Roll, Free Love, and High Times in the Wild West* (New York: Dutton, 1994), 106–7.

7. Bob Dylan, *Chronicles: Volume One* (New York: Simon & Schuster, 2004), 271.

8. http://www2.gol.com/users/davidr/sloan/aboutsongs.html.

9. *Lovejoy's Nuclear War* documentary, dir. Daniel Keller, 1975.

10. http://nvdatabase.swarthmore.edu/content/montague-massachusetts-citizens-stop-nuclear-power-plant-construction-united-states-1974.

11. http://www.freep.com/story/news/local/michigan/2016/10/09/detroit-fermi-accident-nuclear-plant/91434816.

12. http://www.nytimes.com/1979/09/24/archives/nearly-200000-rally-to-protest-nuclear-energy-gathering-at-the.html.
13. http://people.com/archive/from-bruce-to-bonnie-the-hottest-acts-in-rock-warm-up-the-no-nuke-crusade-vol-12-no-15.
14. Nash, *Wild Tales*, 270.
15. http://www.gmpfilms.com/rollingstone.html.
16. http://www.rollingstone.com/culture/news/steamed-clams-hold-nukes-at-bay-19770728.
17. https://reaganlibrary.archives.gov/archives/speeches/1982/60882a.htm.

CHAPTER 10

1. Paul Maher, Jr., ed., *Tom Waits on Tom Waits: Interviews and Encounters* (Chicago: Chicago Review Press, 2011), 361–62.
2. Ibid., 384.
3. https://www.hollywoodreporter.com/news/occupy-wall-street-protests-tom-morello-260993.
4. http://occupywallst.org/about.
5. https://www.washingtonpost.com/lifestyle/style/occupy-wall-street-inspires-a-new-generation-of-protest-songs/2011/10/14/gIQAANnqpL_story.html?utm_term=.9f315a282ec9.
6. https://www.hollywoodreporter.com/news/occupy-wall-street-protests-tom-morello-260993.
7. https://www.rollingstone.com/music/features/james-mcmurtrys-hard-truths-from-the-heartland-20150430.
8. Brian Coleman, *Check the Technique: Liner Notes for Hip-Hop Junkies* (New York: Villard, 2007), 359.
9. Ben Westhoff, *Original Gangstas: The Untold Story of Dr. Dre, Eazy-E, Ice Cube, Tupac Shakur, and the Birth of West Coast Rap* (New York: Hachette, 2016), 80.
10. Ibid., 96.
11. https://www.usnews.com/news/articles/1993/05/23/the-untold-story-of-the-la-riot.
12. http://www.rollingstone.com/music/news/j-cole-mourns-michael-brown-in-somber-new-song-be-free-20140815.
13. http://www.rollingstone.com/music/news/how-blacklivesmatter-changed-hip-hop-and-r-b-in-2015-20151216?page=2.
14. http://www.rollingstone.com/music/news/vic-mensa-takes-on-police-brutality-in-devastating-new-video-w446322.
15. https://www.washingtonpost.com/news/monkey-cage/wp/2018/01/21/one-year-after-the-womens-march-on-washington-people-are-still-protesting-en-masse-a-lot-weve-counted.
16. http://ew.com/music/2017/01/21/womens-march-alicia-keys-girl-on-fire.

17. https://www.npr.org/sections/allsongs/2017/01/23/511186649/a-flash-mob-choir-at-the-womens-march-turned-this-unknown-song-into-an-anthem.

18. Marc Spitz, *Nobody Likes You: Inside the Turbulent Life, Times, and Music of Green Day* (New York: Hachette, 2007), 161–62.

19. http://www.mtv.com/news/1637459/green-day-hope-to-force-change-by-sponsoring-prom-for-gay-teen.

20. https://www.jwtintelligence.com/2016/03/gen-z-goes-beyond-gender-binaries-in-new-innovation-group-data.

21. https://www.advocate.com/arts-entertainment/music/2014/04/26/country-star-kacey-musgraves-angers-homophobes.

22. https://www.hollywoodreporter.com/news/hamilton-broadway-cast-addresses-mike-pence-audience-work-behalf-all-us-949075.

23. https://www.buzzfeed.com/louispeitzman/the-story-behind-the-immigrants-we-get-the-job-done-video?utm_term=.ucYLVdg08N#.kseNrwxQVd.

BIBLIOGRAPHY

Adams, Deanna R. *Rock 'n' Roll and the Cleveland Connection*. Kent, OH: Kent State University Press, 2002.

Adler, William M. *The Man Who Never Died: The Life, Times, and Legacy of Joe Hill, American Labor Icon*. New York: Bloomsbury, 2011.

Aldridge, Alfred Owen. *Man of Reason: The Life of Thomas Paine*. Philadelphia: Lippincott, 1959.

Allen, William Francis, Charles Pickard Ware, and Lucy McKim Garrison, eds. *Slave Songs of the United States: The Classic 1867 Anthology*. New York: Dover Publications, 1995.

Baez, Joan. *And a Voice to Sing With: A Memoir*. New York: Simon & Schuster, 2009.

Barton, William Eleazar. *Old Plantation Hymns: A Collection of Hitherto Unpublished Melodies of the Slave and the Freedman, with Historical and Descriptive Notes*. Boston: Lamson, Wolffe & Co., 1899.

Baxandall, Rosalyn Fraad, and Linda Gordon, eds. *America's Working Women: A Documentary History, 1600 to the Present*. Sarah F. Yoseloff Memorial Publications. New York: W. W. Norton, 1995.

Berson, Misha. *Something's Coming, Something Good: "West Side Story" and the American Imagination*. Milwaukee: Applause Theatre & Cinema Books, 2011.

Branham, Robert James, and Stephen J. Hartnett. *Sweet Freedom's Song: "My Country 'Tis of Thee" and Democracy in America*. New York: Oxford University Press, 2002.

Cantwell, David, and Bill Friskics-Warren. *Heartaches by the Number: Country Music's 500 Greatest Singles*. Nashville: Vanderbilt University Press, 2003.

Cantwell, Robert. *When We Were Good: The Folk Revival*. Cambridge, MA: Harvard University Press, 1996.

Carlin, Peter Ames. *Homeward Bound: The Life of Paul Simon*. New York: Henry Holt & Co., 2016.

Carson, Rachel. *Silent Spring: 40th Anniversary Edition*. New York: Mariner Books, 2002.

Carter, David. *Stonewall: The Riots That Sparked the Gay Revolution*. New York: St. Martin's Press, 2004.

Cohen, Ronald D., and Will Kaufman. *Singing for Peace: Antiwar Songs in American History*. New York: Routledge, 2015.

Coleman, Brian. *Check the Technique: Liner Notes for Hip-Hop Junkies*. New York: Villard, 2007.

Collins, Gail. *When Everything Changed: The Amazing Journey of American Women from 1960 to the Present*. New York: Little, Brown and Company, 2009.

Crawford, Richard. *America's Musical Life: A History*. New York: W. W. Norton & Co., 2001.

D'Ambrosio, Antonino. *A Heartbeat and a Guitar: Johnny Cash and the Making of "Bitter Tears."* New York: Nation Books, 2009.

Davis, Angela. *Blues Legacies and Black Feminism: Gertrude "Ma" Rainey, Bessie Smith, and Billie Holiday*. New York: Pantheon, 1998.

Dray, Philip. *There Is Power in a Union: The Epic Story of Labor in America*. New York: Doubleday, 2011.

Dunaway, David King. *How Can I Keep from Singing?: The Ballad of Pete Seeger*. New York: McGraw-Hill, 1981.

Dylan, Bob. *Chronicles: Volume One*. New York: Simon & Schuster, 2004.

Eisenstein, Sarah. *Give Us Bread but Give Us Roses: Working Women's Consciousness in the United States, 1890 to the First World War*. New York: Routledge, 1983.

Else, Jon. *True South: Henry Hampton and "Eyes on the Prize," the Landmark Television Series That Reframed the Civil Rights Movement*. New York: Viking, 2017.

Faludi, Susan. *Backlash: The Undeclared War against Women*. New York: Crown, 1991.

Fineman, Howard. *The Thirteen American Arguments: Enduring Debates That Define and Inspire Our Country*. New York: Random House, 2008.

Foner, Philip S. *American Labor Songs of the Nineteenth Century*. Urbana: University of Illinois Press, 1975.

Friedan, Betty. *The Feminine Mystique (50th Anniversary Edition)*. New York: W. W. Norton, 2013.

Gaar, Gillian G. *She's a Rebel: The History of Women in Rock and Roll*. New York: Seal Press, 2002.

Garland, Jim. *Welcome the Traveler Home: Jim Garland's Story of the Kentucky Mountains*. Lexington: University Press of Kentucky, 1983.

Ginsberg, Allen. *Planet News*. San Francisco: City Lights Books, 1968.

Gitlin, Todd. *The Sixties: Years of Hope, Days of Rage*. New York: Bantam, 1987.

Guralnick, Peter. *Dream Boogie: The Triumph of Sam Cooke*. New York: Little, Brown and Company, 2005.

Gurman, Hannah. *Hearts and Minds: A People's History of Counterinsurgency*. New York: The New Press, 2013.

Hajdu, David. *Positively Fourth Street: The Lives and Times of Joan Baez, Bob Dylan, Mimi Baez Farina, and Richard Farina*. New York: Farrar, Straus and Giroux, 2001.

Halberstam, David. *The Fifties*. New York: Villard, 1993.

Halker, Clark D. *For Democracy, Workers, and God: Labor Song-Poems and Labor Protest, 1865–95*. Urbana: University of Illinois Press, 1991.

Hansen, Drew D. *The Dream: Martin Luther King, Jr., and the Dream That Inspired a Nation*. New York: Ecco, 2003.

Hernandez, Tim Z. *All They Will Call You*. Tucson: University of Arizona Press, 2017.

Hilburn, Robert. *Johnny Cash: The Life*. New York: Little, Brown and Company, 2013.

Kaskowitz, Sheryl. *God Bless America: The Surprising History of an Iconic Song*. New York: Oxford University Press, 2013.

Kauffman, L. A. *Direct Action: Protest and the Reinvention of American Radicalism*. New York: Verso, 2017.

Kennedy, John F. *A Nation of Immigrants*. rev. ed. New York: HarperPerennial, 2008.

Knopper, Steve. *MJ: The Genius of Michael Jackson*. New York: Scribner, 2015.

Kopkind, Andrew. "The Dialectic of Disco: Gay Music Goes Straight." *Village Voice*, February 12, 1979.

Kurlansky, Mark. *1968: The Year That Rocked the World*. New York: Ballantine, 2003.

Lieber, Jerry, and Mike Stoller, with David Ritz. *Hound Dog: The Lieber & Stoller Autobiography*. New York: Simon & Schuster, 2009.

Maher, Paul, Jr., ed. *Tom Waits on Tom Waits: Interviews and Encounters*. Chicago: Chicago Review Press, 2011.

Margolick, David. *Strange Fruit: Billie Holiday, Cafe Society, and an Early Cry for Civil Rights*. Philadelphia: Running Press, 2000.

Marsh, Dave. *The Heart of Rock and Soul: The 1001 Greatest Singles Ever Made*. New York: Plume, 1989.

Marx, Groucho. *The Groucho Letters*. New York: Simon & Schuster, 1967.

Mayfield, Todd, with Travis Atria. *Traveling Soul: The Life of Curtis Mayfield*. Chicago: Chicago Review Press, 2016.

McAfee Brown, Robert. *Unexpected News: Reading the Bible with Third World Eyes*. Louisville, KY: Westminster John Knox Press, 1984.

McDonough, Jimmy. *Shakey: Neil Young's Biography*. New York: Random House, 2002.

Miller, Neil. *Out of the Past: Gay and Lesbian History from 1869 to the Present*. Boston: Alyson Books, 2006.

Miller, Scott. *Strike Up the Band: A New History of Musical Theatre*. Portsmouth, NH: Heinemann Drama, 2006.

Nagy, Evie. *Devo's Freedom of Choice*. New York and London: Bloomsbury Academic, 2015.

Nash, Graham. *Wild Tales: A Rock & Roll Life*. New York: Viking, 2013.

O'Hara, Craig. *The Philosophy of Punk: More Than Noise!* Edinburgh and San Francisco: AK Press, 2001.

Palmer, Robert. *Rock & Roll: An Unruly History*. New York: Harmony, 1995.

Portelli, Alessandro. *They Say in Harlan County: An Oral History*. New York: Oxford University Press, 2012.

Ritz, David. *Respect: The Life of Aretha Franklin*. New York: Little, Brown and Company, 2014.

Robeson, Paul. *Paul Robeson Speaks: Writings, Speeches, Interviews, 1918–1974*. Edited by Philip Foner. New York: Brunner/Mazel, 1978.

Robinson, Earl, with Eric A. Gordon. *Ballad of an American: The Autobiography of Earl Robinson*. Lanham, MD: Scarecrow Press, 1997.

Romalis, Shelly. *Pistol Packin' Mama: Aunt Molly Jackson and the Politics of Folksong*. Urbana: University of Illinois Press, 1998.

Rosenfeld, Seth. *Subversives: The FBI's War on Student Radicals, and Reagan's Rise to Power*. New York: Farrar, Straus and Giroux, 2012.

Selvin, Joel. *The Summer of Love: The Inside Story of LSD, Rock & Roll, Free Love, and High Times in the Wild West*. New York: Dutton, 1994.

Shapiro, Peter. *Turn the Beat Around: The Secret History of Disco*. London: Faber & Faber, 2005.

Shaw, John. *This Land That I Love: Irving Berlin, Woody Guthrie, and the Story of Two American Anthems*. New York: PublicAffairs, 2013.

Silber, Irwin. *Songs of Independence*. Harrisburg, PA: Stackpole Books, 1973.

Smith, Judith E. *Becoming Belafonte: Black Artist, Public Radical*. Austin: University of Texas Press, 2014.

Smith, Nicholas. *Stories of Great National Songs*. Milwaukee: Young Churchman Co., 1899.

Spitz, Marc. *Nobody Likes You: Inside the Turbulent Life, Times, and Music of Green Day*. New York: Hachette, 2007.

Springsteen, Bruce. *Born to Run*. New York: Simon & Schuster, 2016.

Spruill, Marjorie J. *Divided We Stand: The Battle over Women's Rights and Family Values That Polarized American Politics*. New York: Bloomsbury USA, 2017.

Tolliver, Trevor. *You Don't Own Me: The Life and Times of Lesley Gore*. Milwaukee, WI: Backbeat Books, 2015.

Ward, Brian. *Just My Soul Responding: Rhythm and Blues, Black Consciousness, and Race Relations*. Berkeley: University of California Press, 1998.

Westhoff, Ben. *Original Gangstas: The Untold Story of Dr. Dre, Eazy-E, Ice Cube, Tupac Shakur, and the Birth of West Coast Rap*. New York: Hachette, 2016.

Wilkinson, Alec. *The Protest Singer: An Intimate Portrait of Pete Seeger*. New York: Knopf, 2009.

Wynette, Tammy, with Joan Dew. *Stand by Your Man: An Autobiography*. New York: Simon & Schuster, 1979.

Young, Alfred F. *The Shoemaker and the Tea Party: Memory and the American Revolution*. Boston: Beacon Press, 1999.

Young, Ralph. *Dissent: The History of an American Idea*. New York: New York University Press, 2015.

Zinn, Howard. *A People's History of the United States: 1492–Present*. New York: Harper & Row, 1980.

INDEX